"I say someone even after will remember us."

Sappho

Light and Leaven

Women Who Shaped Augustana's First Century

Ann Boaden

Ꭺ

Augustana College · Rock Island, Illinois

ISBN 978-0-910184-40-3

For Dr. Dorothy J. Parkander

"This ... I am persuaded of ... that to acquire knowledge the best helper our human nature can hope to find is Love."
Socrates on the wise woman Diotima

FOREWORD

Ann Boaden has long been interested in the record of the many women who have enriched the history of Augustana College. This book is the result of that interest. The author knows her subject well. As an Augustana student herself, as a member of its faculty, and as editor of the college magazine for many years she has been an essential part of the effort to understand the general history of Augustana. In this volume Dr. Boaden has paid particular attention to the work of those female members of the college community who, often against the grain of their times, took essential roles in the development of the school.

This book comes from days and years of careful investigation of the college's history in its archives and other records, from thoughtful consideration of the recollections of people who were themselves parties to the history she describes, and from Boaden's own disciplined reflection on her subject. The author's willingness to do hard work as well as her imagination and creativity will both be clear to the reader.

As the study, writing, and teaching of history have evolved, there have been times when its practitioners have simply tried to chronicle happenings. The idea was to list important events in the order in which they took place. At other moments writers claiming to present things as they actually happened have so filled the narrative with their own imaginings and theories that one has had to use their material with great caution. But like all competent students of the past, Ann Boaden has successfully steered a middle course between these extremes. The result is a book both readable and reliable, both imaginative and substantive. It is a valuable addition to the body of academic material that seeks to present and then to interpret Augustana College's history.

From Inez Rundstrom to Florence Neely, Augustana has been indeed fortunate in the women who have taught on its faculty and contributed to its growth. Now a host of names and faces and minds are alive again in the pages of this book, people who enlivened and graced the life of a school whose direction was for the most part in the hands of men—but a school whose intellectual, moral, and spiritual life would have been far poorer and much more limited if the women whom Boaden considers here had not had the courage and strength to take a role in building it. Ann Boaden herself is one of these women. And now Augustana is greatly indebted to her for her persistent interest in these women, for her research into their lives and work, and for this engaging account of their personalities and accomplishments.

Thomas Tredway
President Emeritus
Augustana College

INTRODUCTION

It began as an epiphany.

Where are the women?

As a member of the (two-person) publications committee of Augustana Historical Society, I review manuscripts on our college's history. I have noticed that as I age, that history, with tide-like inevitability, inches closer to my own time at Augustana. And in the latest submissions, though I've learned a lot about the institutional story—the external story, available in minutes and memos, correspondence and catalogues—I've felt something missing. Through all the care of preparation and documentation in these studies, something wasn't right, wasn't *there*.

It was the women.

Of course, institutional history, at least at Augustana and at many American colleges and universities, is the record of what men did because it's the men who were running the places, especially in the years before 1970. But I knew from my own experience that there was another story, an internal story, and that story had everything to do with women, with the kind of power women exerted even if they didn't sit in the president's or the dean's offices. I knew that the women I encountered shaped my experience at Augustana and beyond that, my life; I knew, too, that I wasn't alone in feeling this way, and it wasn't only women who shared that perception. Many students, male and female, attest that some of the most important questions they asked and the answers they groped toward and the things they've found to be of lasting importance in their lives, they owe to women they encountered, in the classrooms, in the dorms, in the practice rooms, backstage and onstage. So it seemed to me that to really tell the story of Augustana we needed to know about its women—what they received and what they gave to the school, and what challenges they had to encounter for these things to happen.

I mentioned this insight to retired Dean Betsey Brodahl one after-noon, adding: "Someone needs to write a book about Augustana's women." She looked at me with her keen dean's eye and said: "Yes. Someone does."

And that is how this project was born, long ago.

As I began my research in the chilly (but warmly welcoming) archives of Augustana, I found I was asking the same question I'd begun with:

Where are the women? For even though women have attended the college since the 1870s, even though they've held sway in classrooms, in student groups, and in academic arenas beyond Rock Island, we have scant records on them. This discovery was a bit daunting. But it was also inspiring. It showed that this book did need to be written. These stories did need to be uncovered and told. And doing so was endlessly exciting.

I confess to having approached this work with a certain trepidation. I'm not an historian. My doctoral work is in literature, and I've studied writing and been more or less a writer all my life. Given those credentials, given that I'd embarked on what was an historical study and that it was to be published by an organization called an historical society, I found, as I accumulated notes and notebooks year by year, that I wasn't at all sure just what was the best way to present the material I've found.

A couple of things helped. One was preparing a series of articles on the first three women graduates for a journal that assumed an intelligent and interested lay audience. The articles were well received, and in fact earned an award (from an historical society!). The second thing that helped was another remark of Betsey's: "I hope you'll include yourself; you're an Augustana woman." At the time I quickly and blushingly dismissed such an idea; I'm not the kind of iconic Augustana woman who has shaped lives and destinies. But then it occurred to me that in another way I was certainly an Augustana woman. I've benefited by all the women who went before and who created the place where women could learn and grow and locate the dreams for their lives.

And so the format of this book is a little different from your typical institutional history. I guess you could say it's in part an embedded memoir of my own journey in discovering the early pioneers, and in encountering the later generations who've given me the privileged life (to quote Betsey once again) that I enjoy. It's certainly not an exhaustive study. Here's the plan I've followed: I've tried to create a context for each generation of women from the earliest (in the 1880s) to 1960, considering aspects of national history, and particularly women's place in higher education during each era. In doing so I've been deeply indebted to the definitive study by Barbara Miller Solomon, *In the Company of Educated Women.* And then I've explored the way Augustana and Augustana women were situated within that larger story. What unfolds is increasing expansion of possibilities for women in the academy, as women, women's abilities, and women's "place" came to be perceived differently over time.

It seems that Augustana followed this general pattern fairly closely. So to tell the story of its women is in some sense to tell an American story, perhaps in some ways a generic story of women's progress. But no story, I suppose, is really generic. Specifics of place and time give each institution its own shape. And within that shape, individual characters move and live: impress with their personalities, the sound of their laughter, the color of their dreams. To read institutional history in Board minutes and president's reports, in yearbooks and student newspapers, is to discover these personalities shining out like points of light. So in each of the historical sections, I've focused on a few of those individuals, individuals who contributed especially significantly to the story of Augustana's women. Most are "firsts," showing, by their lives and achievements, new visions that I and others have profited from. And because I've hung around the college for quite awhile, I've been blessed to know some of our wonderful "new" women. I've sketched just a few of these women, most of them students I've worked with during the past few decades, who have also contributed to this book. You'll find those sketches preceding each of the major textual divisions.

A few words about my principles of selection. It quickly became evident that I couldn't cover in detail all the women who contributed in various ways to the shaping of Augustana: the faculty, the students, the often unsung wives and secretaries and housemothers and dieticians and custodial crew. So I've limited my consideration to the college itself, to the faculty, and to some of its student leaders. The most clearly identifiable history makers, in other words. I've touched only briefly on the three related-but-separate programs: the secretarial school, the Conservatory, and the school of nursing. This may seem a puzzling choice in view of the fact that these programs attracted large numbers of women—were, arguably, originally designed in part to serve the perceived needs of women. Certainly in doing so they offered women of their time solid training in careers then open to them. However, these programs functioned as self-contained educational units, each with its own course roster and administrative system, all offering more what we would call skills instruction than a complete liberal arts education (the fact that Regina Holmen made institutional history in 1922 by graduating from both the Conservatory and the College demonstrates how separate the bodies were seen to be). And they tended to reinforce certain traditional understandings about women's roles and needs. That, I believe, is evident when we look at curricular history.

These separate-but-equal "woman-slanted" programs have since been either dropped or absorbed into college majors. Women no longer study secretarial science; they study business and economics. Women interested in the healing arts study medicine to become physicians. Women—and men—study music in the context of an overall liberal arts program. This development suggests that by focusing attention on the college itself I can better tell the story I want to share.

And then a note about my cut-off point: 1960. Though, as I've noted in the Afterword, certain of the fifties patterns persisted throughout that decade, the sixties were the dawning of change, and some of the women who made that happen remain active contributors to the college today. Others have only recently retired. Their story awaits its chronicler.

What these more recent Augustana women showed us, with increasing clarity after 1970, was a whole different kind of women's movement that emerged throughout the country. In the vibrant feminism of the last third of the twentieth century women go beyond demanding their rightful place in academic disciplines as they've always been studied. Rather, they create new approaches to those disciplines. They insist that we think about gender in different ways, ways that cross academic fields and encourage, even perhaps require, interdisciplinary study. The women who brought this vision to Augustana and continue to share it with students and colleagues have helped reshape the ethos of the college, making it a better, fairer place to study and work for both men and women. And after them, a new generation of young, brilliant, deeply committed women scholars extend their work to new generations of students.

Yet such pushes for equity and beyond are not, perhaps, as new as they might seem. In fact, they enflesh Augustana's deepest core beliefs—in social justice, in the sacredness of each personality, finally, in a God who does not privilege one gender above the other. The beginnings of the "new" Augustana can be traced back to T. N. Hasselquist, the second president, who actively sought to bring women students to campus.

I hope you enjoy meeting these women as much as I enjoyed finding out about them. And that they become as real to you as they've become to me. I am filled with admiration when I look at their stories, and with a deep humility. I hope you will share in those feelings, too. And I hope you will see this book as I do—as the first, but by no means the last, word on a neglected, essential part of the Augustana story.

I have many people to thank for their part in making this book a reality. Dr. Richard Arnell generously supplied me with materials about Grinnell College for my section on Henriette Naeseth, and Dr. Paula Arnell gave me much valuable background on School of Expression in which her mother, Mabel Arnell Youngberg, studied and taught, as well as memories of her own college days. Alexandra and Harold Benedict helped with research from the inception of this project. Special Collections librarians Jamie Nelson, Sarah Horowitz, and Donna Hill, and Swenson Center staff Jill Seaholm gave prompt, willing, and efficient research assistance, without which the book couldn't have been completed. Mike Haeuser, Archivist at Gustavus Adolphus College, supplied valuable information on Inez Rundstrom, as did Mary Pryor of Rockford College on Emmy Carlsson Evald. Many alumni/ae allowed me to interview them about their Augustana experiences. I thank them all, and hope that the result will give some recompense for their generosity and enthusiasm. Thanks also to Peggy Anderson, Dr. Thomas Banks, Martin Katz, George and Pat Olson, and Pastors Nancy Jaster, David Miley, and Richard Priggie. Several people read the book in manuscript and offered thoughtful suggestions: Dr. Jeff Abernathy; Jane Easter Bahls, Dr. Michael Nolan, Dr. Dorothy Parkander, Dr. Thomas Tredway, and Dr. Roald Tweet. Their words and wisdom have made the book stronger, and whatever weaknesses and errors remain are mine. I am grateful to Augustana College, President Steven Bahls, and former Dean Jeff Abernathy for granting me a sabbatical leave to complete the writing of this book, to Augustana Historical Society for supporting the project, and particularly to Dr. Michael Nolan and Kai Swanson for shepherding the book through the press. Kurt Tucker of the Augustana Communications staff worked his technological wizardy on the design of the volume. But most of all, I'm grateful to the women, past and present, whose stories honor Augustana and gift the teller.

Ann Boaden
Summer 2010

TABLE OF CONTENTS

THE EARLY YEARS: PROMISE AND PROGRESS

Jamie Nelson's small office, tucked away in the climate-controlled warrens of Special Collections, is chilly. But not as chilly as if would be if it weren't filled with papers. Papers stacked on the floor, papers in sprawling, layered mounds on her desk. Jamie is head of Special Collections at Augustana, and as her office shows, does the work of ten people.

Talking to her, you can see something of how she does it. She's quick and efficient. She speaks rapidly, incisively; there is a central, essential clarity about her words, her efficient movements, her approach to her work. Her eyes, direct and blue, look straight into yours when you ask a question (which she can always answer). Despite that crowded desk, she's available to seek and fetch the materials people need. She brings me old books with their friable pages, gray boxes of carefully-labelled documents, chunky and tall bound volumes the color of wine. She has the historian's passionate reverence for history and the words and artifacts of history, a passion completely undiluted with sentimentality. When she tells me we have little material on Augustana's women, and that this situation needs to be rectified, I know again how deeply important it is that these stories be told.

And I open the books. Looking for the women.

CHAPTER I

The Early Years:
Promise and Progress

"Girls were scarce in those days—.…[T]heir first appearance awakened an awe and dread such as Adam must have felt when his eyes first lit
on Eve."[1]

The oldest catalogues are in Swedish. Their pages are browned and
brittle; when you sit at the table in Special Collections, resting the crum-
bling cardboard bindings on gray foam pads to prevent their breaking altogether, the edges crumb in your hands. They smell of dust and history.

I think of those who first wrote and read them, who turned these
pages when they crackled and smelled of new ink.

I think of the dreams that clashed and meshed.

*Their portraits look sternly and uncompromisingly from past to future:
Esbjorn—hair slicked across a high forehead, frosted sideburns to the chin, eyes
cold and direct behind round spectacles. Hasselquist, gazing somewhere beyond
the photo's frame, into the light that whitens half his beard, and casts shadows
that define the strength of cheekbone and nose.*

*They rose, perhaps, in their dark clerical suits and stiff white collars, as
they disputed; perhaps leaned across the table between them, perhaps thumped
the wood with fist or open hand. For this was something both cared about passionately: the future and character of Augustana College.*

As Lars Paul Esbjorn and Tufe Nilsson Hasselquist, Augustana's first
two presidents, debated over the kind of institution Augustana was to
be, the position of women wove through those often intense conflicts.[2]
Esbjorn, increasingly homesick for Sweden (an attitude that Hasselquist
scornfully dismissed), wished to retain the Swedish character of the college,
while Hasselquist insisted that "a complete American College"[3] would be
the way of the future—and of survival. For him that meant raising aca-

demic standards to match those of other American colleges. And some evidence indicates it meant the admission of women.

Historian Oscar Fritiof Ander conjectures that as early as the Paxton years (1863-1875) Hasselquist may have envisioned a coeducational institution, "suggested by the fact that he does not use the [Swedish] word sons [in the Catalogue copy for 1872-1873] but the general term '*flere*,' meaning more [students], and in 1871-1872 five girls were attending the college, although they were not officially registered."[4] Hasselquist was obviously paying attention to developments in the American academies that would most have interested him. Particularly in the Midwest during the 1840s and 1850s small church-affiliated colleges were being organized as coeducational institutions, for reasons both pragmatic and principled. Belief in the equality of souls mandated equal treatment for both sexes, and if that included education, maintaining one institution was clearly more economical than setting up two separate-sex schools.[5] By the 1880s Hasselquist was actively recruiting women students.[6] His efforts weren't overwhelmingly successful; the Catalogue for academic year 1883-1884 lists seven "non-matriculated female students" in an institutional body of 206 (37 Seminary—for which in any case women were then ineligible—79 college, 83 preparatory).[7] Not until the Conservatory of Music and the Commercial departments were added to the curriculum, in 1886 and 1888 respectively, did "the number of women students become encouraging."[8]

That slow growth rate isn't too surprising. In recruiting women students Hasselquist was entering something of a battleground. This situation, of course, never bothered the doughty churchman/academician. Boundingly robust, superbly confident, he remained a fighter into his seventy-third year. When Synod leaders attempted to force his resignation from the Augustana presidency, the white-haired, white-bearded old man, tall and erect, strode into the Synod gathering, mounted the platform, and declared in a resonant voice that had, in its day, taken *Messiah* solos, "I will not resign. You have no one to fill the place. Who can do better than I? I have nothing for which to resign, and I will stay until I move to a place a little east of Moline [the cemetery]."[9]

With this spirit he took on his own Swedish-American community, and, to some extent, the culture at large. The Swedish farmers who'd immigrated to break the Midwest prairies and till their rich soils, often distrusted higher education. Reading and writing and ciphering would suffice for their children's needs in life, they believed. In fact, many argued "that education was detrimental, and that their children would become lazy and consider themselves too good for farm work....As for the girls, if they could cook, sew, sing in a choir, and play 'Gubben Noak' (a simple piano piece played with one finger), they were considered accomplished by their neighbors."[10]

The culture at large, on both sides of the Atlantic, tended to reinforce this view of education for women. Religious denominations may have been creating coeducational colleges in the American Midwest, but the general consensus was pretty much that higher education was unsuitable for women and they for it. (In fact, many of the coeducational colleges offered separate courses, or less than the full liberal arts curriculum, for their women.[11]) Various rationales were summoned for this conclusion, but they all boiled down to the assumption of female inferiority, both physical and mental. For example, a paper by a respected French physician "proved" women incapable of advanced study by measuring their brains and finding them, not surprisingly, physically smaller than those of men.[12] In America a retired Harvard Medical School professor concluded (after observing seven Vassar graduates) not that women weren't bright enough to handle college courses, but that studying would deplete their "limited energy" and thereby "endanger their 'female apparatus.'"[13] Such theories provide happy targets for ridicule today.[14] But at the time they convinced many who wished to buttress exclusionary views with "objective" evidence. And while admitting women to their colleges, churches often endorsed, even promoted, the idea of female inferiority by defining "equality" as equal in worth but different in character. Woman's place was in the home; her duty, her glory, her unique calling, was to sacrifice personal ambition for service to her family. As we'll see, even a quite emancipated woman such as Inez Rundstrom (Augustana's first woman graduate, class of 1885) encouraged the image of women as "home builders" whose particular vocation was "to lighten the load of others"[15] rather than to seek their own fulfillment.

A look at the numbers of female college and university students in the late years of the nineteenth century bears out this assessment of women's abilities. In 1870, just five years before Augustana moved from Paxton to Rock Island (when Hasselquist was "advocating coeducation"[16]), of the 582 degree-granting institutions in the country, 12 admitted women only, and 29 admitted women along with men. In 1890, by the time Augustana had graduated its first two women, 1082 degree-granting institutions included

20 that admitted women only and 43 that were coeducational.[17] The pattern speaks clearly: women simply didn't belong in college.

But Hasselquist invited women. In part the additions of the music conservatory and the commercial department, effected under his presidency, were designed to attract more women students. The first brochure from the Commercial Department stated as its aim "to give young men *and women* the best possible opportunities of acquiring such a knowledge of business as will enable them to utilize, to the best advantage, the means and opportunities within their reach [italics mine]."[18] This statement suggests not only that women were welcomed to Augustana, but that they might envision for themselves a life other than, or at least in addition to, that of domesticity. By the time he died in 1891, weary from unremitting work and personal bereavement, Hasselquist was able to see a recruitment of women so successful that "it was considered necessary to build a girls' dormitory"[19]—and Ladies Hall, under the supervision of Marguerite Shuey Foss, opened.

And so the women came. Their names are recorded in pages that thin and break as I turn them.

Augustana's first three women graduates represent more than names in a catalogue and elements in an historical movement. Each forged a remarkable life for herself—a life that put her education to use in ways which nudged at boundaries for women. None followed the usual course of marriage and family. All, at some time in their lives, taught in college. Inez Rundtrom spent a long and distinguished career at Gustavus Adolphus College. Anna Olsson, who headed a household of four adults, attained international recognition as a writer in the early twentieth century. Anna Westman was the first woman faculty member at Augustana.

These are their stories.

"A True Scholar and a Genuine Saint": Inez Rundstrom

Her early photos suggest a practical visionary. The determined chin lifts over the high-necked dress; the eyes, clear and straightforward, gaze with both eagerness and serenity into the future she was to enter.

She entered it as the first woman graduate of Augustana College. Her name was Inez Rundstrom.

She was raised on the prairies of Lindsborg, Kansas, and ended her life as an icon at Gustavus Adolphus College in Minnesota. That in itself was an achievement in the years between 1869 and 1953. Perhaps even more remarkable, in a world that often pitted faith against reason, her intellectual activity was informed by a deep spirituality. At her funeral service (March 5, 1953) Dr. Edgar M. Carlson, then president of Gustavus Adolphus College, and a major figure in the life of the Augustana Lutheran Synod, praised her "penetrating intellect" and "goodness of character and spiritual fervor" which, he said, were "welded together in one." She was, according to him, "A true scholar and a genuine saint."

Inez Rundstrom in her college years

To forge such a coherent identity was somewhat unusual for women students in the late nineteenth and early twentieth centuries. Conflicting needs and demands hampered their development. Society, and usually their families, urged marriage, child-rearing, and domesticity as their appropriate sphere, and the pietistic Swedish immigrants regarded higher education as not only unnecessary but dangerous. Yet some women, perhaps more than we can know now, felt in mind, heart, and spirit a hunger for wider worlds—of ideas, of growth. As Anna Olsson, the second woman to graduate from Augustana, put it: "…[T]he time I can devote to study is extremely limited, so many household duties occupy [me]….I must not complain, however, although it sometimes seems very hard for me to give up my studies. Give up!—I cannot do that…In the midst of my daily toil, often when washing dishes, sweeping, etc., the wish becomes so strong, the wish that I could sometime be able to study…that I have a hard struggle before I can quiet the storm in my heart."[20]

But Inez Rundstrom seems to have escaped this dilemma. She may owe her emancipation in part to her father, Dr. John Rundstrom. Born in Rostanga, Sweden, in 1835, he received his medical education there, emigrated to America with his wife Maria Charlotta, and settled briefly in Water Valley, Mississippi, where Inez Carolina was born October 15, 1869. The following year he moved to the pioneer Swedish colony of Lindsborg, Kansas. He served as its sole doctor, though the wide practice of midwifery may have eased his load. But clearly he was a busy man. In addition to his medical responsibilities, he was appointed Special County Clerk as part of a three-man team charged with organizing the new county of McPherson, Kansas.[21]

He was a long-bearded, majestic man, a man of vigor, competence, strength, and quickness—of action and of temper, a man who seemed to prefer forging new frontiers to living within established communities of place and thought. (He kept moving, from Kansas, to Michigan, possibly as far as Cuba.) When his wife died in 1876 he took on the then-somewhat unconventional role of single parent to two young daughters—Inez, seven, and her sister Ellen, a toddler of three.

More unconventionally, he raised his girls to exercise their minds. He obviously believed in women's education. His friend Ernest Skarstedt, reporting on a visit to the Rundstroms, notes "the extraordinary intelligence and knowledge of the then 10-year old girl [Inez]."[22] This vignette suggests a proud father who not only supported his daughter's studying but encouraged her to demonstrate what she knew. Only four years later he was to send her the long 550 miles by rail to Augustana—an amazing expression of respect for and faith in her mind (not to mention her character). Inez Rundstrom's subsequent career clearly vindicated his faith. Sharing her home in his last years, he could see firsthand her impact as scholar and teacher in the Gustavus College venue. After his death in 1921, at his specific request, Inez Rundstrom and her sister Ellen Werner established a scholarship for women students at the college—a fund named for his wife rather than for himself.[23]

Support for study is one thing—and an important thing. Time and energy are other issues. As the older daughter in a motherless household, Inez Rundstrom necessarily would have assumed domestic responsibilities, as did her friend and fellow Lindsborg denizen Anna Olsson. There would have been household help, of course: a housekeeper in charge, assisted perhaps by a newly-arrived girl from Sweden. Still, the duties wouldn't have been easy, as Anna Olsson's account[24] shows. The fact that Dr. Rundstrom gave the property to his housekeeper in payment for her work when he moved from Lindsborg[25] suggests that what she did was no "light housekeeping." And the girls of the family would have been expected to do their share in handling those duties.

Today's Lindsborg is a charming town. Under a clear summer sky it seems an irenic piece of the past untroubled by the complexities and tensions of 2010. Large houses dating to the last century, many bearing shutters and window frames painted in light Swedish blue, line tree-shaded streets. Even on a hot June evening it's quiet; few air conditioners hum, no radios blast rap. Instead, people sit on front porches, talking quietly or simply keeping silence in the silence of the day's end. Downtown, shops with Swedish names and merchandise cluster, and beautifully and wittily painted Dalarna horses, big enough for children to mount, guard each corner from their concrete plinths. The pace is leisurely. People stroll. The new young president of Bethany College pledges enthusiastically to keep alive what alumni say they centrally cherish—its Swedish-Lutheran heritage.

That's Lindsborg in the early 21st century. The Lindsborg that Rundstrom knew was very different. Between 1870 and 1883 it was the wild west; the 80-acre Rundstrom homestead, in fact, boasted one of the first houses west of town.[26] In the human world violence lurked at the edges of each day and night: tensions persisted between displaced native American Indians and white settlers; justice sometimes took the rough and ready form of lynching. Rundstrom's own barn, built sturdily from blocks of native sandstone and perched on a "lookout" hill, featured windows funneled outward into holes from which guns could be fired—a small fortress.[27] In the natural world, cyclones, rattlesnakes, wolves, and swarming grasshoppers threatened fragile human structures on the long stretch of prairie. To keep those structures habitable demanded hard labor: raising and butchering animals, fetching water, carding wool, sewing, baking, hanging curtains and wallpaper—in addition to the ongoing tasks of sweeping and washing.[28]

Rundstrom appears not to have resented these duties. Rather, for her they seemed to be the natural responsibilities of women. In a talk she gave to the Young Women's Luther League at Gustavus Adolphus in 1925, she defines women as "home-builders" and deems it "a women's [*sic*] place to lighten the load of others"[29] and to take "joy in working."[30] And if she said this, particularly to young women students, we know she believed it. As all who remembered her attest, she spoke from the heart, her words the coin of her values.

Perhaps one reason why she could accept the role she outlines was that she wasn't chained to it. Going to Augustana emancipated her from enforced domestic drudgery at an early age.

Even though a long train ride over stretches of prairieland separated Lindsborg from Rock Island, Augustana was the logical choice for an intelligent, studious young woman of Swedish origin with ties to the Augustana Synod of the Lutheran Church. The religious orientation may have prompted Rundstrom's father to send his gifted young daughter there, though his spirituality seems to have been peculiarly his own: Skarstedt called him "somewhat of a mystic,"[31] who studied and occasionally practised hypnotism. So perhaps the Swedish connection as much as the church affiliation prompted Dr. Rundstrom to select Augustana for Inez. But whatever her father's aspirations for her, it's clear that Inez developed a deep commitment to the church that lasted and grew throughout her life.

So she packed her trunk, this young girl of fourteen, said good-bye to her Lindsborg home, and set off on the long journey eastward. The hopes and dreams she carried with her seem amply demonstrated in her subsequent career. She wanted the life of the mind. And she wanted, or learned to want, the life of the spirit.[32]

What greeted her when she arrived at Rock Island?

Undoubtedly a freshly cleaned and aired room in one of the large Augustana Lutheran parsonages. As late as the 1920s and 30s it was still the custom for the pastor to open his home to any of the extended Swedish Lutheran "family" who happened by—for a day or a year, or, as it sometimes seemed to the pastor's family, a lifetime. Perhaps Olof Olsson, then on the Seminary faculty, and a friend from Lindsborg days, gave her room and board. His daughter Anna, just three years Rundstrom's senior and soon-to-be fellow student, could have helped her adjust to the new surroundings.

Perhaps, after dinner on the first day of her arrival, they'd have walked the campus. Anna Olsson enjoyed climbing Zion Hill, and from it the young women would have been able to look over the town. They could see, or imagine, the gleaming line of the Mississippi River, and above it, the vivid midwest sunset. The first college building, its square central bell tower rising dark against the sky, sat to their right on the southeast side of the campus. Already the all-purpose building was too cramped for the growing school, and a major construction project was underway. Only seven years before, cows had wandered across the campus, but now a fence kept them out—and kept the shoes of Augustana faculty and students clean.

Perhaps the vision of wider worlds opened to Inez Rundstrom as she stood at the top of the hill and saw the world spread beneath.

She joined a college of 79, with, as we've seen, six other non-matriculated female students. Her anomalous situation was intensified by the age difference between herself and her fellow students: the average age for first-years at that time was 23. These circumstances seem not to have fazed her.

She'd have sat in straight-backed, front-facing wooden chairs, taken notes on lectures, and studied, often by memorization of textbook material. According to Netta Bartholomew Anderson, Class of 1894, and Esthena Randolph, Class of 1921, women weren't then allowed to participate in "recitation" periods, so she'd presumably have sat listening as fellow students spoke.[33] It's tempting to wonder if she felt impatient at knowing answers she was unable to give aloud, or whether her professors somehow maneuvered around the restriction.

The schedule was rigorous and rules of conduct strict. Regular attendance at religious services was mandatory. And if she indeed roomed in a pastor's home, she'd have participated in daily devotions with the family. To pass her courses she'd have produced essays on various set topics. A classmate, Philip Dowell, records in his meticulously-kept college diary a "List of subjects and persons writing on them" for their senior finals. "Miss Rundstrom," he notes, tackled the comprehensive subject inspired by a line from Goethe—"*Und Hochmuth ist's wodurch die Engle fielen, Woran der Holle Geist den Menschen fast*" (and it was through pride that the angels fell, whereby the devil [evil spirit] seized mankind)—on Wednesday (April 29). Two days later, along with four others, she addressed the topic "*Hosruli [?] bestod Runnebergs storket somskaid* (What made Runeburg[34] a great poet?) for her Swedish essay.[35] It's unclear whether this was a collaborative effort, or whether each student produced his or her own paper. Either way, Rundstrom obviously took on some pretty challenging subjects—and passed.

But she didn't spend all her time crouched over her books. Dowell describes an evening supper party on May 6 of their senior year, a sort of celebration at the end of the mathematics examination, which of course Rundstrom would have taken. The host, Greek professor Anders O. Bersell, comes across as a genial soul, if Olof Olsson's somewhat romanticized description of Augustana classes is to be believed: "In our lovely Helas" [Olsson writes] "Prof. Bersell holds sway, and with calm confidence he masters the many involved and enjoyable creations of this culture."[36] At this event Bersell wasn't quoting Greek lyrics presumably, but even so the entertainment would scarcely excite college students of the twenty-first

century. However, for their less sophisticated nineteenth-century counterparts, the supper ("a very good one"), the impromptu music making
(which included a cornet duet and singing with organ accompaniment),
the word games ("soon given up"), and the declamation of pieces such
as "the beginning of a Dutchman's speech, a verse in Swedish dialogue—
'Fritiof och Bjorn'," and a piece "about a drunkard having taken his last
glass," were highly satisfactory: Dowell records that "we dispersed about
10:30 all quite well pleased with our visit." Exactly what part Inez played in
this partying is unclear; after the drunkard's last glass Dowell writes simply: "Prof. Bersell, Miss Rundstrom, and some more."[37] But that she was
included in the festivities, and by her own choice, is obvious.

In the spring of that year she collected her degree and made institutional history by doing so.

And then the wide world glimpsed from Zion Hill opened to her.
Records don't tell whether she contemplated a more predictable woman's
route, marriage and family. We know only that her studies took her to
the Universities of Stockholm and Uppsala, Sweden, from 1887 until 1892;
to the Sorbonne and the College de France in 1898-1900 and 1908- 1909;
to the American universities of Minnesota, Chicago, and Wisconsin. And
that during her forty-eight-year tenure at Gustavus Adolphus College in
St. Peter, Minnesota, she led a life in which intellectual vigor and spiritual
energy were, in Carlson's words, "welded together."

Her studies earned her a doctorate, granted in 1900 by Augustana
College, six years after she joined the Gustavus College faculty. She taught
mathematics, not, at the time, the most conventional discipline for
women. As department chair she cared deeply about the future of that
study at Gustavus. Toward the end of her career, speaking to a young colleague she hoped to retain, Rundstrom said, "If you will continue what
I have tried to do all these many years, and if you stay as long as I did,
our college will not have to worry about the mathematics department for
almost a century!" That colleague, a middle-aged man when he reported
the conversation, added, "The printed word does not reveal the sincerity of
her voice; the pride in her heart at having found the 'right young man' to
replace her...."[38]

But much as the mathematics department concerned her, it wasn't
her sole interest or her only contribution to the life of the college. An agile,
wide-ranging intelligence shows in her many presentations to student and
faculty groups on subjects as diversified as Swedish art, French literature

(which she also taught), and Biblical studies. And just as she "welded together" the worlds of mind and spirit, so she seemed effortlessly to negotiate the demands of the academy and the duties of the home, the emerging and the traditional roles for women.

A report in the student newspaper *Gustavian Weekly* illustrates this balancing act. She spoke to a student Mathematics club about Sonya Kovalevski (1850-1891), the premier woman mathematician in the late nineteenth and early twentieth centuries, a gifted scholar who struggled against gender bigotry to pursue her studies and ultimately became the first woman elected to the Russian Academy of Sciences. Rundstrom had become acquainted with her at the University of Stockholm, where Kovaleski was teaching. The young scholar must have been awed by Kovalevski, then garnering honors in mathematics unheard of for women, and besting the top men in the field to boot. And Kovalevski was interested in both mathematics and literature, producing highly praised short stories and novels—another link between her and Rundstrom. After this lecture on a woman who broke barriers and demolished stereotypes, Rundstrom "served a delicious lunch." In her life, apparently, exploration and tradition, science and domestic science interwove comfortably.

She was one of those legendary teachers every institution boasts: revered by students and colleagues alike. Aina Abrahamson, who knew her as a teacher in both mathematics and Bible studies, remembers her "kindness and capability."[39] "...[H]er scholarship was profound but never forbidding," President Carlson said in his eulogy. "...She was a woman of refinement and culture" whose "brilliance...came from both her mind and her heart...." Abrahamson can attest to this; she still keeps a verse written in Swedish to "Mrs. Hulda Abrahamson & daughters from Dr. Inez Rundstrom, 1932" expressing affection and joy in their friendship.[40] President Carlson concluded that "Gustavus Adolphus College has had no more devoted teacher in its history"—a rather extraordinary affirmation, since the school was nearly a century old at the time!

Honors accumulated throughout her professional life. As she began her forty-seventh year of teaching, Gustavus feted her at a celebratory dinner, a tribute that coincided with Augustana's conferring an honorary Doctor of Letters on her, to mark the fifty-fifth anniversary of her graduation. And in 1940 a new women's dormitory at Gustavus was named Rundstrom Hall, the handsomest building on campus during his student years, according to one forties Gustavian alumnus.[41]

Yet in many ways her profoundest teaching came in sharing her "spiritual fervor"—in conducting Bible classes (always large) at a local church; in leading campus prayer groups; in counseling students one-on-one. She herself felt that these activities formed her greatest contribution to the mission of Gustavus as a Christian liberal arts college. This reflection seems important to understanding her legacy, because the faith she shared was a tested one. Given her way of life and choice of vocation, she faced struggles in a world that too often thought in prescription rather than in possibility. As Carlson said, her faith "was childlike but not naïve...."[42]

The eyes of the young woman are circled by spectacles in her later years. But her vision, it seems, was undiminished. Friends and students who dropped in for tea in her "small but delightful apartment" during her post-retirement years could enjoy good conversation, a "pleasant, informal, and unpretentious" living room filled with books and art objects from her various travels,[43] and presumably her memorable cooking as well. To all outward appearances, Augustana's first woman graduate found both place and empowerment.

Scrubbing Floors with Sophocles: Anna Olsson

...I have thought so much of my school and classmates this evening.... Oh! that the happy school-days would return!... I ought to work twice as hard now to make up for the time I spent on my lessons. But no one knows how very hard it is for me to give up my studies altogether.... Give up!—I cannot do that![44]

Anna Olsson wrote these words in her journal in 1890. She was twenty-four. Two years earlier she'd graduated from Augustana College; now she was living in the small Illinois town of Woodhull, keeping house for her widowed father and her three younger siblings. Just the year before, 1889–1890, her family had made the grand tour of Europe, and images of that life-changing experience stayed with her. An imaginative young woman with a keen feeling for beauty, she couldn't escape comparisons between the glories of the old world and the hard, narrow life of the new. "I ought to be satisfied, <u>I have seen Rome!</u>" she wrote. But the hunger of the mind would not be easily stilled; domestic chores, however necessary, made poor substitutes for Sophocles. They tired the body but left the spirit restless. And this restlessness, this conflict between aspiration and duty, forms a recurrent theme in her early journals.

She was born in Värmland, Sweden (August 19, 1866), but the life she knew in childhood was that of the American west. Like her friend Inez Rundstrom she grew up in Lindsborg, Kansas, where her Lutheran minister father had emigrated in 1869, to serve the scattered pioneer settlements of Swedish-Americans.

Ordained at the prestigious Uppsala University in Sweden, Olof Olsson was twenty-eight when he came to America with his wife, Anna Lisa Olsson, and their three-year-old daughter Anna. He was a gentle, scholarly man whose passion for music assisted his spiritual growth. In her semi-autobiographical children's book *En prärieunges funderingar* (variously translated as *I'm Scairt*, *A Child of the Prairie*, and *A Prairie Child's Thoughts*), written in 1917 when she could look back on her early experiences, Anna paints an idealized portrait of her parents; everyone, she claims, loved papa and mama, even those, such as the cowboys and native American Indians, who didn't particularly love each other. In any theological controversy (of which there were many), she asserts, "Papa has the rightest teaching that can be found."[45] Anna would have been too young to understand the ideological issues involved in "the notorious atonement controversy" that

Anna Olsson (bottom left) with her family: sisters Maria (Mia) (upper left) and Lydia, brother Johannes (Hannes), and father, Augustana President Olof Olsson

pitted the ideas of Paul Peter Waldenstrom against the more traditional views espoused by Olof Olsson—and indeed drove Olsson to a rigid conservatism he later admitted was too severe.[46] The child Anna heard only the pounding of fists and hollering of ministers who disagreed with her father; saw only the suffering of the "Papa" who brought a vision of love and comfort to his hardworking and often homesick fellow Swedes, and who shielded her against the excessive pietism that brooded over her home like a storm on the prairie.

The immediate source of this view was "farmor," Olsson's mother (his parents emigrated with him). Farmor, always dressed severely in black "like a preacher," is "*so* strict," the young Anna says. "She thinks that almost everything is Sin."[47] Through Farmor's uncompromising stare Anna sees God as a stern judge, and life as a set of tricks and snares which only strenuous attention may enable the individual to avoid. Of course activities such as smoking, drinking, and card-playing incur instant, unquestionable, and unrelenting divine wrath. But more innocent activities can be potential minefields as well. When, for instance, Anna makes a doll out of a cucumber and pretends to baptize it, she's terrified afterward lest she go to hell for blasphemy. And instead of being told that this rather imaginative play doesn't really constitute blasphemy, she's "reassured" that she need only ask God's forgiveness for this "sin."[48]

In the dress code Farmor lays down for her daughter-in-law and granddaughters—no crinolines, no rosettes on hats or ruffles on skirts, and certainly no earrings[49]—she almost out-Brocklehursted Brocklehurst, the severe (and hypocritical) clergyman in *Jane Eyre.* Olof Olsson himself bore the scars of her aggressive piety. When as a child and a lover of music, he made a violin for himself, Farmor, who "thought it was SIN to play the violin…, broke it all to pieces."[50] But unlike Brocklehurst, Farmor was utterly sincere. On one occasion, when she confuses the days of the week and ends up knitting a pair of socks on Sunday, she berates herself with the same severity she deals out to others.[51]

Against the extremities of this view, Papa and Mama provide a softening influence. Even though they can't tell her that baptizing a cucumber doll *isn't* blasphemy, they can reassure her that God will forgive (with Farmor it's a more problematic issue). And when Farmor bewails the sinful socks, Anna reports that papa and mama "only think it is funny." Still, despite these evidences of gentleness to young and old in their innocent errors, Olof Olsson can't be seen as religiously liberal in a modern sense. In the atonement controversy, he embraces the conservative position, even to the point of excommunicating parishioners whose views differ.[52] And in his household, even his sometimes-rebellious youngest daughter Lydia (who does wear earrings) frowns, in a very properly pietistic way, on wine at dinner and on the loose conduct of a recent Augustana graduate seen taking part in an opera.

Besides treading the difficult path of virtue, the child Anna found much to frighten her in her growing-up years. As both she and Inez Rundstrom could testify, Kansas was a raw and inhospitable environment during the years they lived there (1869–1883 for Rundstrom; 1869-1876 for Olsson). Anna describes the many things that "scare" her[53]: a "pretty ribbon" on her father's desk that turns out to be a poisonous snake (fearless father kills it).[54] The "black funnel of a cyclone that reaches from the sky to the river and spins around so fast, so fast," leaving an aftermath of "dead hens lying in the water puddles." Grasshopper swarms thick as rain.[55] Her father's frequent absences visiting his parishioners and her mother's fear of the "scary" things on the prairie undoubtedly contributed to the anxiety of a watchful, sensitive child. And beyond fear of the threatening physical environment, worry about her own future loomed. She yearned to know more than the small local Swedish school could teach her. "I play that the attic is my study, even though there are no book shelves in it and no writing desk and no chair...only spider webs and a wasp nest and two dead grasshoppers," she recounts. But "when I am grown up I shall have a room full of books."[56] Later, in her teens, she notes in her journal that after hearing a lecture on "the importance of the mind" she felt "like I wanted to study more than I think I have ever felt before....I thirst for a knowledge of philosophy."[57]

She was luckier than most women of her day with such a thirst and such a dream. "Papa" (whom she revered throughout her life) certainly supported her academic aspirations, not only at Augustana, but later, during her post-graduate "grand tour" of Europe, when he showed her "testimonials"—what we'd call her college transcript—to one of the professors at the University of Zurich. Anna reports ecstatically on the professor's verdict: "He said that with [these credentials] I could enter the university as a regular student. Oh! How my heart did jump at such a prospect!"[58]

Unlike Inez Rundstrom, who left her father and sister in Lindsborg to study at Augustana, Anna Olsson came with her family. She was just ten when her father, somewhat reluctantly, it appears, accepted a professorship

in the Augustana Seminary, and they took the train journey Rundstrom
was to follow a few years later. Anna describes it from the child's point of
view, an experience alternately pleasant and startling: the train "is a long
cradle that rocks first to one side, then to the other. Then it shakes and we
hit our heads against the small sofa we sit on." The new venue produced
a similarly mixed reaction. Accustomed as she was to clean prairie air, the
"bad black smoke" from factories in nearby Moline—"smoke, smoke,
smoke, all day long"—seemed almost intolerable.[59] However alien it felt at
first, though, the Moline-Rock Island area quickly became home. And the
heart of that home was Augustana College.

She attended first the Academy (a preparatory high school)[60] then
associated with the college, and after that enrolled as a degree candidate at
Augustana. In those years the College offered various disciplinary options,
the forerunner of today's majors, called "courses." The term signified not
individual classes but rather a course of study. Two courses were offered:
either the scientific or the "philosophical." Anna chose the Philosophy
Course, which emphasized what we would now call the humanistic disciplines—languages, literature, history, and, of course, the philosophy
which, as she said, she "thirsted" for.

Determined to take full advantage of her education, Anna set herself a
rigorous daily schedule. This sample from 1883, when she's still listed in the
college catalogue as a "non-matriculated female student," is typical:

Study: 6–7
Morning work: 7–8
Botany: 8–9
German: 9–10
Sewing: 10–11
Practice instrumental music: 11–12
Geology: 12–1
Vocal music: 1–2
Study: 2–3
Mamma: 3–4
Latin: 4–5
Sewing: 5–6
Practice instrumental music: 7–8
Study: 8–9[61]

On other days, "sacred history," philosophy, and physical geography filled the slots.

Reviewing this daunting agenda, which makes a Ph.D. candidate's life look like a walk in the park, one wonders when the seventeen-year-old girl found time to eat, much less to enjoy any sort of normal social life. Granted, the proscriptions for female behavior were stringent; an advertisement for "Ladies Hall" stated emphatically that "girls…who care more for fun and shallow enjoyments than for real knowledge and culture and solid worth, are not wanted here."[62] Even so, Anna's activities seem almost obsessively earnest. Perhaps the plan represented an ideal more than defining actual practice. Still, to judge by her subsequent academic success, she can't have deviated from it much or often.

And what kind of a reception would such a serious woman student have met at Augustana during the late 1880s? According to one woman, Netta Bartholomew Anderson, who matriculated the year Anna graduated, not a very cordial one. As she recalled fifty years later, "…we [women] were not welcome as students and in fact were only tolerated in classrooms…. [W]e were frankly told that while they loved us as girls, they did not care for us as students."[63] She doesn't make clear who "they" were—presumably both faculty and students.

Anna's experience seems to have differed considerably—at least in her recollection. But she records those school memories just two years after her graduation, so clearly the events haven't vanished altogether in the sentimental mists of old age. Anna remembers "the beloved hill, on which stands the dear, old school-building….the old bridge….my old stump, where I used to sit and learn my lessons….What a sweet memory school times are! It was such a happy time, in spite of hard work, and long lessons….How I <u>do long</u> for the time when 'we clamb the hill thegither!'" It's hard to imagine that the kind of discrimination Netta Anderson records would make for a "happy time" and "sweet memories," or that she'd quote Burns' line "we clamb the hill thegither [*together*]"—italics mine—[64] if she'd felt herself a barely tolerated loner disconnected from the social and intellectual life of the school. Perhaps her own experience of what Anderson called the "old world tradition of regarding education for women a waste of time and money" made her grateful for her opportunities, rather than resentful of the discrimination that might have made her only grudgingly accepted. Or possibly a gentler, more acquiescent nature disposed her to relish what she was able to do, rather than rebelling against what she felt excluded from.

How much her college experience meant to her can perhaps be judged by what happened to her in the middle of it. In that rigorous schedule noted above, each day includes an entry poignant in retrospect: "Help mamma" or simply "mamma." Those entries came to an abrupt end in 1887 when her mother died. The event shook the family. Her father, always sensitive and fragile, was devastated. He looked to her for practical, and we may imagine, some emotional support. So amid her own grief Anna was now expected to assume her mother's position: domestic manager, surrogate professor's "wife," guide and disciplinarian to her younger siblings, sisters Maria (Mia) and Lydia, and brother Johannes. She took these responsibilities seriously, as Lydia's teenage journals make clear. (They also make clear that, though fundamentally good-hearted, Lydia was a typical adolescent.) Unspecified problems with the youngest child and only boy, Hannes, made additional demands. Small wonder that the death haunted her: "Today it is four years ago since our dear mama died. That night comes so vividly before me now, as I sit here writing by the dining room table," she records in her journal on March 18, 1891. She lost both mother and her own girlhood.

Yet, despite these seismic shifts in her life, she managed to graduate from Augustana in 1888—just a year after her mother's death. In a college whose enrollment totaled 66, she is the only woman listed as a degree candidate. Her commitment to study in the midst of personal crisis tells much about her passion, and, perhaps, about her sources of consolation. In the life of the mind she could find not just forgetfulness but order and context for her personal suffering. And it suggests, too, that Augustana supported her in these intellectual and spiritual excursions.

Her mother's death, however, created an acute tension between the life of the mind she longed to pursue and the domestic "womanly" responsibilities she was compelled to assume (and to some degree certainly wished to assume). The crowded agenda of her school days negotiated between these two roles: the scholar (geology and Latin and study) and the domestic woman (sewing and help mamma). And the conflicting demands tormented Anna, often to a pain she could barely articulate. Clearly it included both yearning that she couldn't deny or fault, and yet a guilt for the dissatisfaction that yearning produced. The year abroad—Holland, Germany, Switzerland, Italy, and of course Sweden—glorious as it was, was shadowed by this conflict. "Oh! I am so delighted with Europe!" she exclaimed[65]—with its art, its culture, its opportunities for attending lectures in philosophy and literature. But immediately after recording her joy in the possibility of "entering the university [of Zurich] as a regular student," she adds, "If it were not...that I would be unable to attend to my duties at home, I would immediately enter!"[66] The competing pulls between study and home duties intensified after her return to the United States, when Olof Olsson became pastor of Bethany Lutheran Church in Woodhull, Illinois.

Woodhull is a charming small town that looks almost the same today as it did in 1890. Its narrow streets criss-cross among tall last-century houses. Midwestern skies preside with both drama and serenity over roof-tops, apple trees, lilac bushes, and cornfields. Anna would have walked along the shaded streets, savored "the apple blossoms and the soft green grass" of May and the "snow cover[ing] the ground and the ever-greens right outside the house" in winter.[67] In the deep silences of the country night, she'd stay up late, reading and writing in her journal.

Pastor Olsson's church still commands the corner of 3rd Avenue and 4th Street. Here he was called to rebuild a congregation torn by schism. In this demanding assignment, he needed domestic stability.

So for Anna, though Woodhull meant rural beauty which her heart embraced, it meant also hard labor, and intellectual and cultural aridity. "In the midst of my daily toil, washing dishes, sweeping, ironing, baking, the wish to study becomes so strong that I have a hard struggle before I can quiet the storm in my heart....My feet pain me very much....I have not sat down all day....There is a great difference between 'Rome, April 3, 1890' and 'Woodhull, April 3, 1891.'" It seems unlikely that she received much active support or encouragement in her dreams of study. Students remem-bered Olof Olsson as "an esteemed fatherly friend" who offered considered and "tender" advice. But Anna's journal entries suggest that, while conven-tionally affectionate, her father was absent from her inner life. That is per-haps understandable. Struggling to heal a congregation, finishing a book of his own, fragile physically and still mourning his wife, Olof Olsson would have had little time or energy for listening to the dreams of a daughter whose future he undoubtedly believed would center in the domestic scene. Anna talks of making shirts for her father, not of discussing the fact that she's reading Sophocles—in German.

Part of the "storm in her heart" revolved around faith: what God wanted her to do, how she could discern God's will. "Some years ago I... said I had no wish to try to teach, but now—I would like to try very much," she confides to her journal.[68] "But I must wait until my chance comes. If it is God's will that I shall get a position, I shall get one." She continues to wish for more knowledge of philosophy, for what worlds it can open to her, for how it can school her dreams and desires, and she records her delight in discovering a pamphlet by the Swedish philosopher (and ardent Christian) Karl Pontus Wikner (1837-1888) that assures her "philosophy is no empty thing, no Phenomenon, that has its origin in a vain mind, but that it is a thing divine. And now,—is there any hope for me…to have a glimpse at those truths which philosophy reveals to us?"[69] Where, in her present life which stretched into a monotony so seamless that "we often forget what day it is,"[70] where was the voice of God?

The answer seemed clear in March 1891, when Olsson, weary but willing, agreed to become Augustana College's third president on the death of T. N. Hasselquist. Anna was ecstatic. This was what she had hoped for, prayed for, schooled herself to wait for. It was homecoming. And it promised the life she wanted.

Did it fulfill that promise?

Her journals end here, and none of her subsequent writing tells.

The administrative stresses of the presidency weakened Olof Olsson's already precarious health, and in May of 1900 he died. The following autumn Anna and her siblings moved into the new house built for them just a block east of the Augustana campus. Here they lived out the rest of their lives together.

Like Inez Rundstrom, Anna Olsson eschewed the then conventional role of wife and mother (in fact, none of the Olsson children married). Olsson's reasons for this choice seem more ambiguous than those of the scholar-teacher Rundstrom. One story that circulated among Augustana friends was that Olof Olsson had exacted a promise from his children to remain single, presumably because of some genetic defect he wished not to be passed along. Yet such a story is hard to credit in view of what Anna and her sister Lydia record in their journals. Both explicitly imagine marriage for themselves, Lydia with a specific person, Anna in more theoretical terms. She sets out in her journals what she deemed the ideal husband: "I should wish that he would let me be the sharer of all his little and great joys and sorrows. And I want him to let me keep up some of my studies, and to teach and study with me (when he is not too tired of course). In the meantime I would keep the home pleasant and when any concerts or lectures take place, I should want him to remember that his wife wanted him to take her and go sometimes. Now, I don't think I am unreasonable....If I ever get married, and get a good husband, and by that I mean a <u>noble, educated,</u> man <u>loving with some feeling</u>, I shall try (and I don't think it will be very difficult) to be so <u>good</u> to him. I wonder if I ever shall find such a man...."[71] Anna was almost 24 when she wrote this—"one more year," she laments, "and I will be an old maid!"[72] If indeed Olsson had wished to prohibit his children from marrying, one would imagine he'd have gotten around to mentioning it sooner.

A likelier story is that Anna didn't find the man of her dreams, even though, according to Lydia Olsson's journal,[73] she received proposals from a variety of distinguished suitors, several of whom went on to become leaders in church and college. "I don't know anyone I should trust enough to marry," Anna muses during that twenty-fourth summer. Trust enough for what? To really share with her "all his little and great joys and sorrows"? To "let [her] keep up some of [her] studies" which "I...love...so much that it would almost break my heart to have to give them up entirely"?[74] Perhaps her ideas of marital equality were simply too advanced for her day and for the men who courted her. Perhaps by the time these opportunities presented themselves—when she was about 27, if Lydia's account is to be trusted—Anna was absorbed in her own professional aspirations. Or possibly she believed duty as well as affection required her to stay at home and care for her father and her three siblings—each of whom, in various ways, seemed to need special tending. In 1890 she had written that "I love my sisters and brother and papa too much to part from them yet."[75] By the time her father died ten years later, Anna was in charge; the new home became the Anna Olsson House (even though it would be nearly twenty more years before she could exercise the political and economic power of the vote), and her journal confidences had ceased. Whatever her thinking, despite the compelling reasons for women to marry at that time—social position, economic security, the bearing of children—she chose to remain single.

So her status suggests not default but determination. And possibly, sacrifice.

In her home at 3012 – 8th Avenue, Anna Olsson launched and conducted her career.

She didn't continue her study of philosophy—at least, not professionally. Except for a few short periods of teaching English at Augustana, she maintained no formal association with academia. Instead, she became a writer. She wrote fiction and what we now call creative nonfiction, in both Swedish (under the name of "Aina") and English, principally for children. Her work appeared in church-related periodicals such as *The Lutheran Companion* and under the imprimatur of the Augustana Book Concern and other houses specializing in Swedish-American literature.

For most literary historians today her reputation rests on *En prärieunges funderingar*, mainly for its historical-cultural significance.[76] The book belongs to a genre produced during the high tide of Scandinavian immigration, mid-to-late nineteenth century, when first-generation immi-

grants sought to capture for those still in the "home" country some of the experiences they encountered and the struggles they faced in the new land.[77] Anna's vivid accounts written from the child's viewpoint give direct, accessible pictures of the immigrant life. The book succeeded well enough that in 1927 she translated it as *I'm Scairt*, an attempt to replicate not only the child's voice but her sometimes uneasy seesaw between Swedish and English. A translation produced at Bethany College in 1978 (titled *A Child of the Prairie*) gives a better impression of the text and of Anna's literary skills. She was proud of the book; she gave it to friends, carefully preserved their appreciative thank-you notes, and knew one

Anna Olsson. Her book *En prärieunges funderingar* brought her international recognition.

of the greatest honors of her life when Archbishop Nathan Soderblom and his wife sought out the author of *En prärieunges funderingar* on a visit to Rock Island, to tell her how much they had enjoyed the book. Anna made at least one late attempt, six years before her death, to interest a major periodical (*Reader's Digest*) in reissuing it.[78]

Her short stories demonstrate a command of craftsmanship in their well-controlled pace and rhythm, but lack the complexity of first-rate fiction. Stereotypical characters, strong reliance on dialect, and predictable, heavily moralistic denouements are their stock in trade.[79] In none of them do we find the conflict of her own life embodied with the passion that fills her journals. Whatever resolution she reached, as she sat at her desk covering long pages with her beautiful shaded handwriting, she reached in the silence and privacy of her own heart.

And yet she may have left a clue. "…when I write these lines, I forget that I am in Woodhull," her journal records, "I am brought back to Roma, I see the Cupola of St. Peter, I enter it and I go to each statue…. As I stand there, the marble seems to get life,…to tell me a tale of the wonders of the world,…of the beautiful in art…."[80]

As a writer, as a woman, Anna Olsson loved the wonders of the world and the beautiful in art. To write of "the silvery-white frost on the walls [that] shone so beautifully when the lamp was lit…the sun go[ing] down behind the Bluffs…candles in the church windows…the lights of the village gleaming through the rain and mist…Papa's choir singing…."[81] was perhaps to forget privation in the moment, to live the life of richness her mind and spirit craved, and to be brought, as her father was brought by music, into the presence of divine mystery.

Those who recall her in her age picture a gentle eccentric, a tall angular woman who, with her sister, would sometimes ice skate down the river to attend services at First Lutheran Church in Moline; whose pride refused gifts of food, even when (as was frequently the case) Olsson means were straitened; a woman who, with her sisters, revered her father and his memory.[82] Perhaps that reverence explains why, when she was interviewed by an Augustana student in 1939, she wanted this message passed along to "school girls": "It is more fun to bake a nice loaf of bread than to get a good mark in Greek."[83] That doesn't sound much like the young woman who vowed she could never give up studying; who found housework a weary interposition between her and her books. But her father had loved and served Augustana, she had loved her time there[84], and perhaps in the changing world of the thirties she opted for caution and tradition rather than for risk and challenge. Still, it's a little disappointing to hear this statement as the gathered wisdom of her later years.

Doris Quist Anderson, Class of 1941, spent afternoons of her childhood in the Olsson home; her mother was a friend and neighbor. Anderson recalls being allowed to play with the exquisite china and crystal objects displayed in the china cabinet: "I could take them out and put them on the dining table. I was very, very careful, but still—it was wonderful of them to let a child do that."[85] I wonder if Anna was recalling her own childhood on the prairie, when beautiful things were rare and prized, and seeking in this way to give another little girl the gift of beauty—beauty that could reshape a life.

Anna Olsson died February 15, 1946.

"Struggling for a College Education": Anna Westman

She's like a face seen through opaque glass. The contours are there; the features indistinct. Her story is implication rather than data. And that's ironic, since Anna Westman occupies a special niche in Augustana College history: she was the first woman on Augustana's faculty.

She was born Anna Lovisa Wessman on January 7, 1863, in Saby, Jonkoping, Sweden, one of seven children. Unlike Inez Rundstrom and Anna Olsson, she didn't have the advantages of a professional-class background; her father, Anders Wessman, was a farmer. The family emigrated to Chicago in 1868, when Anna was five; her younger brother Axel Theodor was born there. Then, like many of their countrymen, they made their way west, to the rich prairies and the booming factories of Illinois along the Mississippi River. So it's likely that the children grew up doing their share of hard work in cold winter mornings and hot summer afternoons.

She was twenty-three, older than either Rundstrom or Olsson, when she enrolled in Augustana's Preparatory Department. Two years later she matriculated at Augustana College. She was late coming to advanced education because she'd struggled to manage tuition payments (at that time a whopping $41 dollars a year),[86] and possibly also fought resistance from a family unused to the idea of higher learning for women. By 1885 her mother, Ulrika Kristina Westman, was a widowed seamstress living in a boarding house a few blocks from the railroad tracks in Moline, Illinois, the town immediately east of Rock Island. At Mrs. Westman's unexpected death four years later her landlord described her as "very poor."[87] Anna clearly could not have expected or received much financial help from her.

But somehow she made it to college. And once there, she elected the "scientific course"—that is, major. Her choice of study is noteworthy because it was somewhat unusual for women of that era; the ability of the "softer sex" to handle traditionally "masculine" fields such as science was still being debated both in and out of the academy. Yet Augustana evidently did not discourage her from undertaking this program.

The rigorous, balanced curriculum she embarked on was part of a legacy left by the distinguished Swedish scientist and professor Josua Lindahl, who came to Augustana in 1880 and went on to become Illinois State geologist eight years later.[88] Westman's courses would have included natural history, physics, chemistry, anatomy, and geology; one of her classes would actually have been historical geology, long before the church-versus-academy furor of the Scopes trial.

Ultimately Westman chose to concentrate on mathematics. So she would have studied with the legendary Andrew Woods Williamson, professor of mathematics and astronomy, a teacher respected for his knowledge, loved for his generosity to students in need, and appreciated for his eccentricities, such as talking and gesturing to himself as he strode across campus, and keeping a pocketful of salted peanuts to munch when the spirit moved him. His pedagogical method stressed reasoning skills rather than rote memorization; his idea of education emphasized awakening the imagination to undreamed-of marvels. He shared President Olof Olsson's view that mathematics is a "great" study which "embrac[es] all the external universe"—a universe whose grandeur reflects God its creator. Students, even mathematical novices who tried his patience, remembered the force of Williamson's personality and the strength of his vision.[89] An excellent student such as Westman, spending many hours in his classes, could hardly fail to be impressed by what he offered.

Anna Westman with her graduating class of 1892

And a vision large enough to encompass life in both its beauty and its brutality was something she soon came to need. In late November of 1889, her mother, returning from a visit to a downtown tailor for whom she did "piece work," was killed in a freak accident.

It was a little after 5:00 on a Saturday evening. Early winter dusk had set in. Carrying her bag and lifting her skirts to make her way across the railroad tracks at the Fifteenth Street crossing, Ulrika Westman was concentrating, perhaps, on the work ahead of her; the promised payment (would it cover the cost of the week's groceries?); her weariness at the end of a long week; the rails she had to cross, gleaming faintly ahead of her. She didn't hear the box car switching tracks, didn't hear the flagman's shout:

"Stop! Look out for the cars!" The box car hit her. It was a "flying car," detached from the engine, and it had dragged her about sixty feet before the brakeman could stop it. When the railroad men and a passing witness ran to the body, they found grisly mutilations.[90]

The graphic details of her death that appeared repeatedly, and with almost ghoulish zest, in the local papers must have given Anna great pain. But perhaps, as she walked into the First Lutheran Church on the following Thursday afternoon for Mrs. Westman's funeral and saw pews "completely packed with sympathizing friends of the bereaved family," and looked to the altar, lined with "very beautiful floral tributes,"[91] she would have found comfort.

How the event affected her in practical terms is hard to tell—probably not much. She was already used to scraping together money for her education, possibly even, if any funds were left over, helping a younger brother studying music in Chicago.

But in 1891 her situation eased. A position opened as "Lady Principal" of Augustana's dormitory for women, and Westman was named to it. Obviously her scholastic performance and personal responsibility led the college to make this choice. Possibly Williamson, always concerned for the needs of students, had suggested her. So in her senior year Anna Westman found herself in charge of a dormitory descriptively—and prescriptively—called Ladies Hall (see below). Regulations included studying diligently, observing strict curfews, and confining one's social intercourse to women only.

That appointment began Anna Westman's professional association with Augustana College. But it wasn't a smooth journey.

To begin with, she initially refused the job offer.

An impoverished student attending a college whose own finances often teetered precariously toward debit should have found this offer a pretty good deal. But, in the elegantly theological language of the Board of Directors Minutes, Miss Westman "declined the call." What was she thinking?

Two issues apparently drove her decision. One was concern about the location of Ladies Hall, then situated against the hill and ravine on 35th Street, a remote venue that threatened safety and "invit[ed] misdemeanors." But the other issue was financial. A month after noting her refusal, the Board Minutes report that the committee in charge of "engaging" the Lady Principal "succeeded in getting Miss Anna Westman to reconsider her action, and [she has] now accepted the former call extended to her."[92]

Not, actually, quite the former call. In addition to free room and board, the new package included tuition and a salary of fifty dollars a year. The wording of the Minutes sounds as if "Miss Westman" drove a tough bargain.

It's an extraordinary exchange. Still a student, the only woman in her graduating class, she refused to accept the terms of the men who ran the college. Evidently she placed a higher value on her service and her needs than they were originally prepared to recognize. And she stuck to it. It's tempting to imagine the reactions of those men, a stern and frowning lot with mouths that looked as if they'd been driven in with a staple gun. Were they shocked? Outraged? Did they concede reluctantly? Or did her demands call to their sense of justice, of fair play? Easy as it is to look at their rigidly joyless photographs and see social and political inflexibility, we need to keep in mind something perhaps as extraordinary as Anna's demand: they hired her as the first woman faculty member *after* this exchange.

From all we can tell, she was good at her job as Lady Principal. Certainly she'd have faced some challenges in upholding the high standards of conduct set out in the Ladies Hall prospectus. The journals of Lydia Olsson, President Olsson's youngest daughter, suggest that decorum was occasionally resisted.[93] However, Lydia, at that time a flirtatious teenager little interested in study, was perhaps not typical of Ladies Hall denizens.

Whatever disciplinary issues Westman faced, her guidance seems wisely to have balanced moral and intellectual earnestness with the spirited fun necessary to healthy young women. They may have studied diligently—Anna certainly did—but they also formed parties to skate on the river, make Saturday excursions downtown to buy shoes and dress material, or, in cases of budgetary shortfall, just to window shop. They attended lectures and concerts together, and for relaxation gathered in the evening for Parcheesi (after the obligatory 7 p.m. devotions), or to talk and giggle and dream their way through sewing circles. Even after Westman had joined the faculty she continued to make one of these parties. "The girls" would gather "up at Miss Westman's room" for nuts, apples, and candy as they sewed.[94] And Westman wasn't above joining in on college pranks. Around Halloween of 1896, for instance, she and the Olsson sisters put on "ugly dresses, shawls, and clothes on their heads and call[ed] on" one of the professors.[95]

And certainly the obstacles she'd struggled against and the grief she'd experienced in her life had equipped her with courage. In her journal Lydia

Olsson recounts that one night at 11:00 (after lights out) a "mean fellow who scares the girls" threw rocks at Westman's window. Anna dressed, went to the window, and talked to him. By the time a couple of available men, including Hannes Olsson who lived in the other part of the house, had been summoned and organized themselves for action, "the fellow had evaporated."[96]

Disciplined, quietly spunky, firm, committed to study and *en rapport* with undergraduates, Anna Westman would seem naturally fitted for a career in college teaching. Perhaps Professor Williamson recommended her for a faculty position. (Maybe it was no accident that another gifted mathematics major, Inez Rundstrom, Augustana's first woman graduate, ended up teaching at Gustavus Adolphus, where Williamson himself had spent three years.) What seems obvious is that Westman's academic credentials would have been outstanding to enable her to join the traditionally all-male faculty.

Her accomplishment is even more impressive in view of her background. The first woman faculty member at Augustana College came from a large and poor immigrant working-class family—a ground-breaking and history-making event, indeed.

She graduated in 1892 and began teaching the following fall. She was designated as "instructor of mathematics" in the college catalogue, and as "assistant teacher" in the Board Minutes. These terms seem to be interchangeable. But the term used for her during her second tenure, "assistant," appears to mean something else.

She taught at Augustana from 1892-1894, and from 1896-1897. At that time Augustana included a post-graduate program, and Westman took advantage of this opportunity for advanced study. From 1892–1893, in addition to her teaching responsibilities, she studied for the A.M. in English, with minors in Italian and Philosophy. There's no record of her having completed that degree, but she must have used it in teaching. Evidently her mind was comprehensive, her interests eclectic, and her energy high.

So much seems reasonably clear. But from here on questions shadow her story.

Her duties for 1892-93 included continuing to serve as Lady Principal as well as teaching. For this work she received free room and fifty dollars a month. Her salary equalled that of another new male hired in her rank (professors at the time were making anywhere from eight hundred to twelve hundred dollars a year)—though, of course, her male counterpart would have had neither the dormitory duties nor the free lodging. Teaching loads, also, were comparable: 12 hours for "instructors" or "assistant teachers." Professors were handling up to 27 hours. (In terms of Anna's story, it may be noteworthy that her former professor, Williamson, found his loads so staggering as to require periodic rest breaks to restore his health.)

The point here is that Anna seems to have been hired as a "regular" faculty member, without gender discrimination.

The following year, 1893-94, Anna's salary was raised to sixty dollars a month, and her teaching load increased to 36 hours for the year—19 in the first term, 17 in the second. And her academic responsibilities were widened; now she taught not only arithmetic and algebra, but also English and history. And this, apparently, proved to be too much. There's evidence that, like the chronically overworked Williamson, she'd become ill. Still, when offered a position for the next academic year, 1894-95, she tried to negotiate. She "declined the call extended to her unless the Board saw fit to increase her salary or reduce her hours of teaching one half."[97]

Anna Westman and Augustana classmates—probably at their 15th reunion

And this time the Board didn't see fit.

Again, the facts provide more questions than answers. Had she gone too far with her demands? Did her gender influence the Board's decision? That may be too facile an hypothesis. Other professors routinely petitioned for salary raises from the notoriously frugal college, and not all of those petitions were rejected. Some were.

Or was the reason for the thumbs-down simply a financial one? Was there no room for negotiation? Or was Anna too young, too new in her academic career, to merit stretching the budget to meet her demands?

The Board Minutes express no regret at her leaving, as they sometimes do in the case of faculty who resign. And the Board worked quickly to secure a replacement for her: the same meeting that reports her letter asking for these concessions reports the calling of her (male) successor.

Again: what was Anna thinking? That negotiation had worked once, and she'd try again? That she was of sufficient value to the college that it would accede to her demands? Or did she understand bargaining to be simply part of the hiring procedure?

Whatever the story, it was handled decorously in the local press. The *Rock Island Argus* reports: "The board of trustees of Augustana, at a meeting held Friday, issued a call to Joshua Larson of the class of '89, to fill the position made vacant by the resignation of Miss Anna Westman."[98] As in the Minutes, the announcement from the Board is purely neutral, no expression of disappointment for her leaving or of gratitude for her service is recorded. But the article goes on to say, "The many friends of Miss Westman will regret to know that she has been compelled to take this step on account of ill health." It's interesting that despite this unspecified illness, she seems to have been prepared to carry on with the teaching if her compensation were increased.

And in view of both her compromised health and her monetary problems, her next move seems rather astonishing. She went off to the University of Berlin for part of her "gap" year. What she hoped to accomplish there (apart from personal and intellectual enrichment) isn't clear. Evidently she was finding restored health, though not by lounging around in some pricey spa. In fact, she was "working very hard...with my French and soon I shall begin German lessons." This activity seemed to agree with her. Writing in March of 1895 to her friend Netta Bartholomew, she confides that "I hardly dare say it, for fear the saying of it will break the charm, but for the last two or three weeks I have been feeling remarkably well. I can read and study all day long without the former consequence."[99] And what did she expect to do with all this earnest study when she returned to the States? The March 1895 letter suggests the puzzling possibility that she believed she'd be resuming her teaching at Augustana: "Since I am beginning to feel my old energy returning, I am at the same time beginning to long being back to my work in America," she writes, adding that she'll no doubt soon feel "real homesick." What work did she mean?

By 1896 she is back at Augustana, listed as an "assistant" in the English Department. The Board Minutes are silent on how this happened. But perhaps the Board had nothing to do with this arrangement. In the early years of the college, "assistant" seemed to be rather an amorphous term—students, for example, were often listed in the catalogue (in the faculty section) as "assistants." Both Conrad Bergendoff, later to become Augustana's fifth president, and Fritiof Fryxell, who would return to his alma mater to create the geology department, spent part of their undergraduate years in this category. So perhaps the arrangement with Anna was a private one. Her friend Netta Bartholomew was the daughter of Dr. Edward Fry Bartholomew, whose voice, both literally and figuratively, was a powerful one on the faculty. And Dr. Bartholomew chaired the English Department.

Not surprisingly, Anna returned from her sojourn so financially strapped that she offered the college library an American Encyclopedia worth $130, "she to allow part of the same to be applied to the payment of her board and room-rent at the school."[100] In these circumstances, any job would doubtless be welcome.

At the end of her second term on the faculty, in 1897, however, Anna Westman left both Augustana and academia. And, ill as she was, she pulled up stakes and moved to Cleveland, Ohio. She was thirty-four, middle-aged at a time when unmarried women were deemed old maids at twenty-five, and as far as we know, alone in the world.

Was she "real homesick" when she left the place she'd lived most of her life? Why did she go to Cleveland? She came from a large family, and perhaps had relatives there. If so, she didn't live with them. Whatever her reasons for moving, she made an entirely new life, working first as an accountant and later, until her death, as a retail florist.[101]

Or perhaps that life wasn't entirely new. In some ways Cleveland may have offered different ways of pursuing old interests. One of her housemates, the blind singer and voice teacher Almeda C. Adams,[102] could have provided her with intellectual and aesthetic stimulation, a sort of grown-up version of her Ladies Hall days. If indeed Adams were the "enchanting, whimsical, amusing speaker" she's depicted to be in a brochure from the Redpath Chatauqua,[103] she and Westman must have enjoyed satisfying conversations. Westman was deeply moved by music; she herself was an amateur singer, a member of the women's Philodi quartet at Augustana. And her brother's advanced study of music suggests an inherited ability, perhaps from their father who was a drummer in the Swedish army. Possibly Adams introduced her to her own musical circles, and to other women who shared intellectual interests. She and Adams may have discussed an exciting project Adams was contemplating, which came to fruition two years after Westman's death: the Cleveland Music School Settlement, created to "provide high quality music education to students of all ages regardless of their ability to pay." (Originally supported by wealthy donors whom Adams managed to interest, the school still flourishes.)[104] Clearly the two women shared a passion for education and for giving opportunities to gifted students of modest means. However, if she knew about it, Westman did not live to see the success of this plan: she died August 1, 1910.[105]

The final enigma of Anna Westman's life offers perhaps a shaft of light on what may seem a bleak and inconclusive story. She appears to have left Augustana without bitterness. She returned, bespectacled and chubby-cheeked, with a rather wild upswept do of her now-white hair, and an engaging, alert smile, to what was probably her fifteenth class reunion (the photo bears no date). She looks neither ill, nor angry, nor cynical—just, perhaps, gently ironic.

It seems odd and a little sad that the first woman faculty member at Augustana taught for so very short a time, and that her professional tenure was marked by tensions with the institution. And yet in that time— not even one student generation—she left behind the legacy of her vision for equal educational opportunity, and a loving appreciation for her own efforts to realize this vision. The following announcement first appears in the Augustana College catalogue for 1912–1913:

The Anna Westman Stipend

On February 10, 1911 [one year after Westman's death], the sum of fifty dollars was received by the college faculty, accompanied by a communication from a lady who wished no public mention to be made of her name, stating that she obligated herself "to donate annually, for an indefinite period of years, a sum of money to be used as a benefit to one or more deserving, industrious lady students pursuing studies in the Collegiate department of Augustana College, the beneficiaries to be chosen by a committee of College faculty."

It was further stated that "this fund shall be known as the 'Anna Westman Stipend,' being given as an appreciative memorial to Miss Westman, who was the friend and helper of young women struggling, like herself, to obtain a college education," and further, that "this fund shall be announced annually on January 7ᵗʰ, the date of Miss Westman's birth, or as soon thereafter as is possible."[106]

The anonymous donor maintained this stipend for a decade.

It's a moving tribute. It honors a woman committed to education for all women, "regardless of their ability to pay," and suggests that Westman herself made education possible for the women she knew and taught. It implies, also, that, at least in the donor's mind, Augustana College was a fitting place for women to pursue the kinds of dreams Anna Westman helped them to shape.

Fairview Academy: Mother's Family Business

Just before the first women began to enter Augustana College, provisions were being made for women's education across the street from the Rock Island campus.

It happened partly by default, partly by deliberate commitment to a vision. Professor Henry Reck, who'd joined the English faculty in 1871 and became instrumental in assisting the growth of the college whether in finances or flowers (he landscaped the Rock Island campus and appealed for fencing to keep the cows from trampling his plants), contracted "a

The legacy of Fairview Academy: high culture and hi-jinks. Fairview encouraged both earnest study and celebration of life, a vision embodied by these Augustana women students of a later generation.

lingering illness" and died in October of 1881. He left his widow and five children in severely reduced circumstances. Not that their situation had been precisely affluent before his death; they occupied living quarters in the first Old Main, an all-purpose building that housed classrooms, library, chapel, and band practice rooms, plus six professors and their families, as well as students. As Conrad Bergendoff comments, "one wonders at the close quarters of faculty families, but since 'house' was included in the salary arrangements, the economic factor outweighed the domestic deficiencies."[107]

At her husband's death, or slightly before, Anna Reck sought to augment their meager income by teaching neighborhood children, especially girls, from the Recks' basement apartment in Old Main. Her husband had returned to his home in Pennsylvania shortly before he died,[108] perhaps to seek more skilled medical attention than the river towns could provide, perhaps to explore ways of securing some help for his family. Whatever drove him, the parting between the husband and wife that fall day, each no doubt trying to encourage the other with words of hope and faith, must have been poignant.

Anna Reck was no novice at teaching. As Miss Anna Merring she'd not only taught in private eastern schools, but opened her own academy in Baltimore.[109] However gifted she might have been pedagogically, though, it's hard to imagine a worse venue for keeping children's attention than a crowded apartment reverberant with droning student recitation, thundering chapel organ, crashing drum-bangs, and the wobbling hoots and whines of band rehearsal. In 1881, however, Anna Reck received a life-saving boost from the Augustana Synod. So beloved and admired was Professor Reck as "an earnest pastor, an able teacher, [and] an enthusiastic supporter of the college"[110] that the Synod granted his widow an interest-free loan of $2,719.38 to build a boarding school for girls.

This action certainly, and rightly, honors Henry Reck. But it also expresses considerable confidence in Anna Reck. And she justified that confidence. She built well both physically and academically. The four-story house perched on the southeast corner of what is now 7th Avenue and 38th Street offered a "striking and picturesque view" toward the far river, and the health benefits of fresh, clear air. From the assembly hall and classrooms on the first floor a long banistered stairway led up to the living quarters. (Girls were known to slide down that banister in bursts of high spirits.[111]) The new institution was named Fairview Academy. And by 1885, the year Inez Rundstrom graduated from Augustana, it was a family business. Mrs. Reck and three of her children comprised the majority of the seven-person faculty.

Fairview certainly aspired to give its students a "fair view" of the world they would enter, whether workaday or academic. According to the first and only catalogue issued in 1885-1886, a discreetly elegant brochure covered in smooth dark teal, Fairview took its motto from Psalm 144:9: "that our daughters may be as corner-stones, polished after the similitude of a palace." "Under the auspicies of the Evangelical Lutheran Church," its object was "to train young ladies, not only intellectually, but also morally, socially and physically, and to fit them for usefulness in whatever sphere of life they may be placed."[112] Anna Reck could understand with painful clarity the importance of an education for women that would give them some direction when life didn't work out as they'd planned.

The Catalogue describes an ambitious agenda of study. Fairview consisted of two divisions, each three years long: the Preparatory and the Academic, perhaps corresponding to junior high and high school today. Students were offered courses in English language and literature, history, Latin, Rhetoric, German, French, geography, geology, Christianity, physiology, chemistry, mathematics, mental and moral philosophy, and bookkeeping, plus optional art and music lessons. And to keep them fit for these strenuous endeavors, Calisthenics.[113] Graduates had to demonstrate proficiency in Latin and either French or German; or, if they preferred to concentrate on modern languages, both French and German.[114] The "young ladies" would be well prepared for a liberal arts college such as Augustana, should they be able to continue their education. And bookkeeping would provide a valuable entrée to the world of work.

Moral as well as intellectual development received attention. Rules were to be followed, but the real aim was "to develop the principle of self-government, the basis of all good government. We try to train our pupils to act from a high sense of honor and duty; to abhor wrong and love right; and at all times to be governed by the principles of a cultured society," says the Catalogue. To this end self-adornment is discouraged. "School is not the place to exhibit costly wardrobes."[115]

Students followed a daily regime Benjamin Franklin would have approved. They rose at six and retired at ten; attended "study and recitation" sessions from 9:15 until 12:15 and from 1:30 until 3:30; began and ended the day with fifteen-minute prayers, and were expected to attend church on Sundays with their "lady principal."[116]

Expenses ran to $170 a year for tuition and board (day pupils paid $40 for tuition in the Academy and $30 for the Preparatory department), with reductions for ministers' daughters and "others at the Principal's discretion." Music or art lessons would cost $40 more, with a ten-dollar charge for use of the piano.[117]

But for all its earnestness of purpose, Fairview Academy didn't shun lively, even occasionally outrageous, hi-jinks. Students and faculty both participated in plays. When male roles were needed, the young instructor Marguerite Shuey was deputed to "run over to the Augustana campus" and round up theatrically inclined men. On one occasion, Shuey (later Mrs. C. W. Foss) remembers, the dramatic offering *du jour* satirized an Augustana Commencement, and Fairview came under suspicion of "too much levity." So to placate the "longbeards on the college faculty" who objected, the next production was "extra pious." Mrs. Foss' description doesn't make it sound overly repentant, however.[118]

Despite—or perhaps because of—such episodes, Fairview succeeded. By 1885 about forty students were enrolled. Though most of them lived locally, a few came from the east coast, and one from as far away as Cuba.[119]

Anna Reck was the driving energy of Fairview Academy. And in fact, she died in its service. In 1886, returning from a trip east on behalf of the school, she was seized suddenly with appendicitis. Her death three days later from peritonitis meant "practically the end of Fairview Academy," Mrs. Foss recalls, "though [her] children kept it going one year longer."[120] The family business had depended upon mother.

That it must have been a dream and not simply an act of expediency seems evident from the clarity and earnestness of purpose expressed in the catalogue, and the efficient organization of the curriculum. So despite its relatively short life, Fairview Academy is worth remembering not only as a legacy of love for Professor Reck, but as a tribute to a woman with courage, energy, and vision, and as a tangible expression of belief in the importance of education for women—a belief endorsed, at least indirectly, by the Augustana Synod of the 1880s.

Ladies Hall

It was a physical symbol of the new college. Now, literally, at Augustana women had a place.

Walk through the center of today's campus, across sidewalks spidering over the Quad. Between Olin's west end and Hanson's south end is about where the first two faculty houses, built in 1878 and 1880 respectively, were located. Both were "rather modest" frame structures, according to Bergendoff; each cost around $1,500.[121] The second building became the first women's dormitory.

Just three years earlier Inez Rundstrom had made her (nearly) solitary way through a largely male college. Now, by 1888, enough women were enrolled either in the college or in the Commercial or Conservatory departments to warrant housing arrangements for them. The numbers weren't overwhelming: ten women in the college by 1891, more in the specialized departments. But to establish living quarters for "lady students who are desirous of acquiring a higher education,…and who prefer a home under the immediate auspices of the College"[122] certainly suggested that, institutionally at least, they were more than tolerated; they were welcomed and provided for.

They lived first in the home recently vacated by Professor Josua Lindahl. The Catalogue for 1890-91 describes it as "a neat frame building on 35th Street." Rooms were carpeted, furnished, lighted, and heated; residents provided their own bed linens, blankets, soap and towels and combs. In this pleasant venue backed by wooded hills "no effort will be spared to make the Hall an attractive home for the young ladies….The Hall is under the supervision of a Matron [the terminology changes from year to year] who lives in the same building and who is studiously attentive to the comfort, health, and general welfare of the young ladies."[123] In the first years, Professor Claude W. Foss and his wife, Marguerite Shuey Foss (she of Fairview Academy fame) served as the studious attendants.

This Edenic niche in the groves of academe wasn't without its own serpents, however. Writing in 1926, when the site of a new women's dormitory was being vigorously debated, Mrs. Foss asserts that "I think the worst possible location" would be 35th Street because the street wasn't cut through, making it too quiet and isolated, especially at night. Surrounded by "public buildings unoccupied [all night] and [to the south] wild woods, a high hill and a deep ravine," the Ladies Hall Mrs. Foss remembered offered "a

Tea in Ladies Hall

most inviting location for misdemeanors, to put it mildly." Under these circumstances, perhaps it wasn't too surprising that after only three years the Fosses resigned their supervisorship and moved to their own house. It's intriguing to speculate but difficult to know what responsibility the girls bore for these potential or actual "misdemeanors," and what that said about the residents of Ladies Hall (and girls generally!). Evidently Anna Westman, still a student when she "was called to succeed me [Mrs. Foss] as Lady Principal," understood the nature of the problems, because "she made her acceptance conditional upon the moving of the girls to a safer place,"[124] as we've seen in her story.

In 1891 Ladies Hall moved across campus, to the third college building, which had been erected in 1881. This, according to Bergendoff, was a "more ambitious" structure—"on the eastern edge of the campus, a double-house of frame with brick veneer"—costing the princely sum of $6,000.[125] Here the "ladies" shared space with President Olof Olsson and his family Anna, Mia, Lydia, and Johannes, who occupied the west wing.

If "misdemeanors" were a problem, the Catalogue copy certainly weighs in against them. "[G]irls…who care more for fun and shallow enjoyments than for real knowledge and culture and solid worth, are not wanted here," it states uncompromisingly.[126] No good-time girls need apply. Conversely, however, the new women's dormitory was hardly a seed-bed of bluestockings. Residents were expected to be…well, ladies. The steely gentility of Ladies Hall excluded "girls…who are unwilling to yield a ready and cheerful obedience to the regulations deemed necessary for the general good, who feel that they are above any rules of government." Such "girls" "are a nuisance in any sphere in life and doubly so at school." Activities deemed necessary "for the general good" included "evening... reading of scripture, prayer, and singing" (begun at 7 o'clock), and strict gender separation: "Ladies rooming at the Hall will not be allowed to have any company of the opposite sex. Those unwilling to comply with this regulation need not apply for rooms." (If you didn't live in Ladies Hall, by the way, you were pretty much on your own, as far as the administration was concerned. They'd assume "no responsibility for lady students rooming elsewhere beyond that involved in good scholarship and general deportment," the catalogue said.[127])

As late as 1915 the regimen was still fairly strict: up at 6 a.m., to the tune of a bell wielded by the "matron": breakfast at 7:00; classes from 8:00 till supper; evening study from 7:30 to 9:00; free time from 9:00 to lights out at 10:30, though if you were cramming for a test, you'd be allowed to study later.[128]

Yet in spite of tight regulations—maybe because of them—the denizens of these first women's dormitories seemed to enjoy living in Ladies Hall. The anonymous writer of a 1915 article, "Life at Ladies' *[sic]* Hall," certainly did. Even an outbreak of rats in 1911 didn't appear to quench the residents' high spirits, though it did make for some sleepless nights.[129] The presence of other women students must have created a certain solidarity, a reinforcement for dreams and goals that few women of their generation were allowed to share and that some frankly mistrusted. There would be sympathy and understanding for those who experienced subtle and not-so-subtle sexism in and out of class. And there was plenty of fun. Lydia Olsson, who lived in the other wing of the house with her family, records in her journals evenings of Parcheesi games, snacks, singing, sewing, and giggling. Perhaps, however much you liked the company of males, it was something of a relief to relax with women friends. Even today, many women prize and guard their evenings with "the girls." On a campus dominated by males, what's not to love about a daily Ladies night?

After The Pioneers

Erin is working in Special Collections this summer. Erin is tall, strongly and healthily built; she's neither wandlike nor chunky. She's simply physically reliable. She has short curly hair that sometimes scrolls over her head and around her face in true hyacinthine fashion, sometimes is buzz-cut to a shapely helmet. She has round eyes filled with light that seem always to look at the world with wonder, both for its magic and for its absurdities. Erin is balanced and at ease in her world. She is a poet. She claimed that identity early on in her college career. It didn't seem the amusing and sad arrogance of the young. It seemed, as it was, natural and inevitable. After this summer she will graduate, earn an M.F.A., publish, and take her place among the gifted young poets of her generation. Her mentor at Augustana is a poet, but I have been blessed to know her as a student and a friend.

She discovers me among the old documents, and she comes and pulls out a chair beside my cubicle, curious and comfortable. "What're you working on?" she asks. I tell her. She's delighted but not gushy. Rather, she listens with a kind of energetic respect as I outline my project. The light in her eyes is keen and steady. She says, "That's great. Let me know if there's any way I can help you."

I think: *Erin, you already have.*

CHAPTER 2

After the Pioneers

Anna Olsson could walk to campus easily. From her home on 8th Avenue it would have been no more than ten minutes from front door to classroom, where she'd stand angular and dignified before her students in their precisely arranged rows of desk, and talk about writing. If she chose to come early she could have climbed her "beloved" Zion Hill, and, sitting for a few moments on her old study stump, watched the evolution of the campus from a primarily male enclave to an institution that was becoming genuinely co-educational. She'd have seen women in sweeping skirts and high collars, strolling arm-in-arm; dawdling in chatty groups; or striding singly and purposefully to class. The men wouldn't have been far away. And she'd have heard the blend of high and deep voices, the counter-point of laughter, maybe even a few snatches of song, depending how early it was and how frisky the undergraduates felt in the morning.

And for herself: what did she feel? Her father had died the previous spring; she and her siblings had moved into the house on 8th Avenue that fall; she began teaching in September. Did she yearn for her old student days, now more than a decade behind her? Did she enjoy teaching? She was never to become a permanent part of the faculty. What dreams, regrets, or anxieties would have passed through her mind as she watched the changing Augustana before her?

What Anna would have seen reflects the story of women at Augustana. After the pioneers made their way through the curriculum and across the platform to collect degrees, the number of women began steadily, if slowly, to grow, and the presence of women in class and clubs alike reshaped the college. In 1893-1894, for example, the year after Anna Westman graduated as the lone woman in her class, eleven women were registered in a total college enrollment of 114. And that percentage of women versus men—roughly ten—holds fairly steady up to the turn of the century. The graduating class of 1894 included four women, among them Netta Bartholomew, who (as Mrs. K. T. Anderson) was to become the first woman elected to the college's Board of Directors, a position she occupied long, faithfully, and formidably. By the new century, the enrollment of 95 students includes fifteen women, and women hold their own as degree recipients, three out of thirty in 1900. (The numbers fluctuate some during the early part of the century, but overall there's a general pattern of slow growth.)

This trend, the gradually increasing enrollment of women at Augustana, parallels that occurring throughout the country, a movement that historian Barbara Miller Solomon, in her definitive study *In the Company of Educated Women*, pinpoints as having begun as early as 1850 and gathered impetus from a number of social forces. These forces, according to Solomon, included the Civil War and its aftermath (1861-1865), which depleted the male labor pool, the new views of society that came with Reconstruction and the altered status of the former slaves, and the growth of new institutions for higher education.

As would be the case during the Second World War, in a country desperately in need of workers gender distinctions lost some of their authority, and women entered the workforce during and immediately after the Civil War. And as Reconstruction attempted to rebuild a fragmented society, much that had "always been so" was being reevaluated—including the position of women.[1] Inevitably, as with any movement which advocates change, it wasn't a smooth process. We've noted previously the ways in which science, religion, and the culture as a whole resisted attempts to grant women equal educational opportunities with men. But, also inevitably, slow changes came. And new institutions of higher learning, such as Augustana (organized just the year before the Civil War began) reflected these changes, to greater or lesser degrees. As we've seen, President Hasselquist was among the proponents of higher education for women—in part, certainly, as a practical means of assuring Augustana's survival in its early, precarious days. But only in part. As a man of aggressive integrity, he couldn't have supported measures that he didn't believe in.

And the women came. However, most of them attended classes in the preparatory department—an education designed to bring students up to speed for college work, but also to provide "opportunities for those preparing for teaching" and for "those desiring a more complete education than can be obtained in the common schools."[2] Other women, as Hasselquist had envisioned, attended classes in the Commercial Department. Students enrolled in this division were allowed to attend Preparatory or college courses free, and many women took advantage of this two-for-one deal. Another option that women often chose was that of the "select course" for students who weren't taking the full schedule of classes geared toward the degree. Students "may select such studies in any department as they are prepared to pursue to advantage...subject to the approval of the faculty," according to the Catalogue.[3]

This was progress. And yet, at Augustana as in the culture at large, social transition and ideological transformation creaked a bit. Esthena Randolph, Class of 1921, provides a light-hearted retrospective: "...[T]he male students looked upon us with their superior manner and condescending ways until lo! they were startled to find that the hitherto considered inferior creatures with their inferior minds, possessed a most surprising aptitude for learning, indeed, even equal to that of a man." Women, she says, could attend classes but not recite because "the faculty realized that by nature man wants to be the predominant one, even in the class-room.... However, they could not endure long the dullness of the recitations and in 1886, they enthusiastically welcomed and with awed admiration listened to the voice of women in the class-room."[4] Randolph's account, playfully exaggerated as it is, does reflect in comic tone what Netta Bartholomew Anderson describes more seriously in her memoir sketch quoted earlier. Discrimination was felt—at least by some women—as real and hurtful. We'll deal with Anderson's story in more detail below. What's interesting about it here is that it gives one view of Augustana's position in the American educational scene. Anderson emphatically attributes the way women were treated at Augustana to the heavy preponderance of immigrants who held old-world views on women's education. Hasselquist's battles, recorded above, support that interpretation. But Anderson's recollection that no such discriminatory attitude existed at Carthage College, where her father taught before coming to Augustana in 1888, may be a bit rose-colored. According to Solomon, mistrust of the educated woman persisted into the 1880s. She notes, for instance, that at Boston University, far from protesting when male students "expressed shock at the idea of having a 'lady professor,' female classmates responded that they were quite content with male professors."[5] Augustana, then, may have been somewhat recidivistic in its attitude toward women's education, and its particular ethnic and pietistic constituency may have contributed to that thinking. But evidence doesn't support the idea that higher educational institutions elsewhere in America had erased or escaped such attitudes.

A decade after Netta Bartholomew's college experiences, the student newspaper *The Augustana Observer* was launched. Its announced goal was "to bring our dear Alma Mater into bolder relief." At that time women were being not only welcomed but invited (on paper, at least). An unsigned article from the first academic year of publication (1902-1903), entitled "What Augustana Is," declares that the college "invites young women as well as young men to come and drink at the Pierian springs of literature, art, and science."[6] Whether the writer of a note in the "college news" section of the previous March had in mind the Pierian springs experience may be subject to question. "The [junior] class now has two lady members," the note reads. "Many more would be welcome." Perhaps the writer had the laudable idea that more "lady members" could support one another in study; or perhaps that they could augment "romantic excursion[s]" such as the one "several young boys and girls made" to Andalusia in a "carryall" on a fine spring day.[7] Or perhaps it was a bit of both.

Whatever motivated the students' plea for more women in the early years of the twentieth century, official college mailings from a decade or so later made clear the coeducational opportunities at Augustana. Post cards featuring photographs of various college buildings note on the flip side "Augustana College—A School of Higher Learning for both Sexes."

During this pre-war period women faculty members also increased in modest numbers. What that meant to Augustana, or to any school, was articulated in 1894 by Berkeley undergraduate Katharine C. Felton, who deplored the lack of women on the faculty: "It is not right...that [a] woman, simply because she is a woman, should be deprived of the opportunity of pursuing the student's life and of supporting herself at the same time." And it was more than a matter of professional equity. Felton believed that having women on the faculty would create "'an incentive' affecting all students 'indirectly.'"[8] Women, this quotation suggests, would be encouraged to aspire to college and university teaching positions by the presence of such faculty models; men, encountering these women, would recognize their professional status. That kind of thinking may have inspired the anonymous donor of the Anna Westman Stipend at Augustana. Deserving women students, gifted and industrious, can indeed influence the character and future of an institution. We know that Inez Rundstrom did in her years at Gustavus Adolphus.

What did these early women faculty at Augustana teach? Unlike Anna Westman, mostly the "soft" subjects traditionally assigned to and associated with women: English, languages, the arts. Anna Olsson, Class of 1888, was named instructor in English, and Cotta Bartholomew, Class of 1900, taught English in the Business Department. Emilie Catherine Mertz, Class of 1898, served as assistant professor of Latin and German; Mary

Searles Penrose taught elocution and physical culture, a discipline that Iva Carrie Pearce handled long and admirably; Edla Lund became the first director (or "directress," as she was then styled) of the Handel Oratorio Society begun in 1880 by Professor Olof Olsson, while Gertrude Housel was "Directress of Orchestra."[9] Mae Munroe established the art department, where she taught for three years before Olof Grafstrom, a Swedish artist known for his massive altar paintings, succeeded her.[10] Yet, despite this seeming progress in intellectual and artistic opportunities for women, as late as 1912-1913 the art department featured a course in "china painting." It's doubtful whether this class attracted significant male enrollment.

Edla Lund: First "Directress"

She was a substantial and dramatic woman, given to turning her head sidewise in photographs, Barrymore-style. The profile is impressive, and expressive. For she went at her work with earnestness, commitment, and energy. As a director she was strict, as a singer she was known for verve and flair that many loved and some found excessive.

Born Edla Ferngren in Stockholm August 8 in the mid to late 1860s (her dates of birth are variously given as 1864,[11] and 1867[12]), she'd trained in piano, organ, and voice at the Royal Academy of Music in Stockholm.[13] Her marriage to Professor Victor Lund of the Bethany Conservatory of Music, Lindsborg, Kansas, brought her to the United States in 1887.

Lindsborg was certainly a Swedish settlement, but in the classed society she came from, not all of that community would have shared her interests and abilities. Or her background. She was a child of the city, of lights and bustling streets loud with voices and the clatter of carriages, of concert halls resonant with superb music. In Kansas the landscape was dauntingly different—the reach and remoteness of it, its primitive beauty, its vast silences. Like the artist Birger Sandzen, another member of the Lindsborg community, Lund must have stepped outside on a summer's day and felt the vivid, intense colors of the new world throbbing against her eyes. Despite her love for her husband, and the intellectual and artistic companionship they presumably shared, she must have known moments of deep homesickness.

Unfortunately that companionship lasted only six years; Professor Lund died in 1893. For a year after his death, raising two small sons, Edla

Edla Lund: dramatic "directress"

Lund embarked on a variety of professional activities calling for both vocal and instrumental expertise: she joined the vocal music faculty at Bethany, and she earned a prize certificate in organ in the 1894 Kansas Musical Jubilee.

But this professional success didn't keep her in America. She went back to Sweden the next year and studied with the then-lead soprano of the Royal Opera, Dina Edling. Why did she go? In days of lengthy and laborious travel, embarking on such a journey, especially with two young children, was a momentous undertaking. Perhaps she needed money—the colleges of the church paid notoriously meager salaries—and thought contacts with the musical elite in Sweden might enable her to command higher prices for her work. Or maybe it was something more personal. Perhaps she hoped for a performance career; or, lacking that, for more sophisticated teaching skills and more serious students in a European capital than in the primitive American west. Maybe she'd had enough of those wide wild plains and hoped to stay in urban Sweden to raise her children there. Alternatively, her plans may have called for returning to the United States where, after a period of advanced training, she envisioned wider artistic opportunities. She did in fact get two job offers from the States, one at the University of Vermillion in South Dakota, the other at the Augustana Conservatory. As a retrospective in the *Augustana Bulletin* for June 1907 puts it, "she was induced to accept [the Augustana position]" in 1895—whether for salary benefits or chances for professional advancement the article doesn't, of course, specify.

It's tempting to believe that Augustana's strong musical tradition was the deciding factor in her choice. That tradition began back as far as 1874, with the formation of the Silver Cornet Band. "We know that music had a large part in all the festival programs from Paxton days," Bergendoff reports; we know, too, that commitment to musical instruction formed an important part of presidential agendas. Hasselquist spoke and wrote about the need for qualified teachers of music; Olof Olsson, himself no mean musician, organized the Handel Oratorio Society in 1880, inspired by a performance of *Messiah* he had attended in London during his family's grand tour. Against his own mother's pietistic distrust of music, Olsson asserted its spiritual power.[14] Musical groups—men's, women's, quartets, trios, instrumental and vocal—figured largely in Augustana's extracurricular life, and incidentally, served as effective fund-raisers for the college as they toured the Midwest and beyond. Such leadership and energy were reflected in the Conservatory faculty, arguably some of the most highly qualified on campus—for example, Gustav Erik Stolpe, who was, in fact, the prime mover in establishing the Conservatory in 1887.[15] Scion of a Swedish family who had served as church organists for generations, Stolpe brought seven years' training at the Stockholm Academy of music to his work at Augustana when he arrived in 1882. He enjoyed a distinguished reputation as pianist, organist, violinist, and composer[16]; unfortunately those gifts were matched with an artistic temperament which ultimately led to his dismissal.

But the Conservatory he'd organized continued its success. And that success was especially important to the story of Augustana's women. By the turn of the century, just five years after Edla Lund joined the faculty, "music was taken for granted as a major expression of college life," and the Conservatory was attracting many students, large numbers of whom were women.[17] The Conservatory, then, achieved what perhaps Hasselquist had hoped for: increased the enrollment, and particularly the enrollment of women. But it did more: it provided an entrée for women into the echelons of higher education teaching, and would enable Lund and others to create successful professional lives for themselves.

So in choosing to accept Augustana's "call," Lund could anticipate institutional support, gifted, committed students, and many opportunities for performance. Whatever dreams she'd realized or jettisoned when she returned to America, she apparently saw the chance for a successful musical career here.

And that's what she achieved, both as conductor and as performer. With a reputedly "rich and fascinating soprano voice"[18] she gave concerts in various parts of the country: Pennsylvania, New York, the Pacific Coast. In 1905 she was a soloist in the Swedish Day celebration at the Lewis and Clark exposition in Portland, Oregon. "By the press everywhere she has been accorded fulsome praise for the charm and finish of her vocalism," claim her biographers Olson and Engberg (rather fulsomely themselves).[19] Her "rich, fascinating, and finished" vocal style did have its detractors; some found it overly dramatic. But that she commanded admiration is unquestionable. At home she conducted not only the Augustana Chapel Choir, where according to Conrad Bergendoff she proved herself a "popular and capable leader,"[20] but also the choir of the First Congregational Church in Moline and the Choral Union of Moline.[21] By 1899-1900, just four years after she'd arrived, she was receiving top prices for her private voice lessons at Augustana: $17.50 for twice weekly half-hour sessions, in comparison with male colleagues who charged $15 and $10 for similar lesson time; only one (male) charged more.[22]

And she was an early leader of the choir tours that became famous in later years, taking Augustana's Apollo Quartette throughout the central West. It's easy to see her, upright and tight-corseted, jolting along on the trains that carried her singers into the plains and huge sunsets she'd have remembered from her Lindsborg days.

These credentials made her a natural for director of the Handel Oratorio Society. What's interesting is that she was in fact chosen over a male. Accolades from the *Augustana Observer* mark her performance in that role. In 1906, when the Oratorio Society celebrated its 25th anniversary, the *Observer* credited her with "[bringing the society] to a height not reached since the days of Gustav Stolpe."[23] This was praise indeed; despite his often tempestuous associations with colleagues and students, Stolpe maintained his musical reputation. Measured against what Augustana considered the best from its immediate past, Lund came off well.

By 1910, though, she needed no more yardsticks. Mrs. Edla Lund is, the *Observer* says, "peerless," and the Oratorio Society under her direction "no doubt the leading musical organization of the tri-cities [Moline, Rock Island, and Davenport].... If you miss the [Christmas] Oratorio Concert," the writer goes on to admonish, "you miss the musical treat of the season."[24]

Her story shows a character defined by courage, confidence, and savvy. In a day when single parenthood was the exception rather than the rule, and job opportunities for women still limited, she took on the role of wage-earner as well as caregiver. Certainly it was a decision involving no small risk, both for herself and for the children she had to support. One small incident suggests that, however brilliantly qualified and majestically self-assured she may have been, she understood that her situation was precarious, at least at the outset. She was just beginning her second year at the

Conservatory when during a choir rehearsal giggling broke out. President Olof Olsson's daughter Lydia was apparently one of the miscreants in this episode; she reports that "Mrs. Lund stopped playing and turned around to me and gave me a terrific look and said [in Swedish], 'What is it you are laughing at—is it something to laugh at?'" Lydia, hurt and "provoked," as she later told Lund, "wiped my eyes and tried to sing, but I did not look up once." After the rehearsal Lund called Lydia aside, apologized if she'd said "anything hurtful [and] asked if I'd forgive her which I said I would. She said she gets kind of hot [emotionally] and thought it nothing to laugh at. Then she told me not to go home and say that she was the worst woman out."[25] This incident certainly expresses the passionate commitment of the musician to excellence; it may suggest also the exhaustion of a teacher after a long day. But in the apology we can perhaps detect also a note of panic: Don't offend the CEO on a job you need to keep. Those sorts of resentments and tensions, she must have known (and may have been specifically told), were what had led to the dismissal of her predecessor, the gifted but temperamental Stolpe.[26] Certainly later on, when her position was more secure, she showed no lack of backbone, criticizing the college community for lukewarm support of the oratorio society,[27] although the praise quoted above, just two years before her retirement as director, suggests warm appreciation.

So beneath the almost arrogant carriage of the head, under the security of critical accolades, there may have been vulnerability.

Besides that, there would have been the whole question of childcare for her two young sons, though at that time the close-knit college community, proud of its music excellence, may have filled that gap in a way more difficult for twenty-first century professional parents to negotiate. But it is interesting to speculate on what sources of strength and support she found. The Conservatory was less male-dominated than the collegiate faculty, so perhaps friendships developed there. And as a woman teaching in a field that attracted many women, she must have had her share of protégées.

Where she found support, how that support defined her sense of self and work, remains speculative. What seems clear is that in the end confidence trumped vulnerability. When, in March of 1911, the Board of Directors issued her the "call" to continue her teaching of voice, sight-reading, and ear-training, and to direct the Chapel Choir and the Oratorio Chorus, she balked. The June Board minutes note that, while willing to go on with the teaching, Mrs. Lund "takes exception to the Oratorio, unless

the Board provides means for the increase of interest among and attendance by the students in general at the institution."[28] The Board did not act
on this request, apparently hoping to negotiate, because the Minutes for
April of 1912 record that they voted to "postpone the calling of a teacher
in voice and leader of the Chapel Choir."[29] But Lund was adamant, and in
1912 indicated that she "wished to be relieved" of her duties, as Bergendoff
tactfully puts it.[30]

Despite her apparent robustness, she did not live to a great age. She
died in her early to mid-fifties; her grave is in Washington State. In 1927
another woman, Esther Mandeville, took charge of the Oratorio Society,
following the path first forged by Edla Lund.

Iva Carrie Pearce: Elo-quent First Dean of Women

*Long hair gathered up into a complication of curls and waves, she looks
wistful, fragile, sensitive—an image she perhaps cultivated, since it appears on
the college's brochure for the "Augustana School of Expression." Later, the hair
trimmed to silver curls around a sweet face, she might be somebody's favorite
grandmother. But this mild, vulnerable look covers a persuasive personality and
an energetic intellect. When in the fall of 1920 she was named Dean of Women,
an article in the* Rockety-I *hailed the event as recognizing "women…as a permanent factor at Augustana"[31] and went on to say of Iva Carrie Pearce that "we
respect her, we admire her, and we love her. May her Christian influence ever
be before us as an example of true womanhood!"*

That influence stood before the women of Augustana for 27 years,
eight of those in her position as Dean of Women. But rather than her
ground-breaking role as Dean, she was probably best known for indefatigable work in dramatics and its earlier incarnation, Oral Expression.

The very terminology sounds quaint today—it was called alternately
Expression, Oral Expression, and Elocution—evoking images of high-
collared ladies behind wooden lecterns, shaping their vowels and conso-
nants with painful precision, and gesticulating with elaborate, practiced,
and eminently artificial sweeps of arm and hand. But the field proved to
be something more substantial than the avocations of leisured ladies. It
provided the seeds not only of dramatics, but of speech therapy as well.

Originally paired with what was called "Ladies Physical Culture," it was introduced in 1897 as part of the Conservatory curriculum "to meet the special requirements of the pupils."[32] By 1899-1900, under the leadership of Mary Searles Penrose, the discipline was called "Elocution and Physical Culture" and described, presumably by Ms. Penrose, as something more than vocal mimicry: "Instead of teaching students to become mechanical or imitative readers, 'the interest is awakened, the mind aroused....' While educating the intellect, sensibility, and will we do not forget that the body influences the mind, and every effort is made to cultivate the grace of body, that it may act in perfect harmony with the mind, through proper exercises, movements, marches, etc.,"[33] a method created by Dr. Charles W. Emerson, President of the Boston School of Oratory.

Pearce followed Penrose in 1906. She enthusiastically endorsed the premises and practices of "Elocution and Physical Culture." In the three-fold brochure describing the "Augustana School of Expression," with her wistful photograph on the front panel and presumably written by her, the "object" is set forth as "the promotion of general culture and the training of the student in a more adequate and effective expression of himself in the business of every day life"[34]—a fair description of the liberal arts vision that centered Augustana's curriculum from its inception. Like Penrose before her, Pearce makes it clear that oral expression isn't about

Iva Carrie Pearce: "awake the interest, arouse the intellect"

parroting cadence or assembling an arsenal of stock gestures: "The pupil does more than learn to recite selections with exaggerated vocal expression and much movement of body. The aim from the beginning is independence of conception and expression."[35] To this end instruction is tailored to the individual student, taking into consideration "physical, intellectual, and moral" attributes, and "work is assigned looking toward the development and enrichment of his entire personality."

Moreover, the study is to be interdisciplinary: the student "is never allowed to lose sight of the necessity of giving expression through his own personality to the varied impressions he is hourly receiving from work in other departments of the college...."[36] Interpretation of this kind means mastery not only of the material and its richness, but of the individual's own public presence: "the first work...to be done is to free the student from self-consciousness [*i.e.,* paralyzing embarrassment or shyness] by opening the channels of voice and body so that he may freely express that which he already knows," the brochure asserts, in what sounds almost like the Socratic view of education. Such crippling self-consciousness can "enslave" the individual, no matter how fine his or her mind.

Pearce may have had first-hand experience of this "enslavement." Born February 27, 1863, she graduated from Monmouth College in 1886 as one of its first female laureates. Strong self-confidence and powerful communicative skills may have been needed to assert herself in a largely male environment. In any case, the discipline of oral expression interested her enough that she took course work in the Columbia College of Expression after teaching in a school for the deaf for several years. By the time she established the School of Expression at Augustana, she's described as "a woman of liberal education and broad culture" who "is singularly successful in developing the character and personality of her pupils" and whose own performances demonstrate a "sympathetic grasp of the author whom she interprets" and a "sincerity and naturalness" in presentation that "mak[e] a strong appeal to thoughtful people."[37]

She was forty-three when she came to Augustana in 1906, and she remained at the college until 1933.

Her life in the academy left little room for the sort of contemplative stillness pictured on the front of the Oral Expression brochure, though. In fact, her achievements demonstrate extraordinary energy and commitment. Besides Bachelor of Science and Bachelor of Education degrees, she earned the A. M. from Augustana in 1920. In 1919 she was appointed full professor, the same year that she became Dean of Women and established the School of Oral Expression. This school became the nucleus of the "dramatics" and oratory departments.

It's easy to picture her in her heyday, stepping with grace and purpose across campus from office to class to rehearsal—but also, to judge by the serenity of her expression in the photos, sitting quietly and listening—to women with concerns, to students presenting readings, to actors shaping characters on stage. As attested by the tribute paid her in the yearbook, she was beloved as well as respected. As late as 1931, just two years before she retired at 70, her zeal and engagement with both her discipline and her students appear unshaken: Pearce was keeping a schedule few forty-some-things could maintain. In the course of the school year she directed six one-acts, one full-length comedy, and Ibsen's *Enemy of the People*, called by the *Observer* "the most ambitious undertaking of the dramatic department at Augustana," so demanding that, in the writer's opinion, "very few casts would dare to undertake its presentation"—and this at the end of the term when exhausted professors and stressed-out students are often simply clawing their way to summer vacation. Nor was this play her first encounter with challenging texts: the year before she'd directed Strindberg's *Easter*. In addition to this, she was coaching students for the National Intercollegiate Oratorical Contest, organizing "dramatic recitals" for the School of Oral Expression, and working with private students, as well as giving her own performances for various local groups.

Pearce, first Dean of Women

And she was doing it all with success. The *Observer* for May 21, 1931, summarizes the year in Augustana theater: gate receipts of $525 (this in 1931, when wages for clerical work could be as low as $5.00 a week); forty-six student participants, and a composite audience of 1,325. Pearce's "excellent direction and zealous efforts have done much to make the year successful," the article concludes.

Admittedly, the majority of plays chosen would strike us as dated, and the level of performances probably seem amateurish. Titles like "Feed the Brute," "Two Crooks and a Lady," "The Wedding," "Forty Miles an Hour," and "Take My Advice," a sampling of the offerings for academic year 1930-1931, aren't exactly theatrical classics. The only really ambitious selection was *An Enemy of the People*, and that represented a real stretch for actors and director alike, as the *Observer* noted. About the acting, one *Observer* review suggests its general quality: "All parts showed conscientious preparation." Still, the sheer volume of work, and the numbers of students involved, remain impressive.

And Pearce's influence went further than her own years at Augustana. Obviously she touched many students in varied ways, both at Augustana and beyond. One of them, the late Mabel Arnell Youngberg, graduated in 1924. Youngberg's daughter Dr. Paula Arnell, an Augustana graduate from 1960, explains that her mother attended the Academy, where she studied privately with Miss Pearce and came to admire her and the discipline she taught with such memorable conviction.

For Mrs. Youngberg the fine rhetoric in catalogues and brochures was real. She learned to understand and appreciate the texts she prepared for reading, to read them, in fact, with an attention and care that she believes she might not otherwise have given. The interdisciplinary aspect of her work was demonstrated clearly: the English and philosophy professor of the day, Dr. Edward Fry Bartholomew, who famously and resonantly read aloud in his poetry classes, occasionally invited Mrs. Youngberg in as guest reader.[38]

Besides class work, co-curricular recitals included both musical numbers from the women's Oriole chorus and oral reading selections. After a challenging dose of *lieder* and arias, audiences must have rejoiced in spoken words they could understand, especially if, as sometimes happened, students like Mrs. Youngberg chose comic entries to complement the more serious works. A favorite in this genre, Mrs. Youngberg used to tell her daughters, was the selection "Moo Cow."

And the speech skills demanded by oral expression linked the arts and the sciences. Speech disabilities could be assisted by the kind of precise training in pronunciation, breathing, and delivery that elocutionary studies provided—at a time when speech therapy as a discipline didn't yet exist. Undoubtedly Pearce's experience in working with hearing-impaired students helped her to understand how speech problems might be addressed by the techniques of elocution.

In addition to her class work, the declamation recitals Pearce presented throughout the surrounding local area served as a forerunner of today's college-community outreach.

When, before and shortly after her marriage Mabel Arnell Youngberg herself taught elocution in Augustana's Conservatory,[39] she drew on her work with Iva Carrie Pearce in formulating approaches, and it's to Miss Pearce that she attributed her lifelong love of reading literature with care and attention. Both of her daughters, Augustana graduates, share in this love: Dr. Paula Arnell as an avocation; Dr. Karin Youngberg, Class of 1958, as a professor of English and occupant of Augustana's Conrad Bergendoff Chair in the Humanities.

After her retirement Pearce continued to give private lessons from her Rock Island home. On April 6, 1937, while visiting relatives in Los Angeles, she died of a heart attack. President Bergendoff, noting her "long and fruitful…service," declared, "With gratitude we recall, together with a host of her former students, her devotion to her work and her enthusiasm for Augustana."[40]

She had lived to see a scholarship in the speech department established in her name, but not, unfortunately, long enough to be present at the dedication of Iva Carrie Pearce Hall in the early 1940s. The building, razed in 1974, was a large house on the northeast corner of Seventh Avenue and 35th Street that served as a women's residence, and home to Augustana bookkeeper Mildred Carlson, until her retirement in 1967. Later it housed the college health service and the department of psychology[41]—no inappropriate use to memorialize a woman committed to the physical, intellectual, and emotional development of her students.

Netta Bartholomew Anderson: First Board Member, Tireless Feminist

Standing before gathered alumni at the reunion of 1944, sensibly shod and fashionably-hatted, Mrs. K. T. Anderson was clearly a woman you didn't mess around with. And as she told her story to that group, you could see in the seventy-something woman the bright, feisty, lively girl who took a strong hand in changing the college she attended fifty years before.

She was the daughter of Edward Fry Bartholomew, who had come to Augustana in 1888 from the presidency of Carthage College. With wide-ranging academic experience and expertise—he taught English and philosophy and published in a variety of fields ranging from *An Outline of English Literature* to the relationship of music to psychology—Bartholomew brought sophistication and urbanity to the college on the prairies, and soon established himself as a faculty leader.[42] His daughter was just ready to matriculate when Bartholomew left Carthage.

And here, according to her account, she found things very different from the expectations she'd formed growing up "in a typical small American prairie college town, where...there was nobody of foreign birth in the whole town with the possible exception of old pastor Kuhl and nobody ever spoke anything but English." In contrast, at Augustana "I was the only American girl among all my schoolmates," and that meant making adjustments to different cultural mores, to hearing "a language I did not understand" and English often spoken haltingly; to eating different foods and experiencing different modes of worship, with "chorales which to my unaccustomed ear sounded so ponderous and mournful, written as they so often were, in minor key and having interminable numbers of verses."[43]

Netta Bartholomew Anderson:
"somewhat of a problem child"

But the biggest surprise to the young Netta Bartholomew was to encounter a gender discrimination she'd been unaccustomed to. As she perceived Carthage, "Our college received women students on an equal footing with men students and there was no thought of discrimination against them because of their sex nor was the matter of giving them the advantages of an education ever questioned." At Augustana, though,

we were frankly told that while they loved us as girls, they did not care for us as students. [The men were] so scornful of "women's rights" about which everybody was then talking, and so given to the old world tradition of regarding education for women a waste of time....I very much resented this male assumption of superiority and this accounts for some of the willful forwardness that made me somewhat of a "problem child" and involved me in some... "firsts."

A few of these "firsts" that this early feminist found herself, in her words, "tangled up in," genuinely broke barriers. Others came about as a kind of natural evolution.

Acting on a dare from one of her few fellow women students, Netta boldly breached the all-male ranks of the Adelphic literary society. It's easy to picture her crossing campus, stiff-backed and long-skirted, arriving at Old Main, perhaps taking a deep breath before throwing open the door and entering the crowded history room—crowded, of course, solely by males. She describes the moment when

the President of the society came to me and gravely whispered that it was customary to initiate new members by requiring a three minute extempore speech...and at the proper time he would call on me....[N]o one can know what agonies of apprehension I suffered before my turn came....[M]y knees turned to jelly as I pulled myself out of my chair, the one lone girl in that room, went to the front and faced what seemed a limitless sea of boys' faces all grinning expectantly at me. There wasn't a vacant seat in that old history room and even standing room was... taken for all who could crowd in had come to see the fun, a girl really trying to make a speech! I have not the faintest idea of what I said in those three minutes which seemed hours but...somehow I got through and it wasn't until later that I realized I had been hazed. The whole thing was intended as a joke, planned by some of the more mischievous fellows, for my discomfiture, who confessed to me afterwards that they never dreamed I would take the matter seriously and go through with it. So in my ignorance of the trickiness of college boys, I earned (and I *mean* earned) the distinction...of being the first hazing victim at Augustana....

She also earned her place in the Adelphic.

Even more significant, she claims to have won for women the right to speak in chapel. When she submitted her name as a contestant in the first college-sponsored oratorical contest, she encountered a long-standing prohibition against women speaking from the chapel platform. The oratorical committee, the faculty, and ultimately the Board of Directors thrashed the matter out, and Netta was allowed to participate. "I have always felt rather proud of my part in this incident," she reflects, because it "marked the end of the prejudice and discrimination against women students....The men ceased to struggle against the tide of female demand for equal opportunity, our right to 'free speech' was settled, we would not be frowned down and from that time on we have been not only accepted but welcomed on an equal footing with men students." It's interesting, though, that she attributes her victory at least in part to the college's unwillingness to offend the new (male) English professor, her father.

Other "firsts" for Netta Bartholomew included participation in the first women's physical education class, and in the Philodoi, the first "Ladies quartette" and forerunner of the Jenny Lind and later Augustana Choirs.[44] These seem to have occurred less from the pressure of women students, however, than as a natural development from their increasing presence.

But overarching these "firsts" was that Netta Bartholomew Anderson can probably be called Augustana's first "feminist." Her aggressive challenges to male domination of the school show a gender-bending energy she brought to other activities throughout her life.

She never actually joined the academy: marriage and family responsibilities in that era usually excluded a professional life. But certainly her many enterprises and projects, after marriage to Knut Theodore (K. T.) Anderson in 1897, amounted almost to full-time professional employment. Like her father Edward Fry Bartholomew she had a vital, eclectic mind. Her interests ranged from geology (she published *A Preliminary List of Mastodon and Mammoth Remains in Illinois and Iowa* jointly with a paper by Augustana's scientific luminary J. A. Udden) to music (she herself was an amateur singer) to history (she was one of the first women admitted to the reorganized Rock Island County Historical Society in 1912 and was promptly elected treasurer) to education (she was the first woman member of Augustana College's Board of Directors and first president of the "tri-cities" alumni association of the college) to church and social service (she was national statistician for the board of Augustana Foreign Mission Societies and active in Royal Neighbors, Rock Island Women's Club, and Bethany Home for orphans). It's a daunting list. Beside this vigorous schedule her husband's accomplishments as vice president of the First National Bank and treasurer of the Augustana Lutheran Church for thirty-four years seem rather modest. No wonder her young son Paul, barely able to write in cursive and with some spelling challenges, sent her a note saying "Dear mama I wish you would cum home todae." Equally unsurprising, she was the first woman chosen for an alumni award from Augustana in 1958.[45]

Her activities seem almost wildly disparate. But they're linked by that early feminism. She was doing things women hadn't always done: studying science, gaining entrée to previously all-male organizations, creating her own agendas. Her work in local history came more and more to center around the pioneer women of the area, women who, like her, but from necessity, had battled to forge new lives. She'd invite "old settlers" to her home to drink tea and share their reminiscences of the early days. Many of her papers and publications dealt with this subject. In collecting these stories she's a forerunner of the "herstory" movement to reclaim and proclaim women's places in history. And she clearly had little tolerance for outworn stereotypes about women. The articles she saved and donated to the college with her papers include one from *Harpers* celebrating the many strong single women of myth and history, and deploring the derogatory term "old maid." It's not difficult to imagine that this article was saved with an eye to later researchers who would explore her files.[46]

Late pictures show her seated centrally among the men of the college's Board of Directors, attired in dark suit, flat hat, and no-nonsense shoes, looking, serene and determined, into the camera. A woman to be reckoned with.

She died as dramatically and decisively as she'd lived, and in the venue to which she'd given much of her energetic attention—Augustana College. It was October 1960, Homecoming. She was 87. Appropriately enough, she'd just entered Westerlin Hall, the then-new women's residence where the Homecoming banquet was to be served, when she suffered a massive, and fatal, heart attack. Betsey Brodahl, Class of 1944, then Dean of Women, remembers being summoned to the apartment of the Housemother with the ominous news that "Mrs. K. T. Anderson was suddenly taken ill." "I looked at her lying there on the sofa and thought, it can't be," Brodahl recalls.[47]

But even the hearts of feisty feminists wear out.

And when they finished school, what did these first Augustana women do with their advanced educations? Solomon describes the dilemma of college-educated women in the years from 1870 until 1920: their education, they understood, had fitted them to take a place in life which would use that education productively, yet they "did not question the belief that they should contain their ambitions within the bounds of domesticity."[48] Competing expectations of wife-and-motherhood versus the larger worlds college had opened to them created tensions within many women graduates. At Augustana, the views of the church on women's place often imposed further claims on the energies and aspirations of women.

Looking at the first generations of Augustana women graduates, from 1885 until 1914, just before the war, seems to bear out this idea that occupations rarely transcended the bounds of domesticity. Most of the jobs listed in the alumni record for those years were traditional "female" activities, such as teaching, library or secretarial work. (When no job description is given and the woman is identified by three names, I'm assuming she's a housewife.)

Of 46 women reporting to the alumni record, 18 were teachers (including music teachers), 10 housewives (including one missionary spouse), 3 college professors, and 2 high school librarians. The rest pursued mostly genteel "womanly" occupations as well: a florist, a postal clerk, a deaconess, a music student, a bookkeeper. Only 3 reported more traditionally "masculine" activities: one a deputy county superintendent, one in "business," and one a soldier. The rest of the unmarried women listed no occupation. If they followed the pattern of early college graduates, they'd have returned home, to take on domestic responsibilities and/or to await marriage.

But that pattern was about to be disrupted. The coming of war brought new possibilities and opportunities for college women.

The First World War:
Vivid Rhetoric, Modest Moves

Carol presents a six-page paper for a two-page assignment, writes lyrical and complex poetry, whips up a wicked latte in the library coffee shop, and has been known to balance a spoon on her nose. She is small and gentle; the wit of her irony is no less incisive for that gentleness. Her smile blends all these characteristics.

Carol is aflame with the curiosity of the scholar, passionately interested in the reach and reconciliation of knowledge. She loves interdisciplinary studies that give us clues to the mystery of our humanity.

That curiosity, perhaps, is what attracts her to the figure of Margaret Olmsted—the quiet depth and strength of her. She writes a research paper about Olmsted that is discerning and appreciative; that places her in historical context; that celebrates what she has given. I read Carol's work and am sorry that Miss Olmsted could not.

CHAPTER 3

The First World War:
Vivid Rhetoric, Modest Moves

You have shown your love of Country and devotion to her by going forth, almost 200 strong, from the halls of Alma Mater. She rejoices in the splendid reports which have come concerning you from the camps. She expects still greater things of you in service and in sacrifice, that victory may come to us in this titanic struggle for the welfare of humanity....she invokes upon you God's blessing!

Students who opened the 1917-1918 College Catalogue would find these words printed across from the title page. If the students were far from home, from the safe Rock Island campus, locked in the private and communal hells of war, it's to be hoped the words strengthened them.

The catalogue rhetoric embodies a spirit ignited a generation previously, in the Civil War, a spirit that addressed loss by insisting that war is no "aristocratic game" played by professional mercenaries and impecunious younger sons, but a "bourgeoise enterprise" which sweeps whole families into valorous acts of sacrifice for noble ends. This paradigm, outlined by historian Drew Gilpin Faust, perfectly fit Augustana. The college saw itself as a family; "the Augustana family" was an expression used so often—up until the 1970s—that it seemed a literal rather than a metaphorical description. So when its students left for war, they were followed with words that read like a letter from mother to child—proud, admonitory, strongly reinforcing the ideal that melds her pride and their action in a shared project. On campus the "children" who stayed behind accepted their role in the great enterprise. Thoughtful women students such as Blanche Searle, chosen Class Historian for 1920, found that "life became not a carefree existence of work and play, but a responsibility for which we would be held accountable."[1]

But something more immediate connected the "bourgeoise enterprise" of a noble war and Augustana's perception of its role. Students who read these lines wouldn't have been on campus when the 1912 *Rockety-I* came out. But faculty would have; and in the resonant phrases of the catalogue they could have detected echoes of yearbook copy that proclaimed a similar faith in Augustana's power to shape a global future. Just as the "titanic struggle for the welfare of humanity" played out on the global stage—a struggle that would birth a new world order—so Augustana was poised for a new era, for a grand destiny. As a victorious America would "regenerate" the world by infusing its values globally, so too Augustana's influence would both mirror and assist the country's.

Augustana's ebullience of 1912 looked both backward to the Jubilee Year of 1910 and ahead to the future that year promised. The *Rockety-I* reprises tangible evidence of the confidence shown in Augustana: a generous gift by the Denkmann family ($100,000) to help build a library, and gifts and bequests, including one from Iowa Senator C. J. Ericson ($12,800—what we would now call a matching or challenge gift, promising the money if a comparable amount were raised). Professor Edward Fry Bartholomew, whose essay "'For a Greater Augustana'" demonstrates unmistakably his training in and love for the Victorians, rhapsodizes that "a 'large Augustana' is in the thought of everybody. It is in the air we breathe, we feel it tingling in the blood, we hear it from every quarter, we see it in the life of the school, we read it in the faces of the entire student body, it rings clear from the lecture stand of every classroom. ....[It is] a clear voice from heaven saying, 'Go forward!'"[2] But for the moment of 1917-18, where many students "went forward" was into war.

The Enemy on the Outside

On a spring evening in 1917 Rock Island citizens could look out of their windows or from their porches and see a group of Augustana men literally "going forward," marching through the streets in a war rally. They went four abreast, in "even lines" with "military tread," heads uncovered, eyes straight ahead, "set determination" in their faces. The sight, according to the *Rock Island Argus*, was inspiring and consoling: "No one," the writer claims, "who gazed upon the body of Augustana College students... need have fear of this country being unprepared so far as men are concerned, no matter what the eventuality."[3] These students were made of the "same stuff" as their heroic forbears, the writer says, "fired by a patriotism born from within them,...free men praying for peace, but soldiers to be, whenever their country calls....They represent the minute men of 1917."[4]

The college band had "unanimously accepted the call to become the Sixth Regiment Band" and would shortly leave for its tour, Godsped by a cheering Augustana.[5]

Energized by patriotism and promise, then, the college sent its young men off to the training camps and the trenches, and monitored their progress with accolades and exhortations from the pages of its publications. Besides the Catalogue, the *Observer* devoted its November 1917 issue to the war, including not only lists of men in service, but essays and analyses of the political situation, ferocious injunctions to patriotism, and more of Dr. Bartholomew's vivid rhetoric. Augustana, he told his readers, "expects a good report of all" her men in the services. "And if the supreme sacrifice should have to be made on the part of any one she feels that it is for a noble cause, and this goes far to reconcile her to her loss" (one wonders if this consolation seemed quite so obvious to the men who were actually risking their lives, not to mention their families). "To one and all Augustana sends a hearty and grateful greeting," Bartholomew concludes. "She misses her absent ones in her classrooms and halls, on her playgrounds and in her assemblies, and her heart goes out after them and breathes upon them her tenderest and sincerest benediction."[6] Apparently the men found these good wishes heartening; their letters to the college include appreciation of the *Observers* they've received and laments for the long gaps between issues (caused by delays in mail delivery to their training camps).[7]

Augustana not only sent men off; it received them on campus, briefly hosting a Students' Army Training Corps Unit of 120 members (the program began in the fall of 1918 and disbanded after the Armistice in November of that same year). The addition was a mixed blessing; students who enrolled got help with tuition cost,[8] but, according to Blanche Searle in her Class of 1920 retrospective, "everything was necessarily subservient to the S.A.T.C. unit…, reveille sounded in the morning, taps in the evening, …khaki was the prevailing color on campus, and Augie spirit and Augie life languished."[9] But it languished more immediately for another reason: the 1918 influenza.

The Enemy Inside

It was a pandemic. It killed more people than any other disease in history.[10] An estimated 675,000 Americans alone died from it, ten times as many as the war claimed. A quarter of the total population was stricken during 1918-1919.[11] So severe was its death count that the average life span in America was depressed by ten years in its wake, according to physician and historian Molly Billings.[12]

It was the "great influenza" of 1918.

It killed "with extraordinary ferocity and speed," notes historian John Barry. It could strike people on the street, on a train platform while they were inquiring about schedules, in a living room around a bridge table. They died within hours struggling, in the words of one contemporary physican, to clear airways blocked with "blood-tinged froth that often gushed from nose and mouth."[13] They died with high fevers, with bones so painful they screamed at a touch, with dementia. In the Quad-Cities Red Cross nurses and volunteers worked round the clock at special influenza hospitals. "Practically every physician and nurse, graduate or student, is engaged in fighting the epidemic," according to the *Rock Island Argus*.[14] Cities adopted desperate measures to control the illness, and the panic associated with its rampage. In many places all public gathering places were closed, even churches. Customers at grocery stores stood on the pavement and shouted in their orders, which were brought out to them. Slitted eyes peered out over ubiquitous face masks. Children, confined in fenced yards to avoid contact with infection, jumped rope to a macabre rhyme:

> *I had a little bird*
> *Its name was Enza.*
> *I opened the window*
> *And in-flu-enza.*

How did it "fly in"? Historians disagree, but that it gained impetus from the war is indisputable. In his book *The Great Influenza* John Barry explains that because the war effort had escalated dramatically, American troops arriving at training camps encountered half-completed barracks designed to hold far fewer than their numbers. Men lived jammed together into the "most intimate proximity," where disease could explode and decimate as quickly as artillery.[15] Overseas in the trenches the disease-carrying rat population was often controlled rather than eradicated because rats took care of the rotting corpses on No Man's Land.[16]

And as the illness ran its wildfire course around the world, medical researchers fought frantically to control it, scrambling to keep up with its swift and savage mutations. Symptoms shifted with Protean-like agility;

some mimicked other illnesses so closely that physicians often couldn't even believe they were dealing with influenza. Perhaps most appalling of all, it was a disease that attacked the young—those between the ages of 20 and 40—with the greatest ferocity. Those, in Barry's words, who had most to live for.

This was the war within. But winning the war without took priority, and in order to do so, morale had to be kept high. Panic would have undermined that morale. So media coverage often underplayed, and sometimes even falsified, the degree of danger. Initially, only in neutral Spain did the illness receive major attention; for this reason it came to be called the "Spanish Influenza" (not because it originated there).[17]

Augustana, of course, offered a prime target for a virus that fed most voraciously on the young. The school followed recommended precautions being observed in the surrounding cities: it banned all large gatherings. "Everything in the way of social activities, class meetings, debating clubs have been at a standstill," the *Observer* reported at the beginning of November 1918.[18] On October 17 the school was officially shut down "except for the S.A.T.C. [Students Army Training Corps]" until November 13. Meanwhile, presumably, the campus was diligently following the Surgeon General's Advice to Avoid Influenza, which included the following recommendations:

> Avoid needless crowding....
> Smother your coughs and sneezes....
> Your nose not your mouth was made to breathe thru....
> Remember the 3 Cs, clean mouth, clean skin, and clean clothes....
> Food will win the war....[H]elp by choosing and chewing your
>   food well....
> Wash your hands before eating....
> Don't let the waste products of digestion accumulate....
> Avoid tight clothes, tight shoes, tight gloves—seek to make nature
>   your ally not your prisoner....
> When the air is pure breathe all of it you can—breathe deeply.[19]

Yet, considered against the overall toll, Augustana got off fairly easily. Or, as the *Observer* for December of 1918 more poetically put it, the Spanish influence "has thus far knocked but lightly on our door."[20] There were nine reported cases of students contracting the illness, but only one death: Walter Grantz from Doggett, Michigan, a member of the freshman class of 1918. His story is a particularly wrenching one; he had gone home to attend the funeral of his brother, who had died from the disease a few weeks earlier, and possibly caught the illness then. Not long after that, his sister died. It's touching to read President Gustav Andreen's response to a letter Gantz wrote notifying the college that he'd be delayed in returning to school "on account of sickness." President Andreen responds immediately: "Be welcome back to Augustana as soon as you can come! I desire to express my deep sympathy to you and the other members of your family on the death of your brother....Wishing you all of God's abundant blessing....".[21] Gantz may or may not have received the letter—or have been well enough to read it.

Augustana counted two faculty members among its casualities: Algert Anker of the conservatory and Andrew Kempe of the Commercial Department.

Students are famously resilient. During this dark and anxious time some of them went home. But others elected to stay, at least during the first couple of weeks. And the women who occupied the half-filled dorms, unencumbered by class meetings and official social activities, found ways to keep up their own spirits and those of the remaining S.A.T.C. boys. On October 26 the *Observer* notes that the "girls" commandeered the dining hall kitchen to entertain the S.A.T.C. boys "who did not have a weekend pass," by popping corn and pulling taffy.[22] And even when the boys were unavailable, the girls enjoyed themselves. "Most any evening one could hear peals of laughter coming from [the dormitory laundry room]" as girls shared stories and jokes over the ubiquitous popcorn—whose smell must have been pretty tempting, too. But their activities weren't all frivolous. Part of the time they spent "put[ting] the numeral on the Service Flag" denoting how many Augustana "boys" were serving in the Military, at that time 420.[23]

Despite the pleasures of this enforced vacation, though, "everyone will gladly welcome the routine of study again when the ban lifts," the *Observer* says—which it did in November—a month after classes closed. And indeed, "everyone went to work with lighter hearts...." [24]

Still, under the celebration lurked sobering reminders of the illness. Vacant seats in classrooms. Lingering coughs. The occasional wig to cover lost hair. And when graduation time came, the full cost of both war and illness showed in a depleted class. At Commencement only 12 of the 23 seniors who marched across the platform to receive diplomas had been together for all four of their collegiate years.[25]

For women—still called "girls"—at Augustana the effects of these war years are somewhat elusive to trace. Unlike what would happen in the next great war, the numerical distribution between genders showed little change. Men still outnumbered women almost two to one. The faculty remained predominantly male. It's difficult to discover evidence that Augustana's women felt the new, enlivening currents blowing through the world beyond Seventh Avenue, Rock Island. There, in the country as a whole, women were finding that the war provided opportunities to enter occupations now vacated by men—and to demonstrate their competence in, and love for, these occupations. As was the case after the Civil War, and would be in the Second World War, the disruption of social patterns, especially of gender roles, offered hope and promise to women in all levels of work—from welders and streetcar conductors and farmers, to physicians and college professors.[26] At Augustana, however, the pietistic tradition, and the strong emphasis on family and familial roles embedded in this tradition, may have made the revolution in social patterns less obvious and less applauded.

Rather, women's activities assumed more traditional, approved forms: in social, religious, musical, and service groups organized during the years surrounding the war. Four local social sororities were created—the then-termed "Hellenic" groups (now called "Greek groups"): Sigma Pi Delta (1909), Kappa Tau (1910), Kappa Epsilon (1913), and Phi Rho (1919)—only one fewer than the men's fraternities formed during those same years. In 1917 Florence Anderson organized the Woman's Club, including both students and staff. These energetic women got right to work; a year later they'd raised $130 at a Red Cross benefit.[27] Women formed their own religious group, the Berean Bible Society, to match the men's Sola Fide Bible Class. Professor Arvid Samuelson directed the Orioles women's chorus as counterpart to the men's Wennerberg Chorus in 1916, and the women's group "was 'given the same standing as the Wennerberg' by the [college] Board."[28] If these modest moves didn't represent quite the social upheaval occurring on the larger national scale, they nonetheless formalized and highlighted women's presence on campus.

Housing, though, was another matter. At the Synod assembly of 1915 the college presented several building needs: new seminary buildings, a new science facility, a new gymnasium-cum-auditorium, and "the matter of a ladies' dormitory." Unfortunately, after a study proved that the dormitory would cost at least $100,000 (for housing 200 women), plans were dropped.[29] It had to be left to the Woman's Missionary Society to raise the funds; not until 1927, and after much heart-burning, was the Woman's Building completed. That story is told elsewhere.

But if women weren't explicitly reshaping the world of Augustana, still, students clearly felt a new world emerging. Writing in a January 1919 edition of the *Observer,* editor Eric Wahlstrom voiced large hopes for the coming year and beyond:

We all feel that 1919 will bring us events that in their consequences will overshadow even the great war itself. We feel that we now have entered upon a new era, a new phase of human development, possessed with unlimited possibilities of expansion. The war has revolutionized human thought and human institutions, the old order of things has been revealed in all its deplorable inefficiency, and mankind today is confronted with the problem of rearing from the wreck of the old a new structure, founded upon principles of eternal justice and truth.[30]

Whether his vision of a brave new world extended to new dreams and duties for women, he spoke prophetically. The next year women were enfranchised. And a new day did indeed dawn.

Quiet Excellence, Long Shadow: Margaret Olmsted

She was quiet, gentle, patient, and rigidly disciplined. She was smaller than most of her students, tidy, unobtrusive, reserved—and devoted to her work. Her ambition was directed not toward attaining administrative power but toward succeeding in the classroom. "What I have enjoyed most is just plain teaching," she said at the end of her long tenure at Augustana. "I like a regular thing to do—a regular life....I like to feel that what I do is worth doing." And though she conceded that "a person needs a little social life," she added significantly, "but if I gave very much of my time to that, I wouldn't feel my life was very profitable."

Trying to recapture her strong, delicate essence nearly a decade after her death, a student wrote: "The strength of character that Margaret Olmsted bestowed upon her students as a professor at Augustana College lives on in those people; we carry the gifts of such…[teachers] …with us.…"[31] This quiet strength was indeed her gift, to her students and to the college, for more than a half-century.

She came to teach in 1921. But her association with the college reached back further. She described that association in an interview with the *Augustana Alumni Bulletin* issued in the spring/summer of 1967, the year she retired from a forty-six year career: "…[M]y brother, two sisters, and I all came here [as students].… Since 1911, there has been only one year that some member of my family hasn't been teaching or going to school at Augustana. I think we've set some kind of record." What held the minds and hearts of the family, Olmsted said, was "Augustana's

Margaret Olmsted: "high scholarship, good character, balance"

standards of high scholarship, good character, balance, morality, and goodness of life."[32] This summary gives clues to the things that mattered to her, the things she would transmit, by her quiet dignity, to her students.

Born February 7, 1894, in Orange City, Iowa, she was the oldest child of Judge Robert Ward Olmsted, scion of an old and distinguished family that included, among others, the famous landscape gardener Frederick Law Olmsted. She grew up and lived her century-long life in Rock Island, much of it in the apartment building downtown that bore her family's name.

Like her more flamboyant colleague Henriette C. K. Naeseth, she came from a family to whom education mattered. Her father (born and raised in Rock Island County) served as superintendent of schools in Milan, Illinois, and in Orange City, Iowa, before being admitted to the bar in those states (Iowa in 1895 and Illinois in 1899). He later served Rock Island County as assistant state's attorney, county judge, and circuit court judge. His obituary notes that "Judge Olmsted…held a great interest in philosophy and read the works of the great authors in that field. He also took a keen interest in the history of cultures," interests he pursued actively following his retirement from private practice.[33] Among Margaret Olmsted's papers is a carefully preserved, neatly typed list of "Books Read by Robert Olmsted" between September 1932 and February 1936;[34] it includes 206 entries ranging from *The Iliad* and *The Odyssey* to the essays of Montaigne to William James on psychology to—somewhat surprisingly—*Gone with the Wind.* He probably encouraged these interests in his children; the fact that his daughter saved the list and presented it to Augustana suggests that she regarded it as important. It's easy to picture the tall, silver-haired man, seated in his armchair, light gathered on the page of his open book, reading away the long evenings of a Midwest winter, his children around him with their own books, or at the dining table, meticulously completing homework. If Margaret's adult behavior is any clue, it was likely a quiet family circle.

Margaret Olmsted says that "my father wanted me to go to Augustana" —an interesting choice in view of the fact that the family were neither Swedish nor Lutheran in an era when those affiliations still mattered. In fact, Olmsted's "different-ness" formed an early source of embarrassment to her, when she invited her father to a Founders' Day program conducted almost exclusively in Swedish. "I felt foolish," Olmsted recalled, "because I knew my friends were asking one another: 'What's Margaret Olmsted doing here? She doesn't understand a word of Swedish!'"[35] Presumably the academic and moral standards she later defined had influenced her father's selection. He didn't, apparently, suggest that his daughter attend his own alma mater, Iowa State College (he was the last surviving member of the class of 1890),[36] because it seems likely that if he had, she would have done so.[37] At any rate, alien as she may sometimes have felt, she went to Augustana, and her siblings followed her. And since three of them were women, Olmsted obviously made no gender distinctions in encouraging higher education for his children. Quite the reverse; as he noted in a speech given at his college, "It is said that an institution is the lengthened shadow of a man. That might be amended to say: men; and in this day and age, to include women."[38]

Another, more personal reason for his choice may have been that he wished to keep his family close to home. His wife, Jennie Fahnestock Olmsted, died just at the time Margaret was graduating from high school (the spring of 1911) and he may have felt protective toward his serious-minded, quiet, brilliant daughter who could, in her words, "straddle... math and Latin"[39] with success. Or he may have needed Margaret at home, to assume (as did Anna Olsson) household and hostessing duties; perhaps also for emotional support in his bereavement. Not until 1928 did he remarry, thereby acquiring the Sala Apartment building through Sala's widow Mary Elizabeth. She died three years later. For the rest of his life Judge Olmsted lived in an apartment in the Sala—then Olmsted—building, with his daughters Margaret and Jeannette.

Unlike Henriette Naeseth and Anna Olsson, Margaret Olmsted left no written records that we know of about her mother, or about her feelings on losing her at so early an age. Obituary records omit even her name, calling her "the wife of County Judge R. W. Olmsted."[40] What connections of shared interests, models of possibilities for women, or support for Olmsted's aspirations Jennie Olmsted provided we can't now recover. Perhaps Mrs. Olmsted was close to her oldest daughter. Or perhaps her long illness—she suffered for seven years from tuberculosis[41]—distanced them. Whatever the relationship, during some important years of her growing up, basically from the onset of puberty until the end of her public school education, Margaret must have witnessed her mother's physical suffering. Perhaps, as the oldest child and a girl, she assumed some nursing duties as well. Even if the Judge had hired a live-in nurse, the weight of her mother's illness would have pervaded the house. And if she'd been confined to the tuberculosis sanitarium in Rock Island, young Margaret would have dealt with the difficulties of an absent mother. Such experiences could well have contributed force to an innate love for discipline, for order and stability, for "a regular thing to do," and to her particular love for the order and precision of mathematics and the Latin language.

Coincidentally enough, Mrs. Olmsted died on April 27—Augustana's Founders' Day. Perhaps Olmsted's invitation to her father to attend the program early in her student days was intended to distract him from grief on a sad anniversary. (If so, the unexpected language barrier certainly must have been effective as comic relief.)

Margaret Olmsted appears to have been close to her father, imbibing his interests, adopting and enacting his values. In a biographical sketch written for the fiftieth anniversary of his college graduation, Olmsted says that he believes "the great words in our language [in creating a worthwhile life] are health, truth, charity, honesty, industry, energy, patience, persistence, tolerance, generosity, reasonableness, self-control, intelligence, moral perception, beauty, poise and sociability."[42] The words seem almost a checklist of qualities associated with his daughter Margaret. As early as her sophomore year in college she began exploring some of these large abstractions. A short story she wrote during her sophomore year, published in the *Observer* (March 1913), recounts the experience of a college boy who battles his conscience for cheating on a final exam which will determine whether or not he graduates. After a sleepless night, he bravely presents himself to his professor and confesses what he's done. Interestingly, the young Olmsted doesn't construct a sentimental ending in which the forgiving professor allows the student to retake the test as a reward for his (belated) honesty. Rather, she leaves his academic fate open-ended: "whether or not he graduated from school, he had already graduated from one plane of moral existence to a higher one."[43] The story is well-written, if a little heavy on allusions to battles in history and literature; the main character John is drawn with sympathy and understanding, and the events build real tension. "John's Battle" suggests that Olmsted had some promise as a writer; she seems not to have been interested in pursuing that ability. Perhaps she felt disinclined to grapple with the emotional and moral complexities demanded by serious fiction; she seems to have excluded such experiences as much as possible from her life.

Like her predecessors Inez Rundstrom and Anna Westman, as a student at Augustana Olmsted "enrolled in what was known as the 'Latin-scientific group'....I knew I liked both subjects," she said, "but felt I could do better in Latin.... Later I took the M. A. in Classics at the University of Illinois" and when she returned to Augustana to teach, "I taught in the areas where they needed help."[44] The assessment is a modest one to reflect forty-six years of teaching Latin and forty-three of teaching math.

In her college years she acquired a reputation for intense studiousness—a quality teasingly alluded to in an *Observer* "comedy section" entitled "Hits and Hints." The April 1913 issue offers a long list of "What They Could 'Cut Out'" and features a number of suggestions to fellow students for curbing certain excesses. For "M. Olmsted" the "thing she could cut out" is "grinding" (*i.e.*, studying hard).[45] That this was intended as a good-natured allusion to her native intelligence rather than a cheap shot at an overachiever is reflected in the inscription under her graduation picture in the 1915 *Rockety-I* yearbook—"Where the stream runneth smoothest, the water is deepest"—and by the fact that her class elected her valedictorian over other high-ranking candidates, including Conrad Bergendoff and Thorsten Sellin.[46] The *Observer* congratulates her warmly, noting that though the competition was unusually keen, "Miss Olmsted was not pushed hard by her nearest competitor."[47] Obviously the "grind" was respected rather than despised.

However much she cherished these honors, Olmsted clearly didn't just "grind" to amass them. Her valedictory address articulates the values that shaped her life. In it she insists on the importance of education as a lifelong enterprise: "A liberal education…implies an ever-growing knowledge. One who seeks to be liberally educated is constantly enlarging and renewing his knowledge and endeavoring to understand more as the opportunity for such increase is offered to him."[48] The carefully correct and gender-exclusive pronouns of her day map what she practiced: she completed her master's degree at the University of Illinois with the valedictory scholarship she'd received, taught high school in the nearby towns of Viola and East Moline for six years, and then returned to Augustana to spend the rest of her career—more accurately, to live out her calling—there. Along the way she took further graduate work at the Universities of Iowa and Chicago. She didn't go on for the doctorate; in her day, in Rock Island, Illinois, few women did.

She taught long enough to encounter generations that would question the "relevance" of classical languages to the practical, immediate claims of the modern world. To that critique her answer was firm and clear: "Latin has never been a dead language. So much of Latin lives in our own English language and in the Romance languages….Knowing Latin would be helpful to anyone, because to live effectively we must know and use our language effectively." Even more, she believed, studying Latin "improves one's ability to think and express himself clearly." And since, "life is becoming more and more complex,…about the only way to simplify it is through careful thinking and planning."[49]

She didn't say a lot about her own vision for teaching. But the "great words" identified by her father provide insight. And in a tribute to another colleague which she helped write, it's possible to trace more precisely how she realized those words in her own classes. The colleague, art teacher Alma Johnson, is praised for critiques that were both fair and constructive; for "deep and personal interest in each student as an individual";[50] for refusing to privilege the gifted over the average. The tribute ends with the passage on the quality and power of love from First Corinthians 13. Students who sat in Margaret Olmsted's classes certainly experienced such fairness and interest. They remember a calm, serene demeanor, and, as Dr. Harry Nelson, class of 1935, emphasizes, her "infinite patience with each of her many students," which, "as a student in her analytical geometry class in 1932, and for more than twenty-one years as her colleague and office partner, I had the privilege of observing first-hand."[51] Endlessly patient, indeed, but never easy. Her meticulously-kept gradebooks reveal a teacher who insisted on high standards and wasn't afraid to fail those who didn't meet them.

And those standards coupled with the indefatigable patience, as student Carol Marquardsen observed many years later, were Olmsted's great contribution. Though she occupied some minor administrative positions,

Margaret Olmstead nearing retirement

she knew what she liked to do, what she was best at doing, and did it—with thoroughness and dedication for almost half a century.

Her personal life was kept strictly personal and very private. But clearly two things mattered to her: her work and her family. She lived most of her adult life in the Olmsted apartments, with her father and sister Jeanette. The survivors listed in Judge Olmsted's obituary include "Miss Margaret Olmsted and Miss Jeannette Olmsted, *both at home*"[52] (italics mine), an interesting way to refer to women in their sixties and fifties, as

if they had yet to make a social debut. And yet it seems accurate. Margaret Olmsted was indeed "at home" in the big apartment, as she was "at home" at Augustana and in the subjects she taught. She showed no inclination to push limits or change structures to secure more administrative power for women. She chaired the mathematics department, and then watched one of her own (male) students return to assume that role. She took conscientious notes as faculty secretary, a job traditionally assigned to women. (As noted previously, in those minutes, at one point she refers to "faculty and *wives* [italics mine]," even though at that time the faculty numbered about 22 percent women.) Her affiliations were professionally appropriate and politically conservative: Phi Beta Kappa, American Association of University Women, Delta Kappa Gamma (educational honorary society for women), classical and mathematical associations. She was active in the Rock Island League of Women Voters—a registered Republican, as was her father.

Being at home meant being in control of her life through regularity and discipline. One of the tenants in the Sala/Olmsted apartment building, a young bride of twenty-one, recalls the almost ritualistic experience of paying the monthly rent. She would knock on the Olmsted door, which would be opened by Miss Margaret or Miss Jeannette, present her payment, be formally thanked and issued a receipt. "I was never invited in," she remembers. "It wasn't part of the pattern."[53] The threshold of the apartment was the threshold of privacy.[54]

It's hard not to wonder what she made of some of the more explicit passages of Latin poetry, of the violence and sexuality of much classical myth. Her classroom texts were unfailingly decorous: the orderly, pristine prose of Seneca and Cicero.

And yet her eyes were open to the world she lived in. Pragmatically and calmly, she purchased a car and learned to drive at 68, an age when some people would avoid tackling major new learning experiences.

Given Olmsted's reserve, it's interesting to consider but difficult to discern her tone when, in the last formal assessment she made of her career at Augustana, she said: "…few students have chosen Latin as their major over the years. And fewer still take their graduate degrees in the Classics. A number of Augustana professors have been able to train their successors or to train valued assistants in their department. There seems no Augie graduate available to follow me."[55] Was it a flat statement of fact, or a recognition tinged with regret? Did she wish for a protégée such as her colleague Henriette Naeseth had found in Dorothy Parkander? Clearly what Augustana was and would be mattered to her. "I hope," she told the *Augustana Bulletin*, "that Augustana's standards of high scholarship, good character, balance, morality, and goodness of life will be maintained."[56] Did it concern or distress her that no one trained by her, imbued with these values, would follow?

An institution is the lengthened shadow of the men and women who comprise it, her father had believed. Certainly his daughter, in her quiet way, cast such a shadow at Augustana.

The Twenties:
Polls and Prohibition, Flappers and—Feminists?

Amy is no flapper. She's radiantly healthy, walks and climbs in the clear Montana air, zooms around in her truck to gigs across the country. She records CDs under the label Raven's Wing, a metaphor taken from one of her own songs for flying free. She has achieved the freedom those twenties women sought with their rolled stockings, short skirts, and unbuckled boots.

Her freedom is grounded in commitment to the vision she's evolved and is evolving. It's political, it's intellectual, it's aesthetic, it's spiritual. Her songs reflect it with both lyrical poignancy and political bite. And wit. She sings the stories of the vulnerable, the searching, the marginalized—often, the stories of women.

Amy was a thoughtful, amazingly mature Phi Beta Kappa student when I first met her in a class at Augustana. Since her graduation she has taught me much about commitment, about the strange and sacred places of the human heart, about the windings of the spirit as it discovers its own path. I am humbled before her energy and vision.

CHAPTER 4

The Twenties:
Polls and Prohibition, Flappers and—Feminists?

It was over!

Triumphant cannons boomed out victory. Parents joyfully assured children that they need never fear war again, that we'd fought the war to end all wars. Stocks soared. Jazz sizzled. The Twenties roared in.

Though Augustana endorsed sobriety, as we'll see below, it certainly showed its own spirit. Modest celebrations attended the return to "normal" life, the demise of the S.A.T.C., marked by a special (non-alcoholic) banquet, vets back on campus, classrooms, music, sports, social groups, and the generation-spanning corny in-jokes.

Indefatigable Gustav Andreen, a.k.a. "Prexy," rode this financial and psychological upswing, setting off on one of his marathon fund-raising campaigns to make sure that needed new campus buildings would be constructed. Bergendoff reports that in quest of support for the new seminary buildings Andreen "had traveled 34,000 miles and spent 77 nights on sleeping cars, between January 1, 1921, and January 31, 1922."[1] Given that strenuous agenda, he must have felt a little disheartened to hear the Board reprimand the college for permitting his extended absences. Rather, the Board believed, a college president should "stay at home and attend to the work for which he was called: office work, a spiritual adviser, and a housefather, a man at the helm to guide the ship."[2] Andreen sagely ignored this directive long enough for the Board to reconsider. Clearly his energy and charisma filled the pledge cards and the coffers, and by 1924 the Board seemed to get it, reversing their position to request that "Dr. G. A. Andreen...use every effort to close this year without a deficit."[3] He succeeded. By 1928 he could report that things were looking good for the campaign. Donations and pledges would cover costs for the most urgently needed buildings, particularly the science hall. A grateful Synod established a $100,000 Gustav Andreen Fund to assure a pension for "Prexy," should he ever find time to retire. And it not only granted him a year's leave of absence to recoup his energies, it paid for him and his wife to travel to Europe and the Orient.

Women especially felt the energy of the twenties. Two pieces of legislation ushered in a new era of empowerment for them: the Eighteenth Amendment (Prohibition, January 1919) and the Nineteenth Amendment (Equal Suffrage, June 1919).

Cold Water Armies[4], On and Off Campus

Many men supported prohibition fervently. Augustana shows that; its active Prohibition League was spearheaded primarily by male students. But in important ways Prohibition nationally and locally was a women's movement. Unregulated liquor sales, women believed, undermined the family unit—traditionally the woman's sphere and responsibility—by producing drunkenness, poverty, and abuse.[5] As Moline's Mary Stewart put it dramatically, "There were sleepless nights, agonizing prayers, and many times was the question repeated mentally, 'What, oh what! can be done to stay the terrible curse [of drinking]'?"[6]

Some anti-salooners answered the question with direct action. From 1900 till 1910, famously, six-foot, 175-pound hatchet-wielding Carrie Nation (who liked to pun on her name, signing herself "Carry A Nation") smashed and hacked at saloons, when her subtler techniques, such as greeting barkeepers with the sinister "Good morning, you destroyer of souls," weren't getting results. Despite her claim that she was acting on personal instruction from God, the effects she achieved were problematic. On the one hand, every stroke of the hatchet was a blow for those "family values" women were supposed to support.[7] On the other hand, such behavior, however divinely sanctioned, was hardly ladylike.

Nation did some of her most spectacular and widely reported saloon-smashing in Kansas City, Missouri. Nearer home, though, the Tri-Cities had long boasted their own anti-saloon campaigners. Inspired by Chicago's Frances Willard, local women formed the Total Abstinence League (going the Temperance associations one step better), and as early as 1874 courageously gathered outside a Moline tavern, not to smash but to carefully record the names of all who entered, in the (vain) hope of shaming the patrons. It wasn't really the women's fault that a street fight broke out between temperance and tanked-up anti-temperance factions, with "shouts, jeers, and profanity,"[8] but the women were blamed for it. They persisted, however, petitioning the City Council not to grant liquor licenses, and testifying against those saloon keepers who violated city ordinances—with limited success.[9]

By the nineteen-teens a new generation took up the temperance cudgels, and Augustana students were among them. They wrote and orated, studied "the liquor issue" in a class famously nicknamed "boozeology,"[10] and formed a Prohibition League[11] which, by 1913, the *Observer* claimed was "the strongest among the thirteen leagues of the State [of Illinois]."[12] Decisively, as the League discovered by polling students and faculty, the campus supported Prohibition.[13] Rather more so than other areas of the country, where the Eighteenth Amendment brewed speakeasys; "private parties" swilled gin and scotch (the amendment didn't make it illegal to drink, buy, or serve liquor, only to make, sell, or transport it[14]), and contraband alcohol was fairly easy to procure. In Chicago, home of many Augustana students, it would take you a scant 21 minutes to locate a venue and purchase a bottle of your favorite spirit[15]—typically not the Holy variety.

The Nineteenth Amendment: Campus Silence

For women, prohibition and equal suffrage began, at least, as linked issues. As Frances Willard put it in 1879, "women who preside over the homes and rear the children, and whose hands turn over the leaves of the Bible, should be placed in a position where they can help to protect their homes."[16] That position, it became increasingly obvious, was enfranchisement. Until women could vote they could exercise little power. In Chicago, for instance, women petitioned the City Council that laws against selling alcohol to minors be enforced. Council members responded that "we do not see the names of our constituents on your petition."[17] In a similar defeat, the Illinois Woman Suffrage Association urged passage of the so-called "Home Protection Laws," which would allow women to vote on whether a given locality could sell liquor. The measure lost in the Illinois General Assembly.[18]

But eventually the push for equal suffrage split from the temperance movement. Suffragists found that tying the right to vote to one particularly divisive issue weakened their position. Ideological matters aside, in pragmatic terms no barkeeper was going to support a measure that would empower those he saw as adversaries.

Though religious pietism joined women's moral and political agendas in working for Prohibition, Augustana supported the measure almost exclusively because of its church relation. For the Nineteenth Amendment apparently didn't excite the campus. Textual silence speaks powerfully here. Bergendoff's careful history of the early 1900s gives attention to matters that engaged student interest—the Prohibition question, discussed above, not to mention the status of football—but makes no mention of that other hotly debated issue, Woman Suffrage, or, as it came to be called in 1890, Equal Suffrage.

In searching for campus feeling about national and international issues, early *Observers* serve as a useful guide, since they envision themselves as news magazines rather than newspapers (that difference in perceived mission has accompanied the publication throughout its long history). They typically open with two or three substantial articles by students, faculty, and/or alumni/ae, dealing with topics such as current events, political observations, or literary and historical subjects, before moving to lighter, shorter pieces of campus news and jokes. And from the period of the late nineties until 1920 the "women's movement" receives only glancing, and mixed, attention. For example, a 1912 article tracing the causes of increased divorce rates, attributes the problem in part to "'individualism,' which breeds selfishness," and which has "brought about the 'Woman's Movement'," another factor in divorce. To be fair, though, the writer does add that the movement isn't altogether harmful, as it has helped women to develop their talents and abilities more fully.[19] A serialized short story from April and May of that same year poses the problem of the "emancipated woman" of artistic genius versus the homemaker, loving and beloved. Which is the "higher" calling for the woman's talent and energy? The male narrator, attending a recital by the violinist he'd like to marry, feels that "every note [she played] was directed at me, to tell me of the glory, the achievements, and the joy of emancipated womanhood; of the meanness, sordidness, and selfishness of arrogant man."[20] However, after a good deal of philosophical discussion about art, the violinist reveals that she played with such consummate skill because seeing her would-be lover in the audience produced an epiphany: "I beheld life in a new, a nobler light, I gloried in my womanhood, the home appeared exalted and the one hallowed spot upon earth. Love became the basis of all higher motives...."[21] So basically, it's good for women to realize their abilities, but it's better to pour those abilities into creating a loving home.

To train women for doing just that, a course in domestic science was proposed. In support of this move the *Observer* reminds the college community that while Augustana aspires to University status (a possibility then being discussed), it "must not forget that this is a co-educational institution"—meaning that women need to be educated specifically to fit the roles they will assume. Other course proposals, in fields such as engineering, law, and medicine, presumably targeted men.[22] The college, in other words, should recognize that its women students have special needs, and should plan responsibly to meet them.

Articles and orations published throughout this decade from 1910 to 1920 deal, in laboriously polished but often abstract rhetoric, with large issues: patriotism, democracy, duty, selflessness, a changing world, a new era. None address the specific issue of equal suffrage, though divorce, child labor, and (of course) liquor are cited as evils the country must eradicate. Two short news articles mention the "woman question." In 1911 a superbly-named Miss Harriet Grim of the University of Chicago addresses the Adelphic literary society on "Equal Suffrage." Though the *Observer* writer begins somewhat jocularly that "Augustana has at last been invaded, and perhaps it is only a question of time before we will have a Woman's Suffrage Club in our midst," he—the writer presumably is male—goes on to praise Miss Grim's "thorough knowledge" and "logical and convincing manner" of presenting her arguments.[23] Apparently they weren't convincing enough; the prospective Woman's Suffrage Club seems not to have materialized at the college. In 1913 Illinois women gained the right to vote in presidential elections;[24] this event is noted in a story about women students forming a debating club: "The girls are to be congratulated—because such an organization surely will be efficacious in preparing them for the proper performances of those functions of citizenship which devolve upon them by the recent state constitutional amendment."[25] (Were they thought to be presently incapable of performing those functions?) And a 1919 *Observer* calendar notes that the women have scheduled a "Sophragette" Banquet. "Leap Year?" the writer queries, clearly equating the suffragist movement with aggressive females.[26]

This relative silence on the part of Augustana students and faculty is interesting in view of the fact that Illinois was, as local historian Kathleen Seusy has termed it, a "hotbed" of political interest; Moline, in fact, boasted the distinction of mounting the only suffrage movement in Illinois that met continuously from 1877 until the Nineteenth Amendment was passed.[27] Illinois was the first state to ratify the Nineteenth Amendment, just a week after it passed the House of Representatives and the Senate [28]—the *Observer* makes no mention of it.[29] And yet many students came from cities in Illinois, especially Rockford and Chicago, where Jane Addams and Frances Willard, as well Emmy Carlsson Evald, daughter of Augustana founder Erland Carlsson, had achieved prominence in the suffragist movement. Even the doughty Mrs. K. T. Anderson, a frequent contributor to the *Observers* of those years, doesn't tout equal suffrage. Had she forgotten how angry she was when the male students of her generation scorned women's rights? Hardly. In an article chastising the college for the current apathy of its literary societies, she rehearses the discrimination she faced when she dared apply for membership in the Adelphic. Even fifty years later the memory of that discrimination stays and stings in her mind. And yet on the Nineteenth Amendment she shares Augustana's silence.

A couple of explanations for this silence seem reasonable here. First: the college student's eternal insularity, which is both salvation and limitation. Alumni contributions notwithstanding, a campus newspaper/magazine is about the campus. Despite the aspirations of Augustana publications to reflect something beyond Seventh Avenue, Rock Island, despite the fine rhetoric of essays and orations, despite the real dangers being played out on the national and international stage, college students of the teens and twenties tended fundamentally to look inward—to campus concerns, to organizations, to records in debate and forensics and sports being made and broken, to professors and classes loved and resented, to social activities. Young energies, both intellectual and hormonic, are lavished on the doings and tellings of the immediate venue. For instance, even though the Prohibition League was "perhaps the busiest organization at our college" in 1914, the *Observer* doesn't trumpet passage of the Eighteenth Amendment.

The other explanation for silence about the Nineteenth Amendment lies in what may be seen as institutional ambivalence toward women's "emancipation." On the one hand, Augustana's strong church connection enjoined both social justice and individual responsibility for gifts seen as God-given.[30] That meant women ought to be allowed equal opportunities to learn and grow, and they ought to make the most of these opportunities. On the other hand, that same church connection tended to endorse traditional distinctions in gender roles. Attempts to wrestle with this paradox are illustrated in the two pieces outlined above. That the writers did wrestle is to their credit and to the credit of their education. It's certainly more than many of their day and ours are willing to do.

And Augustana's women weren't meekly silenced.

Raising Their Hems and Their Voices: Flappers

If your concern was paternal, the flapper was a problem. Otherwise, she was a pleasure. Jauntily feather-footed in her unfastened galoshes [which flapped, creating the nickname], her flesh-colored stockings rolled below the knee and her skirt barely touching it, slender and boyish, the flapper came in to the tune "I'll Say She Does"—and frequently she did.[31]

They were newly energized. They had, after all, fought their own battle, or listened to the stories of their forebears who had fought, for the right to vote in national elections. Like the world war, that battle, too, was about freedom. They no longer had to accept political measures legislated by men alone, and that, as for instance Augustana's Anna Olsson surely discovered, not only affirmed their autonomy, but gave them a certain economic leverage as well. They could claim independence. They could listen unblushingly to Sigmund Freud and Havelock Ellis laud sexual freedom. They could forget that low soft voice ever a fine thing in woman, and speak up, assert their opinions openly, even stridently, choose their behaviors and values (and they did, often to the consternation of appalled parents). They bobbed their hair in men's barbershops, painted their lips and powdered their noses, bought brassieres to flatten their chests, rolled their stockings and hiked up their hems, smoked, and danced the Charleston, that fast knee-knocking fox-trot that many colleges banned because it was considered "overly physical and lacking in grace."[32] (The ban was no more successful than Augustana's ongoing attempt to prohibit more genteel dancing. The Charleston became so popular that in 1923 the dance floor of Boston's Pickwick Club collapsed under "1,000 gyrating Charlestoners" and killed forty-four of them.[33]) The advent of the automobile gave them wider physical freedom as well. And prohibition, far from restraining rebellious behavior, seemed to encourage it. Chugging out to a roadhouse in a shiny Ford Model T, and possibly chugging from the gin flask in the brown paper bag as well, flappers reveled in pleasures that "nice girls" would virtuously eschew.

Although "not all flappers went to college," still, as Barbara Miller Solomon points out, "flapperdom invaded the campus."[34] Their look—and the attitudes it implied—"bedeviled and challenged" college administrators who found their independence threatening. As one observer put it, "What kind of grandmothers will our present day masterful flappers make? Accustomed as they are to their own way, will they be content in 1960 to let themselves be overruled by fresh young things?"[35]

Solomon's research suggests that the flapper was a bit more complicated than this image implies, however. "…[S]trong as well as self-centered…[the flapper was] the woman who liked men but would not be controlled by any man"—the woman "who roused anxiety for her seemingly anti-feminine values on college campuses of the 1920s"—yet at the same time, the woman who "did not abandon the compulsion to behave correctly, to be ladylike, though [she] insisted on [her] individuality".[36] As one flapper put it in 1927, "You cannot heap us all together and announce that in sum total we constitute a problem. We are not one single problem. We are a multitude of problems all different…." [37]

At Augustana, where a still-strong church connection could impose some controls over behavior not possible on larger, secular campuses, flapperdom appears not seriously to have "bedeviled and challenged" dean and president. The bobbed hair and short skirts sported by students and some of the younger faculty seem more concessions to practicality (for women athletes) than to prevailing style. Still, there are indications that Augustana recognized both the threat and the possibilities of the flapper phenomenon. An early (March 1920) *Observer* article discussing "Vulgarities in American Life" (contributed by an alumnus of 1915) cites the "soulless music that appeals to nothing but the feet," and fashions in which "a woman hurts her body [presumably by strapping down her breasts, which in some quarters was considered unhealthy, and]…sacrifices her womanly modesty to the dictates of a [degrading] fashion."[38] A year later, a sophomore student decries the loss of values that the war had been fought to preserve. Materialism reigns, the writer claims, "dress has become extreme in cost and fashion," and "hardness and flippancy," originally needed to maintain a "'stiff upper lip,' have remained in our characters; while the deep emotions, splendid courage and sympathy, have disappeared…."[39] But most specific of all in its condemnation of the flapper style and its underlying affront to morality came in a 1925 editorial reflecting on the winners of the Miss America pageant, then in its sixth year. The editorial, entitled "Miss

America," is a half-column quotation from Armand T. Nichols, pageant head, and ends with an impassioned peroration describing the kind of girls who have won the contest:

The roses on their cheeks have been natural. Their long, lovely hair has known not the henna or the barber's clippers. Their lips have not fallen into the evil ways of lipstick.

The *Observer* editor and his assistant are of course male; no comment accompanies Nichols' obvious attack on the flapper style. (Parenthetically, it's interesting to note, as does Barrington Boardman, that the pageant's first winner Margaret Gorman posted her "vital statistics" as 30-25-32—the perfect flapper figure.) But the fact that Nichols' trenchant comments were included without qualification in the *Observer* implies editorial agreement with them. Add to this tacit disapproval a piece showing a template for the educated woman, featured in 1926, again reprinted without comment, and a picture emerges of what "nice girls" at Augustana should aspire to. Writer John Lord, drawing heavily on the Victorian "angel in the house" model, instructs his readers that "A Woman Should Be…" educated to be "interesting to both her own sex and to men"; useful in the home; with "affections as well as intellect developed" and "soul elevated" beyond cosmetic and sartorial superficialities, and above concerns for social caste. Vitally important, "she should be taught to become the friend and helpmate of man,—never his rival…." because man's instinct is to worship, not compete with, her, and she can use his devotion to raise and purify him spiritually.[40] And when, in 1929, two students died from a scarlet fever epidemic, the man, Paul Munson, is lauded for his leadership in many campus activities, while the woman, Gladys Oberg, is praised for her "unassuming and ladylike" demeanor.[41] It's undoubtedly true that one was a leader and the other wasn't. It's also pretty clear where the official organ of Augustana opinion, carefully overseen by mentoring faculty, comes down on the flapper issue.

And yet. We can find indications that Augustana women in the 1920s, if not exactly lipstick- and gin-toting rebels, did share a more general feeling that "…college represented a time of learning, growth, and hope,"[42] and that part of this feeling involved asserting their own capabilities in the face of traditional male dominance. Esthena Randolph's 1921 essay in the *Rockety-I* satirizing the arrogant superiority of males in the classroom (quoted in the sketch on Netta Bartholomew Anderson) offers a critique, albeit in humorous vein, of previous anti-feminist attitudes, and a healthy sense that women, "considered [by male students] inferior creatures with their inferior minds, possessed a most surprising aptitude for learning, indeed, even equal to that of a man."[43] In 1925 the first "co-eds" were allowed to join the college band, and in 1926 Helen Searle became the "first girl…elected editor [of the yearbook] at a regular election" by the sophomore class. This victory was no small achievement; according to the *Observer*, the editor-in-chief and the business manager represented "the two highest offices a class can bestow upon any of its members,"[44] and Searle took on "intense competition," winning by one vote.[45] In 1926, just a month before the Angel in the House manifesto, an *Observer* editorial comments that "marriage and divorce questions are of more serious import than to be merely debated. *What the girls say* bears directly upon each one's future. Statistics now show that on the average one out of every seven persons will be faced with the question of divorce…." (italics mine).[46] "What the girls say" mattered, not just theoretically, but in practical life-choices.

But probably the most serious challenge to "unassuming and lady-like" behavior came not from rebellious campus flappers, but from women athletes. We'll deal in more detail with women's athletics elsewhere, but here it's worth noting that Augustana women resisted the old models of decorous, subservient femininity—and the second-class status they often imposed—when it came to use of facilities and opportunities in sport. As a student writer in the yearbook for 1926 recounts, "Gym requirements, lockable dressing rooms, and practice hours have all been gained through the steady effort of Miss [Anne] Greve [women's physical education instructor and director of women's athletics, 1923-1934] and some few interested girls. Progress has been made against all the odds of conservative thought, sarcastic word, and common practice."[47]

If they weren't full-fledged flappers, these Augustana women could, when necessary, raise a flap.

Emmy Evald and the Flap Over the Woman's Building

When the former, refurbished Carlsson Hall was rededicated and renamed in October 2008, President Steven Bahls announced that a long-standing injustice had been rectified. That injustice was the story of the Woman's Building.

It began and ended with Emmy Carlsson Evald—whose portrait now hangs over the fireplace in the Great Hall of the building, and whose name is incised on the stone lintel above the door. And in that hall, where faculty and student groups gather, and voices carry, her voice, once silenced, solos over the rest.

A woman was commissioned to be the first person to proclaim the tidings of the resurrection [of Jesus Christ]. "Woman" was the first word uttered by the resurrected Saviour.... "Go tell!" was the Lord's first command to woman.[48]

She was neither student nor faculty, yet she influenced Augustana in lasting and sometimes tumultuous ways. She was born and grew up Augustana. In fact, she and the College and Theological Seminary came into being at almost the same time and by the same agency: Emmy Christiana was just three years old when her father, the Reverend Dr. Erland Carlsson, helped found Augustana in 1860. Her faith—the driving force behind her extraordinarily varied activities—was shaped in Carlsson's Chicago church.

That faith translated into social activism with a strong feminist bent. As a child Emmy observed not only her father's passion for social justice but also the extraordinary gifts of his wife Eva Charlotta Andersson Carlsson. Emmy was later to claim that "no Swedish pastor's wife in America or Sweden has...carried out such

Emmy Carlsson Evald: "Go tell!"

important work, as mother did."[49] She may have been inclined to exaggeration—her rhetoric tends toward the fierce and fiery—but obviously Eva Carlsson influenced Emmy's almost militant commitment to the suffragist cause. Emmy was a charter member of the First International Woman Suffrage Conference in 1902, sharing platforms with luminaries such as Susan B. Anthony, Clara Barton, and Carrie Chapman Catt.[50] In the first decade of the twentieth century she appeared before both a Congressional

Committee on woman suffrage and the Illinois state legislature, pleading the cause of enfranchisement. Long-skirted, corseted, and bespectacled, she minced no words:

> *Do you [men] withhold order and justice because all do not want it? Our Lord and Father, the Creator, did not withhold salvation because there are some who do not want it....Oh men, let justice speak and may the public weal demand that this disfranchisement of the noble American women shall be stopped.*[51]

She would wait another decade before "justice spoke."

But Emmy didn't believe in waiting. Her lifelong mantra centered on active verbs: "Go tell!" While the political bodies dallied over women's fitness to vote, Emmy was busy creating another way to "go tell." And that way was the Woman's Missionary Society—the group that, in 1922, would be commissioned to raise money for a women's dormitory at Augustana.

The Woman's Missionary Society (WMS) was a mover and a shaker in the Augustana Synod, almost from its inception in 1892. Before that time, various women's groups in individual churches—sewing circles and the like—had nourished the church's work on both financial and spiritual fronts. But Emmy Evald envisioned an organization that would unite these groups under one umbrella with one compelling purpose: mission. And that mission expressed her bold feminist slant. In *Mission Tidings*, the WMS periodical she founded and edited, Emmy never lost an opportunity to charge readers with their possibilities and responsibilities. Banner headlines ringingly asserted that

> *Woman's status determines to a very large extent the character of her nation. It is woman who is the measure of civilization. When I find a field too hard for a man I put in a woman.*[52]

Emmy, rightly, called the organization a "dynamo": it sent missionaries, doctors, and educators throughout the world, often into then-remote areas. By 1903 it was paying the salaries of women missionary doctors, sending women to medical schools—even making up a deficit in the men's missionary society funds. By 1926 it had grown from its original fifty to 60,000 members. By 1935—dimes and quarters coming in steadily even during lean Depression years—it had gathered almost two million dollars[53], worth more than ten times that today. By 1946, the year of Emmy's death, the WMS had used those funds to build more than seventy schools, hospitals, orphanages, and women's homes around the world, as well as supporting hundreds of missionaries.[54] And for forty-three years, one woman served as president: Emmy Evald. How close that position was to her heart shows clearly in a reflection she made as she neared 80: "As president [of the Woman's Missionary Society] for forty-three years [I] have been keeping up its work by the grace and strength of the Lord. I praise and thank God for this wonderful opportunity in my life to have served the mission cause and to obey the resurrected Savior's challenge, so dear to me, 'Go tell.'"[55] Dynamic, tireless, and superbly confident, she gained both ardent supporters and disgruntled detractors; both honorary academic degrees and a Swedish knighthood, and threatened lawsuits; both compliments— "American's most outstanding woman of Swedish descent,"[56] "the Jane Addams of the Augustana Synod"[57]—and complaints—"Mrs. Evald has you hypnotized."[58]

But much of this controversy lay in the future when, in 1920, the Augustana Endowment Society suggested that the WMS undertake fundraising for a new women's dormitory at the college. The project obviously appealed to Emmy, weaving together many of her dearest interests: educational opportunities for women, sited specifically within a Christian context; the future of Augustana, which had meant so much to her father, and building buildings, which meant so much to *her*. She quickly assumed chairmanship of the building committee and got down to the work with her customary—or perhaps even more than customary—zeal; I imagine her signature pearls swinging, her glasses almost shooting sparks of energy. A blitz of pamphlets and inspirational speeches ensued. Special "campaign" stationery was printed up with a letterhead that read:

Largest Common Task Undertaken by the Women of the Augustana Synod, Pray and Labor for its Success.[59]

The women who opened this intriguing letter would have read that

The Call is that all the women of the entire Synod should…so co-operate that this Home Mission Task, right at the heart of our Synod, may be realized….Come and help us to build a house that will safeguard the health, the morals, of the daughters of our Synod.

Shall we close Augustana's gates and bid our daughters go elsewhere for lack of suitable living quarters?

And, to loose a shaft right into the heart of Lutheran guilt:

You *are an Augustana Woman! How much have* you *given?* [60]

The goal was $150,000. Thanks to these appeals, in just one year the WMS had collected $121,000 in gifts and pledges. Augustana president Gustav Andreen mused rhapsodically: "What a glorious day it will be when at some great convention of our Synod the women will gather from East and West and North and South in the new and attractive Woman's [*sic*— Emmy wanted it stated in the generic singular] Building at Augustana! How they will rejoice and thank God as they gather in the ample reception room with its open fireplace, and inspect the home that they themselves have helped build to be a blessing for the women students, their own daughters, at Augustana!"[61] It was a dream Emmy happily shared.

Unfortunately, the dream wasn't quite realized. Disagreements, then tensions, then outright conflict developed between the WMS and the college's Board of Directors about the new building: where it should be placed (the WMS wanted it on the hill on the corner of 38th Street and 7th Avenue, the board preferred the location on 7th Avenue, across from the Denkmann Library), who should be hired to draw the plans and build it (each party had commissioned its own firm). Negotiations were attempted. Deliberations, sent into committee, dragged on. Students joined the increasingly acrimonious fray, siding with what they saw as a beleaguered Board. "If the women can agree," the *Observer* said in 1925, "Augustana will soon begin the construction of its new women's hall. If they begin to wrangle, as they have done before, well—there's no telling when its erection will be begun, much less completed."[62] "The large majority of Augustana students" supports the Board's position, the *Observer* claimed, arguing that the Board, who were responsible for Augustana's overall welfare, ought to have final say on where the building would be located—a not unreasonable point, certainly.[63]

Various explanations, some almost caricatures of the growing hostility between the two parties, were offered for the disagreement about location. The Seminary didn't want a building to interfere with their view across the

One of the posters urging contributions to the proposed Woman's Building

river. The WMS wanted a more prestigious location than that afforded by the lower 7th Avenue site. The women's health would be impaired were they to live in the damp atmosphere below the hill. The men resented the women's assumption of control. The women resisted being dictated to.

In the end the proposals of the WMS were rejected in favor of the Board's choice. And the campaign fragmented. Some of those who had pledged support, shunning controversy, withdrew. Others voiced anger and disillusionment with what seemed to them a betrayal of trust. As Mary Andreen, President Andreen's wife and Evald's friend, put it, "Those who had worked hard to push through [the woman's building project] were made to feel like those of unsavory reputations who were not wanted and could scarcely be tolerated."[64] Legal action resulted. The WMS turned the remaining money over to the college. When the Woman's Building ultimately was completed and officially dedicated in 1928, not a single representative of the WMS was present, nor wished to be. A suggestion that the building be named "Emmy Evald" stalled in Board deliberations. Perhaps in a belated attempt to salute Emmy's efforts, the building was named Carlsson Hall (for her father) when it became a men's dormitory in 1960.

What went so disastrously wrong may have roots in both the political and the personal. One student of the WMS, Augustana alumna Jane Telleen, suggests that the organization may have been seen as too powerful; in 1907 it had become a self-standing, independent unit apart from Synodical jurisdiction. After the Augustana debacle, and another conflict in New York City, the WMS was reabsorbed into the Synod.[65] But another cause was undoubtedly Emmy Evald herself. The famous, energetic confidence that drove her efforts and created such amazing results could also antagonize. Emmy wasn't a compromiser. She wouldn't negotiate; she'd sometimes turn off her hearing aid at moments of controversy.[66] Increasingly she was seen by some within her own organization as autocratic and inflexible. Perhaps had she come to the Augustana Board of Directors with a more open, conciliatory attitude, she'd have achieved different results. Or perhaps not. To be less assertive might have reinforced traditional ideas about women's appropriate deference to male authority, and ended, finally, in the Board "knowing best" where the women's place should be—even though the women had raised most of the money to build that place.

However disputatious the circumstances of its birth, though, the Woman's Building turned out to be an elegant living space, according to an enthusiastic account in the *Observer* shortly after its opening. Its appointments are described in almost lyrical detail: Kaplan Furniture Company advising on interior design for that "ample reception room" Andreen envisioned, Shallene Brothers providing the furnishings. Three large rugs, several sofas and armchairs, and curtains and drapes created "a harmonious color scheme" appropriate for both relaxed conversation and special "spreads," for which reservations were required. Besides what's now known as the Swanson Great Hall, two smaller reception areas opened. These, the *Observer* said, complemented the larger room, each with sofa, desk, and chair, and accessories "in keeping with the color scheme in the larger hall."

Woman's Building: exterior and "ample reception room"

They offered greater intimacy; in the delightful phrases of the *Observer* writer, they "afford an opportunity for personal visits, and perhaps confidential talks between parents or visitors and the dormitory girls."[67]

Individual rooms received the same careful attention. They were "beautifully decorated..., [each] fully furnished with a fine rug, single beds, desks, chairs, and dressers. Great care has been exercised in selecting the furniture.... The result is that each room is very comfortable, beautiful, and convenient, and provides an ideal home for its co-ed occupant." The writer assures readers that "there are sufficient means to permit purchase of only the best"[68]—a tribute to the Board's effectiveness in raising additional necessary funds after the WMS had withdrawn from the campaign.

Besides the "co-eds" the new premises housed the Dean of Women's office, and two faculty members, Estelle Mandeville and Anna Viola, both members of the Conservatory. Later English Department chair Henriette Naeseth took up brief, memorable residence there.

But the new quarters were to be women-centered in other than cosmetic terms; residents were to participate in their own governance as well. Dean Dora Carlson headed a newly organized house council to "work... on the question of rules and regulations" for the women who occupied the "finely furnished" venue. Emmy Evald might have approved of that.

Carlsson-Evald Hall is impressive: state of the art in design and equipment. French windows on the north side of Swanson Great Hall open onto a veranda overlooking the tennis courts beside the Bergendoff Fine Arts building. Carlsson-Evald is home to the departments of accounting, business administration, economics, education, psychology, and sociology. And so, as President Bahls has observed, justice has been done. Perhaps a building that asks students to learn about our humanity, to function justly and ethically in a practical world, and to teach tomorrow's citizens to realize their own gifts—perhaps such a building more fully houses the spirit of Emmy Carlsson Evald even than the women's dormitory she never entered.

The Art of a Gracious Life: Alma Johnson

She painted lyrical landscapes, trees tipped with gold, lakes full of light, studies in gentleness and serenity. The subjects and technique fit her character. She was gracious, gentle in both person and pedagogy. And yet there was vision and shrewdness, too, in the white-haired, bespectacled, sensibly-shod lady with the irenic half-smile who looked like the quintessential grandmother.

She came to Augustana in 1926, after an eight-year stint at Luther College in Wahoo, Nebraska. She'd been born in the winter of the year Inez Rundstrom graduated from Augustana (December 21, 1885), and had grown up in a Midwest Lutheran parsonage. Her excursions far to the west and east—to Washington State College, the New York School of Fine and Applied Arts, the Chicago Academy of Fine Arts, and Northwestern University, where she earned her B.S. degree[69]—represent rather remarkable pilgrimages for a daughter of the Rev. and Mrs. George A. Johnson of Rockford, Illinois. Rockford was, at that time, so concentrated a community of Swedish Lutherans that for many years it provided a veritable nursery for future Augustana students, who didn't need to travel far physically or spiritually for their college education.

It's tempting to speculate what Alma Johnson made of these new and different venues, a young woman entering the academy in the early years of the twentieth century: whether she encountered and was challenged by different cultural patterns, or whether her focus on visual expression narrowed her concentration; whether she was aware of the general skepticism about women in higher education, or whether her choice of study—one of the "soft" subjects within the reach of women—secured her a safe place. Whatever her life journeys meant to her, she kept on taking them, to various "art colonies" throughout the United States, and to sites in Europe.

But ultimately, it seems, she brought her vision back home. In 1926 illness forced the retirement of Olof Grafstrom, who had held single sway in Augustana's art department for thirty years. His departure created a large void; he'd been a productive and much admired practitioner as well as a teacher of art. His monumental tryptichs with their muscular Biblical scenes grace the altars of many Midwest Lutheran churches, and when he left the college, according to Bergendoff, "friends gathered funds to keep on the campus one of the finest and largest of his paintings—a scene from Lappland."[70] His pedagogical methods consisted more of demonstration and some touching-up of student work than of verbal critiques; his English remained uncertain, according to his former student Fritiof Fryxell, Class of 1922.[71]

As his successor Johnson presents a study in contrasts. Rather than an assembling of massive forms, her work projects delicacy and intimacy. And rather than correcting, she critiqued. She did so, according to a tribute prepared by colleagues representing the American Association of University Women, with both acuity and love: "her criticism was always constructive, softened by a true evaluation of [students'] work." And she didn't cultivate stars: "her attitude of sincere interest was the same toward students of lesser ability as toward those of greater talent," all of whom, according to the tribute, "loved and respected her."[72] Her vision of Augustana College evidently mandated regard for and patience with every

student. Teaching here was about serving, about showing and genuinely feeling "deep and personal interest in each student as an individual."[73] "Her joy," according to Conrad Bergendoff, "was in opening the eyes of her students to the beauty in the world, and to train their hands in creating something of beauty themselves."[74]

But what earns Alma Johnson her particular niche in college history is that she created the impetus for the Augustana Art Association in 1927. With a slim-to-none budget but with presidential approval she managed to gather a collection which fostered art appreciation not only on campus but for the larger

Alma Johnson: opening students' eyes to beauty

community who could attend exhibits free of charge—and so to form the nucleus for the impressive art collection and for the art history department at the college today. She also assembled a rental library of artworks which faculty and students could, for a nominal fee, borrow to give aesthetic touches to sparsely furnished homes and dorm rooms. "Since her college teaching was done when money and facilities were limited," the AAUW tribute reads, in massive understatement, "she knew how to assemble such a library at little cost."[75]

In the home of her sister, Ruth Johnson Ander, and her husband O. Fritiof Ander, who taught history at Augustana, Alma Johnson lived her serene and gracious life at the college until she retired in 1953. Dinner guests at the Ander table remember Johnson's kindness and her gentle but incisive wit. In January of 1959, after a brief illness, she died in a local hospital. [76]

The Holmen Sisters: Music From the Heart

They were unlike in many ways. In appearance—Regina, simple and understated, long hair drawn into a bun, rosy face makeup-free; Ruth impeccably stylish, the latest fashion accented with jewelry or the vivid sweep of a scarf. In demeanor—Regina reserved and dignified; Ruth outgoing and enthusiastic. In life situation—Regina, married in her twenties, mother of three, centered in her home base of Rock Island; Ruth, single until the age of 74, as much at home in New York City as on the Augustana campus. And yet the Holmen sisters shared what was central to each: a passion for music, for the making and teaching of it. And they shared a strong loyalty to Augustana.

Both graduated from Augustana, Regina in 1922, Ruth in 1928, each at the top of her class. They had grown up in Lutheran country parishes around Kansas and Iowa, where their father, the Reverend Dr. John Algot Holmen, ministered. Later he joined the Augustana Seminary faculty and the family moved to Rock Island. Each sister showed musical gifts at an early age, a legacy from their mother Amelia Christensen Holmen. Mrs. Holmen served as a model for her daughters in the intelligence, sensitivity, and discipline with which she approached music. And by her example she inculcated more personal qualities as well: love, strength, gentleness. Regina's husband Fritiof Fryxell declared that "I worshipped the ground she walked on so lightly," and her grandson Roald was later to write of her, "My grandma lived like candle-light."

Regina Holmen Fryxell

Mrs. Holmen was, in fact, Regina's first organ teacher. The lesson took place on a quiet Sunday afternoon in the Holmens' Essex, Iowa, parsonage. Listening to her mother play the reed organ, little Regina determined she wanted to do that. But she was too young, her fingers too small to reach the notes her mother showed her. The lesson dissolved in discord and in her tears.

But the tears soon ended as she practiced and practiced, and felt her skill growing. By the time she matriculated at Augustana in 1918, she was aflame to learn more about the music she'd come to love. And when she graduated in 1922, she'd learned enough to qualify for the Juilliard School of Music in New York.

Regina Holmen Fryxell: composer, liturgist, teacher, performer

And she'd also qualified for a modest piece of Augustana history. Gifted in words as well as in music, she'd majored in English and French in the College as well as piano and organ in the Conservatory— thereby becoming the first person to graduate with degrees from both Conservatory and College.

That double achievement was to inform her subsequent professional life. In addition to teaching piano and organ at Augustana, serving as church organist into her eighties, and performing recitals, one memorably in Washington, D.C.'s National Cathedral, Regina became a composer. In her many anthems, published by houses such as Fortress, Abingdon, Westminster, and Carl Fischer, she joined word and music with deep sensitivity to both semantic and musical nuance. Undoubtedly her sister Ruth's expertise in voice helped refine her understanding of singable melodies for the scriptural passages and poetry she chose to set.

But her most significant accomplishment, as least as far as the heritage of the Augustana Synod is concerned, remains her setting of the liturgy for the 1948 *Service Book and Hymnal* of the Lutheran Church in America (LCA). This work entailed adapting to the English language, and then to a musical line, the liturgical traditions of the various ethnic bodies that had merged into the LCA. Regina's setting has been used and beloved in many congregations throughout the country. In fact, parts of it are included in the most recent Lutheran hymnal, *Evangelical Lutheran Worship*, which appeared in 2006. As one organist put it recently, "Her work was a gift to us." Augustana recognized that gift when it conferred on her an honorary Doctorate of Humane Letters in 1961.

She gave other gifts as well. Her piano students remember her patience and encouragement. She kept a much-thumbed spiral notebook in which she recorded their names and some personal information about each one. And her passion for music, her belief in its transformative power, has touched lives of people she never knew. That belief survived strenuous testing. She and her husband, Dr. Fritiof Fryxell, who established Augustana's geology department, lost two of their three brilliant sons to traffic accidents. Regina's answer to these tragedies was not tears but music. Her anthems produced in the wake of grief move with quiet depth and authenticity. And in that movement—in lines that haunt with yearning, but resolve to serenity—persons distressed physically and spiritually have found a way to healing. Where do those lines come from, she was sometimes asked. And she'd smile. "Who knows? But you listen [to the music] and let it lead you."

Listening led the first graduate of both College and Conservatory to unite both, triumphantly, in her life.[77] Regina Holmen Fryxell died in 1993.

Ruth Holmen Taylor

She would come to Commencement for nearly thirty years with suitcase packed and waiting by her door at home, ready to board the train for New York City as soon as she'd congratulated her graduating students— many with hugs and tears at leaving her—and doffed her cap and gown. This ritual marked not only the end of each school year; it served as a paradigm of Ruth Holmen's life. It was a life balanced between the ethos of a Midwestern Church-related college, with its celebration of the individual, its stability, its optimism, and the high-powered, competitive, exhilarating world of the New York musical scene. Ruth's amazing achievement was to be fully at home in both worlds.

That achievement was honored in a syndicated feature story that appeared in newspapers across the country when she died. Her heritage of "prairie Swedish Lutheranism," which fused "living from the land and sophisticated appreciation of vocal literature" made her "an American musical guru," a "can-do American, finding the maximum potential in any voice," according to singers she coached in New York. And those voices ranged from the undergraduates who came daily to her studio on

Ruth Holmen Taylor: "an American musical guru"

the Augustana campus, to professionals in the Metropolitan Opera chorus who visited her Manhattan apartment during her post-retirement years.[78] No teacher is universally beloved, but Ruth Holmen probably came as close to that state as any.

Like her older sister, Ruth Holmen earned double degrees, in both liberal arts and in music (she majored in history). And like Regina, Ruth studied at Juilliard, as well as the Eastman School of Music. Before joining the faculty at Augustana in 1948, she taught in grammar and high schools in Kansas and New York.[79] She retired from the college in 1981, married her former voice coach, Bernard Taylor, head of the vocal department at Juilliard, and moved to New York City where she joined him in teaching.

Campus visits from the Taylors were always gala events: long reception lines in House-on-the-Hill, Ruth resplendent in the latest New York styles, looking exotic and often, to dazed Midwest eyes, mildly daring; Bernard Taylor in formal attire. There would be hugs and handshakes for everyone, regardless of whether the Taylors knew you well or not. Both glowed with the charisma they were famous for, and with the joy of their union.

Like Regina, too, Ruth found in her passion for teaching strength to continue Taylor's methods after his death. Even when her own health failed, even when age blurred her senses, "she could still hear the wind whisper—and set it on its right path," one of her New York students claimed. Days before her death at the age of 96 she was still teaching, "singing through her breathing tubes," laughing softly when a student failed to match her tone. "Is it that bad?" the student asked. "No, no," she said. "I could definitely teach you to sing. You just need help with your pitch."

Her step-great-grandson put it this way: she "knew how to bring out the talent, beauty, and strength we all have inside us. She was a gentle enabler....And she was dogged."[80]

THE THIRTIES:
THE DEPRESSION OF EDUCATED WOMEN

Dana could have written the book on depression—of spirits, of professional advancement. Well into her doctoral thesis, with years of research and graduate-student living (or partly living) behind her, she hit an impasse with her chosen subject. Personal and intellectual integrity insisted that she couldn't get around the difficulty. As Annie Dillard notes ruefully, when the bearing walls of a piece of writing won't hold, you've got no choice. They've got to go down. So Dana—who kept bees, built house additions, repaired cars, and whipped up the best four-course meal in Iowa City—took a sledge hammer to her dissertation and, with courage, energy, honesty, and a fair amount of anger, knocked down the bearing walls.

But instead of settling into a lifelong whine at the wasted time and energy, she started all over again. Her second choice of subject was to assure her not only of her degree, but of a place in the history of feminist studies. And to make her a teacher and mentor whose clarity and tested integrity won her the love of her many students.

She taught something else: how to die gracefully. Even when you, at not quite forty, and your friends want desperately to get around it. Physical strength failed, but in Dana's case, the bearing walls—the energy, the honesty, the wit, the love, the investment in life—held. They hold in the memory of her.

CHAPTER 5

The Thirties:
The Depression of Educated Women

When the Andreens returned from their tour of Europe and the Orient in 1929, and the Augustana Woman's Club feted Mrs. Andreen with a welcome-back tea, the college faced a very different outlook for its economic future than the rosy one of the year before.

It's come to be known as "Black Thursday," October 24, 1929, "the most disastrous decline in the biggest and broadest market of history," according to the *New York Times*.[1] Security values plummeting by $6 billion. Brokers on the New York Stock Exchange floor "roar[ing] like... lions and tigers...holler[ing] and scream[ing],...claw[ing] at one another's collars...."[2] Though the crisis briefly and precariously stabilized, by the end of the decade America was in serious economic trouble. In fact, in the Great Depression.

By 1932, about a quarter of America's banks were defunct. More than half of the nation's African-Americans and 40 percent of its whites were unemployed. Two hundred fifty thousand children younger than twenty-one reportedly "roamed the country" in freight trains.[3] Men without jobs stayed at home, if they had homes, watching their families shrink to bone, feeling useless and desperate; otherwise they "curled up on park benches" and stood in "dreary" lines at soup kitchens.[4] Women went out and scrounged what employment they could find—if they could find any. People foraged through garbage dumps. "Brother, Can You Spare a Dime?" was the current hit.

The economic crisis, naturally, generated a crisis for education. Teaching jobs grew fewer, remuneration poorer, firings commoner. Educators across the country objected, fiercely, to slashes in funding for public schools. In Chicago, for instance, a locality known well to Augustana's constituency, public school teachers had worked for eight and a half months without pay when in the spring of 1933 they began a series of high-profile protest marches.[5]

Higher education fared no better. College degrees lost their cachet when jobs became so scarce that New York department stores could require aspiring elevator operators to hold the B.A. An Association of Unemployed College Alumni came into being.[6] Even those who valued the less tangible benefits of higher education couldn't afford it. Consequently, "everywhere college enrollments were dropping."[7]

Augustana, of course, shared that fate. It graduated 70 students in 1928; by 1933 that number was down to 57, though with fluctuations in between. "Both for new and continuing students work had to be found on campus or in community [in order for them to stay in college]," Bergendoff writes. "Dr. [F. O.] Hanson [Augustana's financial secretary] redoubled his efforts…to induce students to come to college…. Salaries had to be reduced." In academic year 1933-34 (one of "deep concern," according to Augustana's Board president), some faculty were teaching at only two-thirds of their normal pay.[8] Board Minutes from the time rather poignantly record what a professor's salary would be, and then note the percentage of reduction. And those donors so energetically cultivated by Dr. Andreen necessarily defaulted on pledges to the new building fund.[9] It also didn't help that the college's financial operations had been managed somewhat casually, often more on hope than on hard-headed budgetary projections.[10]

But while the college overall may have been scrambling for students, the numbers of women seem to have been less markedly affected by the economic crisis. Between the years of 1928 and 1934—the grimmest years at the college, according to Bergendoff's history—women comprise between a low of 27 percent (in the junior class of 1933) to a high of 53 percent (in the first-year class of 1930). The average hovers around the 40th percentile. (It's not uncommon to find that the higher percentages fall in the first and second years, since completing the degree was, for women who might reasonably expect to marry and be supported, less urgent than for men.) In 1933 the Big Sister/Little Sister tea to welcome and orient incoming women students drew an attendance of 150, including "old and new members."[11] These statistics might suggest, as one observer of college history has conjectured, that parents who determined to send their daughters to college and/or women who determined to go somehow managed to pursue their plans in spite of the Depression. Perhaps those campus and community jobs that Dr. Hanson worked so hard to secure helped out with tuition costs (by 1934, at $90 a semester).[12] And the determination to attend college may reflect Barbara Miller Solomon's assessment of women collegians during the twenties and thirties who saw college as a time of "learning, growth, and hope," and felt "very conscious of the possibilities...for their lives...."[13] Certainly an energetic, determined confidence sounds in the various plans, petitions, and deliberations of the Woman's Club for those years (this group is discussed more fully elsewhere). And a notice to alumnae included in Augustana's 1927 yearbook urges action to solidify women's status at the college:

Get busy! Get behind the movement to make it possible for Augustana women to take their rightful place in the Association of Collegiate Alumnae. All that we need now to meet the requirements is a woman on the College Board. Let us elect to the next Synod delegates pledged to put in a woman director![14]

But as the Roaring Twenties sank into the Desperate Thirties, observers of the collegiate scene noted that women weren't attending graduate school in great numbers, nor were college and universities snapping them up to teach. By 1938 Marjorie Nicholson, Dean of Smith College, finds that numbers of women faculty in colleges and universities actually *declined* from 1926 to 1938. And when women did secure positions, they often found themselves placed—and left—at the lowest faculty ranks, with little incentive to produce the creative scholarship that universities rewarded. So the sense of their inferiority was self-perpetuating: schools didn't hire faculty who weren't productive scholars; women weren't productive scholars because schools were slow to recognize their achievements. As a result, according to Nicholson, women in the academy "settl[ed] down to competent but undistinguished service."[15]

Augustana followed this national trend, at least in terms of numbers and rank. Women comprised 22 percent of the faculty,[16] slightly below the national average, which stood between 27 and 28 percent during the same time period. And they did tend to get "settled" in the instructor/assistant/associate categories, with accompanying salary stagnation. Tredway notes, for instance, that Henriette Clark taught in the Department of Secretarial Science from 1935 to 1945 without a raise.[17] Women faculty were typically settled also in traditional "female" fields—subjects such as literature, music, art, or secretarial skills.[18] Only Margaret Olmsted taught courses in the more traditionally male domains of mathematics and classics. And she herself seemingly accepts the norm of male faculty: as we've seen elsewhere, one set of minutes she prepared as faculty secretary refers to professors "and their wives."[19]

Such cultural nuances aside, to be fair in assessing salary and rank discrepancies, as well as those in college committee membership, it's important to remember that no woman until the arrival of Henriette C. K. Naeseth in 1934 had earned the terminal degree. And when she came, both her rank and her salary were commensurate with those of her male counterparts. Thereafter President Bergendoff insisted on equality of rank and salaries for male and female employees, and managed for the most part to achieve this goal by the late fifties.[20]

And certainly the judgment of "competent but undistinguished service" doesn't, most alumni would agree, apply to the women of Augustana in this pre-war period. They were overworked, certainly, but so were many of the men; and "undistinguished" hardly describes the energy, patience, conscientiousness, and love that defined their teaching and helped form the values of their students. In part, Augustana women could escape the "competent but undistinguished" label because the college at that time didn't operate on the cutthroat publish-or-perish ethic. (Marjorie Nicholson famously pointed out that "It is entirely possible to be a scholar and a gentleman; it is intensely difficult to be a scholar and a lady."[21])

The influence of these dedicated, engaged faculty women may help explain why, for women undergraduates at Augustana, the energy and optimism of the twenties seem to have carried over into the next decade. Women's organizations on campus flourished. Presidential reports attribute this vitality to one of those dedicated faculty members, Esther Sundberg, who had replaced Dora Carlson Cervin as Dean of Women in 1932. (Sundberg resigned in 1937, and at the college's urging Cervin returned as Dean that fall.) Sundberg served as advisor for the women's Dormitory Club and House Council, and for the Woman's Club, the latter of which "has done much to foster a closer tie between students on and off campus."[22] She helped organize the Augustana Independent Women's Association for students not affiliated with sororities.[23] Like the sororities, but without restrictions, the "Indees" supplied both social and academic support for their members. The group remained strong through the 1950s.

It wasn't all triumphant progress for women in those years, however. Though women's groups flourished, some traditionally male organizations remained exclusionary. For instance, in September of 1930 the grandly named Augustana "House of Representatives" considered admitting women to membership "if a majority of the House members are in favor of the plan."[24] Apparently they weren't; at least, no follow-up story appears, and all subsequent references to the organization name male members—even though in December of that same year the topic for consideration was "Resolved, that a college course for young ladies should include the art of cookery."[25] Tongue in cheek—or not?

Still, by 1936 the college could proudly claim a big coup not only for present students but for Augustana alumnae as well. Augustana was admitted to the American Association of University Women in that year. President Bergendoff explains that the affiliation had been sought for "a number of years. Its [AAUW's] standards are high:" of the more than 650 colleges and universities that admitted women, only 247 made its "approved list." And of that number, only two colleges out of 90 applicants were admitted after a rigorous inspection. This, Bergendoff says, is good but not surprising news, because "there is…no inconsistency between the standards of the A. A. U. W. and our own…. [T]he Association frankly states as its purpose to win for women 'equal status with men in faculty and student body,'" and "we are interested in giving our women students the best possible education and…providing for them the best possible environment during their college years."[26]

And beyond the undergraduate experience, the futures of Augustana women occupied the college. Dora Cervin, on her return to the deanship in 1937, worked with the Woman's Club to organize a career conference for women students featuring both group sessions and "private interviews," and, according to her report, "we could have used twice as much time for individual conferences."[27] Clearly, Augustana women were keen to realize the fruits of their education in entering the world beyond the academy.

Outside the Academy: What the Culture Told You

But. That world offered mixed signals. If you were a female student or professor in pre-war America, and you liked to kick back on the weekends with popular magazines such as *Look, Life, The Saturday Evening Post,* or even *Business Week,* you wouldn't find a lot of reinforcement for your scholarly or professional aims. And while these periodicals weren't the intellectual's forum, still they, and especially the *Post,* were respectable periodicals that purveyed articles of some substance. During World War II, for instance, the *Post* ran a story on the U.S. Military Geology Unit, featuring its assistant chief, Augustana geology professor Fritiof Fryxell. So accurately did it present the information that even the exacting Fryxell found the piece acceptable. Such magazines, with their articles, images, stories, and advertisements, certainly shaped and were shaped by the general cultural milieu. And almost universally the women depicted were in subservient positions: secretaries to suited and important businessmen, who smiled on them for preparing Sanka coffee; anxious wives seeking to please husbands with Heinz Ketchup or A1 Sauce—women timid, sentimental, mechanically maladroit and financially inexpert. If they're shown in more active roles, they're either linked with husbands ("Mrs. S. Kip Farrington, wife of the famous fishing authority," lands a 720-pound tuna), or lauded for succeeding "in a man's game" (journalism).

For Augustana Synod families, the periodical of choice, received in every household, squarely placed on every coffee table, was *The Lutheran Companion*. Drawing from a then largely ethnic tradition, in which Lutheran piety figured strongly (the ideological descendents of those Swedish farmers Hasselquist battled back in the 1860s), *The Companion* lauded marriage and motherhood. For example: A college "girl" asks Mother whether she should pursue "Career, marriage, or both?" In reply Mother briefly narrates her own easy renunciation of a concert career in favor of the domestic satisfaction she's found. "Perhaps I have been foolish to let what talent I may have had slip so completely away from me, but other interests have always seemed so much more important and have brought so much bigger returns"—*i.e.*, family. Her conclusion: "I wouldn't lose too much sleep over this problem, my dear. Somehow, when you meet the one man, the solution is pretty apt to take care of itself. A career may be all right in spots, but you can't run your fingers through its hair."[28]

And after the matrimony question had been satisfactorily settled, the woman could embark on her true vocation: motherhood. The "mothers of the world," one article claims, play a creative role second only to that of the Holy Spirit:

[T]he mother is the creative force in life.…The mother, like a sculptor, models the child.…This moulding and modeling by the world's mothers is the hope of civilization, and demands all the capacity, devotion, affection and usefulness in a mother's heart and character.…All through the night and the day, all through life, the mother thinks, toils, and lives for her children. [Thus] of all the things on earth the most beautiful is the face of a simple-hearted mother contemplating with limitless happiness the child in her arms. [*The child] represent[s] her in the work of the world* [italics mine].[29]

One could, of course, read this piece simply as a tribute to the mothers of the world. But the idealized portrait suggests, intentionally or not, that this role is the one to which young women should aspire above all others. The last lines in particular imply that the best life for women involves leaving the "work of the world" to your children (presumably male) and keeping your heart simple. Even conceding a metaphoric interpretation of motherhood as mentoring or teaching (which the article really doesn't support), it's obvious that young women are being persuaded through powerful emotional images to shape their identities as care-givers, nurturers, and supporters, rather than as active participants in the occupations of life. As we've seen, even Augustana's first woman graduate Inez Rundstrom, "liberated" for the day by studies in Europe, an advanced degree, a position on the faculty at Gustavus Adolphus, and her single status, still in her speeches to college women essentially echoed these sentiments about the position of the Christian woman. Readers of *The Lutheran Companion* were not encouraged to question the template for their lives provided by the church and by those cultural patterns it supported.

For Augustana women, then, as for college-educated women throughout America during the 1920s and 1930s, who had seen new possibilities opening to them, the culture presented complexities. As Solomon points out, "competing claims" of career or marriage, often perceived as mutually exclusive, created tensions both within themselves and with families whose expectations for their daughters remained as traditional as the material quoted above.

But into Augustana's world came a woman who by her life gave three generations of women students a model of intellectual, political, and personal power. In 1934 Henriette C. K. Naeseth arrived on campus.

"The Great Presence": Henriette C. K. Naeseth

She stepped off the train. Perhaps it was one of those mellow September days when the light lies poised on the hills and patterns of shade cool the streets, and the air smells faintly of dryness and fruit and it is time for thinking of school. Or perhaps it was a sweltering August day. But she would not have been perturbed, except possibly to say "Oh pshaw" as she emerged onto the

Dr. Henriette C. K. Naeseth: a presence that changed Augustana

steamy platform of the Rock Island Depot. A porter would have been sum-
moned to carry her suitcase; somehow she would have made it seem a special
favor. Somehow her ordinary travel dress and mended stockings would have
projected glamour. She'd have walked—strode, rather—out of the depot and
squinted up the hill toward the college, under the brim of her hat. Perhaps she
realized, even then, that this territory was to become hers.

Henriette Christiane Koren Naeseth was the first woman "power
player" at Augustana. Her voice, throaty and emphatic, had weight. In faculty meetings, on committees, in college policy determinations, Naeseth
was someone to be listened to. Today, if you ask alumni from the thirties through the sixties what women, in their experience, most decisively
helped shape Augustana, they'll inevitably begin, "Well, Dr. Naeseth, of
course"—whether they took classes from her or not. Hers was a great presence, and that presence changed the school.[30]

From the first "she brought to the college a vision of new possibilities that were neither parochial nor provincial," her former student and
colleague Dorothy Parkander has said. "What she gave through her gifts
of mind and energetic spirit can't easily be exaggerated."[31] Partly, significantly, her gifts were to women. But even more, they were to the academic
enterprise as a whole. Karin Youngberg, another of Naeseth's students who

ultimately succeeded her as both department and division chair, ranks her with "Bergendoff, Veld, and Fryxell as [a name] synonymous with…quality education at Augustana."[32]

For thirty-four years she chaired the English department. For twenty-four of those years she also served as head of the Humanities Division, which at that time consisted of modern languages—French, Spanish, German, and Swedish, the classics, music, art, and speech, and, as Parkander says, "what fragments there were of theatre."[33] Naeseth was the first woman in college history to occupy so large an administrative role. For almost thirty years she was the only woman at Augustana to hold the Ph.D. degree. She was one of the prime forces in guiding Augustana through the rigorous screening process for admission to Phi Beta Kappa in 1949—a process that required three attempts over nearly a decade before the chapter, Zeta of Illinois, was granted. This affiliation, as subsequent catalogues proudly recorded, represented "a signal honor," both for electees and for Augustana, coming as it did when fewer than ten percent of American colleges and universities could boast chapters of the nation's oldest academic honorary society. She served as Zeta of Illinois' first president and held the office for a decade. She was instrumental in securing recognition for Augustana by the American Association of University Women (A. A. U. W.), a status the college had sought since the twenties. And she helped Augustana gain affiliation with Mortar Board, a national honorary society for senior women (today the society inducts men as well).

She was an advocate for students. Early in her career she emphasized the importance of including student representation on college committees. In her own department she organized and sponsored the Writers' Club, and its publication of student writing and art, *Saga*. Under her firm direction, the group flourished. *Saga* has continued an uninterrupted run from 1937 to the present, from days of galley proof paste up with pungent rubber cement, to desktop tech. And the writing awards have multiplied substantially, thanks to generous gifts from Naeseth's University of Chicago friends.

As the *Saga* awards demonstrate, her influence reached beyond Augustana. She established a close connection with Chicago's English Department. Though some deplored the "in-breeding" this connection allegedly generated, the relationship worked well throughout the sixties to secure Augustana students immediate respect, and generous graduate fellowships, from Chicago, and to supply Augustana with a series of young scholars seeking teaching experience in the then-"gap year" between master's and doctoral studies. This steady stream of young instructors, some of whom went on to achieve significant scholarly and pedagogical reputations, meant that the department was constantly being refreshed as well as maintaining the stability Naeseth imposed. She created a writing/reading assessment examination for juniors that was copied and instituted in several other colleges across the country, before assessment became the academy buzz-word. She conducted her own meticulous scholarship (which we'll look at presently). She was listed in *Who's Who in America*. She was knighted by the King of Norway. And, again before it became a matter of college policy, she understood the importance of community relationships, and forged strong town-gown connections, briefly hosting a radio show on books and playing an active role in many education and arts groups. She served as president for the Rock Island-Moline branch of the A. A. U. W., and as a member of its state fellowship committee. When the local branch reached the half-century mark, it established a fiftieth anniversary fellowship in her honor.

A power player indeed. One reason, perhaps, why she could be so effective was that she apparently felt none of the tensions that often beset educated women of her day as they searched for ways to reconcile domestic expectations with academic aspirations. She was in many ways non-traditional. Unmarried and unapologetic, brilliant and confident, scholarly and glamorous, severe as a don, charismatic as a screen star, at home in classroom and kitchen alike, she represents something of an enigma to those who look back on her professional life. She was a collection of paradoxes. She advanced the cause of feminism without in the least considering herself a feminist. She was a passionate Democrat on an almost exclusively Republican campus without in any way compromising her views of class and ethnic privilege. In short, as another of her former students, the Reverend Richard Swanson, once put it, she was "self-defining." And endlessly fascinating.

She was born April 6, 1899, into a Norwegian family with aristocratic connections and long records of service to scholarship and to the church. And with models of strong, literate, witty women whose spirit shaped her own. Her mother's family, the Korens, could trace its roots to the thirteenth century, predating the Hanseatic League's arrival in Norway. Throughout their history the Korens moved in worlds of ease, privilege, and refinement.

So it was no easy transition for Henriette's grandparents, cousins Elisabeth and Vilhelm Koren, when they left home to pioneer the establishment of the Norwegian Lutheran Church in America. As the young Elisabeth records in her diary on her first New Year's Eve in America, "Last year I began the new year clad in bobbinet, dancing away with roses in my hair. This year I am sitting here with Vilhelm in this bare room [in a log cabin, which they shared with another family], where tomorrow he is to conduct divine services for all these people who so long have lacked a pastor. Still," she adds gamely, "this is best."[34] She was later to preside over the charming parsonage in Washington Prairie that's since become a landmark.

A writer who observed keenly, recorded precisely, and turned a phrase wittily, Elisabeth Koren was determined that her children should be educated. So despite a demanding schedule of housekeeping, gardening, and childrearing, she home-schooled her children "every morning from 9 to 12, much of the time with the youngest child on her arm,"[35] not only in the basic three Rs, but also in religion, Norwegian, English, and German.[36] Life for Elisabeth Koren was adventure and challenge—and the good use of her mind. No wonder her granddaughter Henriette admired her.

Elisabeth's husband Pastor Vilhelm Koren was instrumental in securing the Decorah location for the newly-established Luther College. Luther's Koren library honors that contribution. On the other side of her family, Henriette's father Christian Naeseth taught classics at Luther, and served also as its librarian. And beyond her immediate relatives Naeseth's cousins include ambassadors, one of the nuclear scientists working during the war at Oak Ridge, Norway's Queen Sonja, and *New Yorker* cartoonist Edward Koren. For Naeseth, then, family pride mandated success; family gifts of mind, spirit, and self-assurance guaranteed it. The words of Chicago poet Harriet Monroe[37] might well have been Naeseth's: "From earliest childhood I used to tell myself, and God, that I was to be 'great and famous...'"[38]

Though she respected her professor father, it was her mother, Caroline Mathilde Koren Naeseth, to whom Henriette was most deeply attached. A late-coming, cherished child, Henriette received attention and encouragement for her quick wit, her high—some would say naughty—spirit, and her wide-ranging intelligence. She remembered all her life a three-month siege in bed with pleurisy, reading nineteenth century novels with her mother. She never spoke of illness; she spoke of a winter's idyll.

As she grew up, the intimacy of mother and daughter increased rather than lessening. Henriette's daily letters to Caroline Naeseth reveal aspects of her life and personality not seen elsewhere. Apparently few of her adventures and misadventures—from the price paid for stockings to her candid observations of a male companion to her frustration at job prospects— were withheld from Mrs. Naeseth's sympathetic eye and ear. Students from the 1940s remember well the impact on Naeseth of her mother's death. "We were studying Whitman's 'When Lilacs Last in the Dooryard Bloom'd,' the moving elegy for Abraham Lincoln," recalls Parkander, who graduated in 1946, "and she couldn't finish. She left the room in tears."[39]

Today Decorah, Iowa, retains something of the small-town, closed-community air that defined it more strongly during Naeseth's youth at the turn of the century. On a perfect September day it's a picture-postcard of the good life in the heartland with its tree-shaded residential streets, its houses with steeply-pitched roofs, their dormers scrolled with wood carvings that cross Frank Lloyd Wright prairie style with clean-lined Scandinavian decoration. Set at the foot of river bluffs, it might have recalled a more rugged landscape to homesick, land-locked Norwegian settlers. The main street today is a bit self-consciously charming; you feel the city administrators have read the brochures about tourist attractions and dutifully maintained them. But the Vesterheim Norwegian-American museum and library is clearly a working place, serious about its mission of preserving the town's historical identity and gracious to those who seek out its resources.

Naeseth grew up in one of those Norwegian houses. The neighborhood, very much "gown" in appearance, climbs up and down the swell of the land. A short pleasant walk would have brought Christian Naeseth to the college campus. Henriette Naeseth's memories of her Decorah childhood suggest that it was as quiet and pleasant as those streets, with an ethos as defined and self-contained as its geography. She loved it, considered her place in the world Edenic. She also loved challenging that world, flirting with the Luther college boys, smoking the occasional Sweet Caporal on the street corner. None of her escapades, in her mind, could shake her secure position—a position rooted in family background and in her own superb self-confidence. She was attractive, she was bright, she would command wherever she went. She was, as people have noted, at home in any world she chose to enter.

If Barbara Miller Solomon's analysis of the flapper, quoted earlier, is accurate, then Henriette at Grinnell College fit the definition perfectly. She smoked, "gadded," studied, and broke hearts routinely. Many years later she used to love quoting the first two lines of her poem written for the 1922 Grinnell Commencement exercises: "Youth kicks his heels on a sun-whitened road/His laughter debonair is all his load...." [40] She was the rebel who "kicked her heels," refused male control, who insisted on her own individuality and independence, yet who, as Solomon puts it in describing the flapper, "did not abandon the compulsion to behave correctly, to be ladylike." [41] She wrote poetry and read omnivorously, finished her collegiate career with Phi Beta Kappa honors and as class poet, yet originally planned to major in domestic science. During her early years of teaching, she became engaged to, and disengaged from, a jazz musician.

Grinnell would have been a good place for her to explore and negotiate her identity during those years. Founded in the mid-1840s (and briefly located in Davenport, Iowa), the college began admitting women in 1861 and awarding them degrees in the 1880s. (In contrast, Luther became coeducational in 1936.) With more relaxed church connections than those at Luther or Augustana, Grinnell "secularized the Social Gospel," according to Grinnell historian Alan Jones, [42] and early formed a tradition of encouraging philosophical and ethical exploration rather than doctrinal adherence. [43] This kind of academic atmosphere would have prepared Naeseth for the heady intellectual freedom she was to encounter in graduate school, especially at the University of Chicago. Social opportunities weren't lacking, either, even though the then-new women's dormitories featured closed and locked cloisters, as opposed to the men's open loggia. Strolling across campus under trees "shining with hot gold," as she described them in a poem, Henriette was in no way a cloistered co-ed.

She must have must have taken graduate school by storm. Academic honors swiftly accumulated: Master's degree from the University of Minnesota, doctorate from the University of Chicago; a year on the faculty of Goucher College. But after Goucher, that comet-like dazzle of success temporarily tanked. She joined the faculty at Chadron State Teachers' College in Nebraska. And that, for her, was the back of beyond. Despite her later interest in frontier theatre, she found little to recommend the venue on the plains of Nebraska: uncongenial colleagues, tight budgets, and few chances for cultural stimulation. In June of 1933, for instance, she complains in a letter to her mother of "be[ing] stuck out here, working too hard, & getting so little" (her salary had just been cut. It was, however, later partially restored).

The problem was, of course, the economic climate of the time. As we've seen, funding for public education had been slashed dramatically. With that support eroding, understandably the future for a new professor at a teachers' college would be precarious. The job scarcity in part explains why Naeseth applied to Augustana rather than trying for what her Chicago friends considered higher-powered, more prestigious academic environments. (It probably didn't hurt any, either, that when President Gustav Andreen interviewed her for the faculty position, he kissed her hand. She never forgot that old-world, gallant gesture.) But having committed herself to Augustana, Naeseth resolved to shape it into the best school she could. In this effort she was supported unconditionally by the newly-elected (1935) President Conrad Bergendoff, whose aspirations and academic credentials matched hers.

Naeseth was one of the first active women scholars at Augustana, publishing regularly, especially in the 1940s and 50s. When she began to forge her scholarly reputation, she consulted her own heritage. She was, she said, keenly appreciative of the "double ties that bind an American of foreign birth to two countries."[44] To explore that heritage she translated and wrote original poetry for *American Scandinavian Review* in the 40s, prompted in part no doubt by the family's anxiety and helplessness at the invasion of Norway. One of her own poems, "April 1940,"[45] counterpoints her youthful experience of celebrating *Syttende Mai* (the Seventeenth of May, Norwegian independence day) with the grim reality of the current war:

The Seventeenth of May—
A holiday—a ball game—
Our parochial school marched with Norwegian flags....

We sang "*Ja vi elsker*" ("Yes, we love [our country]," the Norwegian National anthem),
"My Country 'Tis of Thee,"
We didn't think much about it;
We didn't know that in every town in Iowa,
In every American town,
They were not marching and singing on the Seventeenth of May,

Or reciting in Norwegian,
Wearing gay bodiced costumes,
White capped and adorned with silver,
Treasure from the chests
Brought from home in Norway.

We sang hurrah
For the red cross on the blue,
For the white stripes and the white stars on the blue,
For the minister from Norway,
For the senator from Iowa—
And we ran out to play,....

What were they doing,
Our parents and grandparents from Norway?
Giving us their love and longing
And their hope?

A knife turns in that love,...
Which the songs and the flags and the Norwegian words of our parents
Gave us
While we hardly knew it....

In 1942 she translated Nobel laureate Sigrid Undset's autobiographical account of her experiences in World War II Norway, *Return to the Future* (Knopf). The book, a bitter record of Undset's pain at the loss of family and hope, moved Naeseth deeply. Writing to Undset in 1941 to announce the finished translation, Naeseth concludes:

Before 1940 I had no idea how strongly I felt related to Norway, and I am sure many other Americans of Norwegian descent feel as I do. I hope we shall have courage to act, now and later.[46]

Return to the Future was an "immediate best seller in New York," garnering critical raves from *The New York Times* for its "forceful writing..., phrases and maxims which will remain for several generations of people, and for all the countries occupied by Germany in this war, as classic as those of Tacitus." As an *Augustana Bulletin* notice observes, "these comments, and others like them, are indirect tributes to the quality of the translation."[47]

Naeseth's own work expressed this sense of an identity balanced between two worlds. Rather than close analyses of major texts, she chose to study cultural history, in particular the kind of theatre that came to Chicago and to the western frontiers. In this approach she anticipated the interdisciplinary interest of the academy today. Her major work of scholarship, a meatily-annotated volume entitled *The Swedish Theatre In Chicago 1868-1950*,[48] testifies to this interest, as does the final work she was engaged on, a study of Norwegian-American social reformer and playwright Marcus Thrane. Her work is thorough, meticulous, and exhaustive, but it is not, nor does it set out to be, incisive or dynamic. Its goal is to compile data from a careful scrutiny of records, venturing few interpretations of these data. Her voice as scholar is magisterially neutral. The large and sometimes flamboyant gestures of her personal life, the wit and passion of her classroom presentations, define the personality that commanded her immediate sphere: Augustana College.

Augustana proved to be a good fit for Naeseth. It provided her a venue where she could be, if not in the larger sphere, at least locally "great and famous," an environment she could mold, and a place whose destiny came to matter to her. It mattered enough that she dismissed the advice of friends and colleagues from larger academic venues, who urged her to move on.

At Augustana, especially during her heyday in the forties and fifties, she was clearly Someone, a breath from an exotic world. Statuesque, commanding, she swept across the campus on long elegant legs—"Legs" Naeseth was her sometime-sobriquet. Her classroom rigor was daunting and legendary: the pages and pages of reading she assigned, her gimlet blue gaze from the lectern, her abrupt (but always majestic) departure from unprepared classes, book and door slammed shut. Yet her charm, her interest, her unwavering support for students created love and spurred effort. When she walked out on you one day, you prepared extra carefully for the next session. Students called her The Queen.

During the forties her weekend forays into Chicago were legendary. On those occasions she'd arrive for her Friday morning class not just with the usual scarlet lips and nails, but also sporting the latest of hats, ready to step onto the Rock Island Rocket as soon as the session concluded. Students whose idea of a good time was a Coke date at the College Drug imagined with awe the world she'd be entering, the adventures that awaited her. And that world was a refreshment and a stimulant for her mind and spirit. She'd often be the *raison d'etre* for elegant dinner parties given by her close friend, English professor and Dean of Humanities at Chicago, Napier Wilt. Around the table at his spacious Hyde Park apartment conversation ranged widely and eclectically—books, theatre, politics, music, food. Guests would include both established academic luminaries and younger faculty such the genial Southerner Gwin Kolb, who published studies of Samuel Johnson and counted Eudora Welty among his friends.[49] And whenever it fit the weekend schedule, there would be an afternoon at Comiskey Park; Naeseth was a passionate White Sox fan.

Yet even as she occupied this large stage with éclat, she never neglected her immediate responsibilities. And they were enormous. As was the case with many professors in small colleges, she carried a heavy and diverse teaching load: Shakespeare, writing (basic and advanced composition and fiction—all with large enrollments), several courses in American literature, and the Scandinavian novel, as well as the many directed and independent studies tucked in around the edges of crowded faculty schedules. But, as her successor Roald Tweet has observed, she was equal to it. In particular, she was suited to teach the "biggies"—Shakespeare, Melville, Whitman: "They were up to her and she was up to them."[50]

She was also "up to" a daunting agenda of extracurricular work. Hers is sometimes the only woman's name on important college committees such as Educational Policies. She appears regularly in the *Observer* throughout the forties and fifties, speaking to various campus groups, hosting teas, sponsoring guest lecturers. And through it all, to the end of her tenure, she neither postponed nor omitted a letter of recommendation for faculty or student. Happily for Naeseth and her sanity, she'd always been a quick study, and she was the quintessential multi-tasker. She could manage to grade papers, writing comments in her swift, decisive longhand, while she listened to two baseball games on two different radio stations—and followed each one play-by-play.

Her "homework" at Augustana reached beyond her own professional activities. She expanded course offerings and supported innovative pedagogical styles in the English department. She was an aggressive advocate for faculty members under her supervision, calling attention to salary inadequacies and "inhumanly exhausting" teaching loads, and, on at least one occasion, forcibly stopping inappropriate demands for a young single female instructor to assume unpaid domestic work.

She had her detractors, of course, as do most commanding personalities. Her authority was fierce, formidable, and absolute. The deep gravelly voice could blister as quickly as it could commend. Legends abound of her deliberate breaches of decorum, of her rumbling *basso* commentary from the back of the room during faculty meetings, a latter-day Greek chorus. On one occasion when a speaker had orated at length and finally declared that "I have just one final word," Naeseth was heard to drawl, not quietly, "Ye gods! *Any* word will do!"[51] But at the same time, her "contagious zest for life,"[52] punctuated by her signature "Ha *ha!*" when she was delighted or amused, gained her friends and admirers literally worldwide.

She was a sociable spirit. Parkander calls her "a true humanist,…not concerned with the private exploration of the self, nor…exclusively with the intellectual self. Her concern was the self in society."[53] And that meant opening her spacious Long View apartment to faculty and students alike. No student from the fifties or sixties forgets Writers' Club and English major teas there: the masterfully set serving table that backed against a window giving onto the central courtyard of the building; the gleaming silver coffeepot; the thin china cups; the daffodil patterned spoons. "She taught us more than literature; she taught us to live gracefully," one student has said. Even Writers' Club picnics were upscale. She would never countenance ordinary hot dogs.

Nor were new faculty neglected. "She was almost alone in recognizing that new faculty needed to be welcomed," Parkander recalls, "and she gave dinner parties to suggest that Rock Island was not a barbarian outpost. She was an excellent cook…. [Salt was never set on her elegant tables; her dishes, from stroganoff to sweetbreads, were always perfectly seasoned]… Her table was dressed in the most beautiful linen I've seen outside of museums. Her specialty was a dessert: hot fruit pancake. If you chose, as a guest, to follow her out to the kitchen you could see her pour batter into a pan sizzling with butter, watch to catch the precise moment when fresh peaches were poured on top, then see the pancake folded, sprinkled with powdered sugar, cut, and served."[54]

Especially for women students of the forties, fifties, and sixties the encounter with Naeseth could be life-changing. Many whose goals had reached no further than the A.B. degree were encouraged, in ways both intangible and practical, to go further, to form and realize dreams they hadn't conceived when they entered college. Naeseth's "great presence,"[55] her stature, and her unfailing support made it possible for these women to dare a whole new world.

To the end of her tenure, that presence held, even when physical fragility shortened the commanding stride and sometimes turned the magisterial temper to querulousness. As her career wound down and the sixties burst upon the country, younger faculty sometimes chafed under her authority, and in various ways, subtle and not so subtle, subverted it. Yet as late as the 1970s, after her retirement, a couple of wild-haired students who joined her and Tweet on a trip to Chicago came back as smitten with that presence as their forebears in the forties and fifties had been. She died November 25, 1987, still and forever The Queen.

Henriette Naeseth made one other significant contribution to Augustana College.

At the Commencement exercises of 1946, one of her favorite students whom she'd mentored, encouraged, and supported—and who had just graduated at the top of her class—came up and shyly touched the sleeve of Naeseth's doctoral robe.

"I want one of those," she said.

Her name was Dorothy Parkander.

Sailing Headfirst Into Walt Whitman
for Dr. Henriette C. K. Naeseth

After a fall term diving
with her Moby Dick pin
and wintering beside her fur coat
at Walden, I was ready for
the spring semester
and Volume II. Behind the podium
she had grown into a mythic figurehead
on the prow of East Hall's American Literature
and sailed her course
toward warmer latitudes. That's when,
one morning, she stepped on deck,
paused, nodded, beamed
a Henriette smile and chanted:

I celebrate myself, and sing myself,
And what I assume you shall assume,
For every atom belonging to me as good as belongs to you.

Before I could recover
myself, she was singing
the solitary poet's long, wave-sweeping lines of free verse,
drawing me closer
to his new, bold, ocean-rolling rhythms.

I, years later,
see a mighty presence, a woman
of honed intellect, a professor,
so tall and straight and stern,
whose teaching style
of *passion, pulse and power* breathed
life into every lecture, fear
into every failing heart,
and bravado into every blue book.

I am large, I contain multitudes, she chanted
in one reading, midway, and then before
the whirlwind unit test:

I too am not a bit tamed, I too am untranslatable.

Dick Stahl, Class of 1960
Quad-Cities Poet Laureate Emeritus

THE SECOND WORLD WAR:
GIRLS AND WOMEN, TASKS AND POSSIBILITIES

This is a not-so recent story. But it's one I want to tell.

Bunny is a warrior and a victor—for peace.

I first met her when I was a young, inexperienced professor and she an eager student. That was thirty years ago. She is one of my best friends today.

She took most of my courses. I can't remember what I taught her. What I do know is how much she taught me: about discipline and commitment, about love for learning, about the sacredness of laughter, about the centrality of grace and the reality of healing. These are lessons she has continued to teach, more profoundly each year of our deepening friendship.

Bunny has fought many battles: against illness which continues to dog her energies; against loss; against spiritual and emotional pain. Gritty, gallant, and irrepressibly funny, she has won, again and again.

She is ordained today. She entered ministerial studies in her fifties, her family successfully raised, her marriage enriched by each partner's delight in the growing gifts of the other.

If we still had a Victory bell, I'd ring it for Bunny.

CHAPTER 6

The Second World War:
Girls and Women, Tasks and Possibilities

In the midst of gathering storm clouds Augustana has gone steadily on through the past year [1941], believing that thus far, at least, its best service consists in seeking to help its students understand the kind of world in which they will have to live and work. Undoubtedly the liability of many men students for military training in the near future has had a sobering effect on the student body.

Conrad Bergendoff[1]

We all filed out from the chapel in Old Main, crossing Seventh Avenue, on down the hill and over to the Rock Island Depot. We had sung hymns together, we had listened to the distinctive cadence of Dr. B[ergendoff], with his usual carefully chosen words which would that day reflect this singular occasion. Maybe we even joined together on "O Dear Old Alma Mater." This was a special morning chapel service because another group of our fellow students would soon be inductees. As one all-school body we were there with them to wish them Godspeed. There had been personal farewells on preceding days, but this was Augustana, their school, saying good-bye.

Would some return to eventually join us as alums? Some did, but on that day we could only hope.

Betty Fridlund, Class of 1944[2]

While wars devastate and decimate, they can also animate. That, historians have long noted, has been true of the major wars involving the United States. As we've discussed previously, American conflicts as far back as the Civil War, in taking men from their home front occupations, thrust on women the responsibilities their spouses, brothers, and fathers had previously assumed. All grieved for partings; some lamented the lack of male support and friendship. Many others found unsuspected strengths and abilities that were to challenge and reinvent their worlds.

That pattern was true of the country at large, and replicated in the microcosm of Augustana College during the war years.

People remember where they were when the announcement came, the appalling, unbelievable news that America had been attacked. They were doing ordinary things—writing Christmas cards; paying bills.

Dr. Wendell Lund, who'd graduated from Augustana in 1927, was rocking along in a train between Washington and Detroit, admiring his compartment companion, who happened to be actress Rosalind Russell. In Rock Island, geology professor Dr. Fritiof Fryxell, Augustana Class of 1922, was home building a block-fort with his youngest son.

Students were winding down the weekend or frantically doing studying they'd put off for two days.

But with the news all other activity was shelved. Students gathered around radios, listening intently as out of the static came the voice of President Roosevelt announcing that Pearl Harbor had been bombed, that America was now at war. Monday lectures were interrupted to deal with the news. The event changed world history. It changed Augustana College. And it changed the histories of individuals.

Though Augustana had reflected the overall mood of the country in supporting an isolationist policy in the earlier years of the war, the attack on America caused a swift about-face. Now students and faculty alike who had opposed U.S. involvement in the war became its eager champions. As Thomas Tredway observes, "Until late 1941 [the] position [of the college] seemed to be that the struggles in Europe and Asia were not the country's concern and that involvement must be avoided. After that the war was seen as a struggle against the nihilism which threatened the foundations of western culture and society; the role of the college in the war was seen to be to aid the national effort so far as possible and to continue to stand for the fundamental values which the school had always represented and taught."[3] And that wasn't just institutional rhetoric. An Augustana soldier's letter quoted in the 1944 *Rockety-I* echoes that same sentiment:

To me Augie means all that is worth fighting for, namely Christian democracy in action. Moreover, I believe that Augie is training and will continue to train men and women with living faith that will enable them to build a more peaceful and creative world....'we'll win for Augustana'....

The yearbook editors, both women, presented this letter "lest we forget that in this present world cauldron of bitterness, smoky confusion, and hate, there is still a center for our memories, our hopes, our ideals, our faith....Augustana."[4]

The college responded in practical as well as ideological terms. Dr. Fryxell and Dr. Lund became major players in the Allied War effort, Lund as head of the key Labor Productions Division of the War Production Board; Fryxell as Assistant Chief of the Military Geology Unit in Washington, D.C. The dean of men,[5] the director of athletics, the head football coach (football was suspended for want of a team in the war years), a music and an English professor all entered military service.[6] By war's end Augustana had contributed one thousand twenty-one people to the effort. Sixty-eight women were included, twenty-six as nurses, forty-two in various branches of the service.[7] One of them, Victory Pearson, Class of 1940, enlisted in the Navy the year following Pearl Harbor, and as Lieutenant Pearson participated in a ceremony to launch the *U.S.S. Augustana Victory* in 1945.

On campus recruiters from the Army and Navy arrived immediately. Some students left for service at once; others enrolled in a plan that enabled them to continue their college education until they were called. The Selective Training and Service Act of 1940 created "the first peacetime draft in U.S. history."[8] All men eighteen to twenty were registered.[9] Families and

U.S.S. Augustana Victory

friends watched anxiously for draft notices to show up in campus or home mailboxes. Excitement and uncertainty sharpened daily mail checks. The 1943 *Rockety-I* highlights this moment in history and in the students' day with a full-page photograph of students clustered around mailboxes, and with the accompanying text: "Just a few days prior to this writing, many of our classmates received their induction notices....[But] the fellows took their calls in stride and left with a spirit of willingness and even of anticipation that overshadowed the feelings aroused by leaving school so abruptly, and by cutting off so suddenly friendships of long standing."[10]

President Bergendoff was not altogether unprepared for the mass exodus of young men. Early in 1941 educators representing the American Council on Education, the National Education Association, schools from throughout the country, as well as various government officials—1,200 strong—had met to consider how schools could best serve the war effort. And what they noted was the beginning of a movement by (mostly) young men from the classroom into both military service and industry. Representatives of the American Council on Education reported that 17 percent of college students and 9 percent of faculty had, even before the official declaration of war by America, followed this exit pattern. An immediate solution to the loss of faculty was that "married women who taught formerly will have to be called back into teaching for the emergency."[11]

But after the official declaration of war in December the situation became critical. "Immediately higher education was challenged…shaken by what was happening," according to Bergendoff.[12] In response to the government's call for each college to create a plan for dealing with the realities of war, President Bergendoff prepared two pamphlets, "Augustana in War Time," later included in the college catalogue. Basically they warned against radical change and emphasized that the academy could best serve the effort by holding fast to those "riches of mind and spirit which war cannot destroy."[13]

As was the case with schools throughout the country in these destabilizing days, Augustana faculty meetings devoted much discussion to the balancing act of holding fast to those riches of mind and spirit while introducing curricular and calendar changes that would support the war effort. Other institutions provided models to consider: a shortened degree program (three years instead of four), lower admissions standards to keep enrollments steady during a time of increasing attrition, new courses specifically designed to address what was going on in both theoretical and practical terms.

Augustana considered such changes and adopted some of them. New courses were introduced: Spherical Trigonometry, Conservation of Natural Resources, Economics of War and Defense, Industrial Chemical Calculations, America at War. A special section in the War pamphlet, "Women in the National Crisis," offered courses in Red Cross First Aid, Home Nursing and Hygiene, and Household Economy. "A Civilian Pilot training program had already graduated fifty-four boys [by 1941]."[14] Physical education offerings were increased in response to concerns that young men were entering military service unfit for active duty. Physical education professor Leroy Brissman reported that in 1942 thirty percent of new recruits required four months' additional training to get in shape. Though the recommendation from a Naval spokesman of three to five hours of P. E. a week generated considerable conversation—where, Augustana faculty asked, would it all fit into an academic schedule already full of requirements?—still in the end an enhanced P. E. program was adopted.[15]

Despite these curricular adjustments, it's clear both from Faculty Meeting minutes and from Bergendoff's reports that overall "Augustana resisted [major] changes," steadied by Bergendoff's own firm, serene vision. As he wrote, "...[W]e have believed that one of the accomplishments of higher education in wartime might be to keep calm and clear in the turmoil and confusion of the times."[16] Still, it's worth noting that the faculty endorsed, and Bergendoff wisely did not countermand, some flexibility in scheduling for students who needed to take courses privately, or to finish early. In a few cases, when the faculty determined that circumstances warranted, students were allowed to graduate without the precise number of required credits.[17] Similarly, the obligatory high school diploma was waived for war veterans whose service had prevented them from finishing high school; they were allowed to take entrance tests for admission to college.[18]

But these were, largely, modest and cautious adjustments. What held firm was Bergendoff's central belief in the importance of the liberal arts not just to address but to help heal a broken world.

According to Tredway,[19] the curricular revisions conducted during Bergendoff's presidency, in particular the new post-war "Augustana Plan," had as their foundation a core curriculum "based on common assumptions about what constituted a solid undergraduate education in mid-twentieth century America,"[20] and in fact reflected the kind of curriculum Bergendoff had inherited when he assumed the presidency in 1935. Tredway notes that Bergendoff believed "the most fundamental of all educational work was to gain a knowledge of the past,"[21] and the humanities were the way to that knowledge—a knowledge that wouldn't simply confer skills on its possessors, but would "contribute to the preservation of our heritage of culture."[22] An important element in the culture to be preserved was religious experience, specifically, Christianity, as Augustana's constitution of those years emphasized: one of the two purposes of the college, it stated, was "To teach youth the way of life determined by the revelation of Jesus Christ in the Word and the Church."[23] But for Bergendoff, the importance wasn't just a matter of following a rubric set down by his predecessors; it was part of his vision. Knowledge, as he said, was a circle of related disciplines; to remove one aspect of it, the spiritual, would leave the circle incomplete.[24]

How that aspect of human experience was expected to be conveyed can be seen in Bergendoff's response a decade later to religion instructors who refused to make their courses "bomb shelters" for religiously-raised students. Rather than teaching Christianity in such as way as to deepen and confirm faith, some of these instructors subjected it to the rigorous intellectual scrutiny that had begun a century earlier and grown in depth and sophistication in the interval. Such teaching often drew protests from pastors and parents alike. The college was accused of destroying students' faith (the same charge that would be routinely leveled at some of the faculty in the 1960s). To one instructor who presented Christianity as a subject for study instead of revealed truth Bergendoff wrote: "The world hardly needs to be told more of what not to believe—men are hungry for what to believe."[25] Given this attitude in the fifties, it's clear that a decade earlier, the Church, and all that it stood for in terms of both theology and social convention, was largely upheld.

And that had implications for the role of women in the pre-war forties. As we've seen, women collegians in the twenties and thirties were receiving mixed messages from the general culture and the culture of Augustana. As we'll see later in this chapter, women students were carefully guarded and protected, and what concerned college officials, according to Tredway, "seem[s], by later lights and depending on one's perspective, antiquated, quaint, or hopeless"—for example, that female students be reminded to draw their shades when undressing,[26] or that tablecloths be purchased for the women's dining hall so that "girls who have had very little opportunity at home [would] gain...in the correct ways of social living."[27] As late as 1954, Bergendoff—who had recruited gifted women to teach in postwar Augustana—expressed the opinion that "certain courses [for women] would be desireable, as in home-making."[28] Many women and their families concurred with this view. Even graduates who envisioned careers usually chose traditional "womanly" occupations—jobs that could be easily surrendered, or accommodated, to marriage and family, such as teacher, secretary, or nurse. Others attended college not necessarily expecting to finish, should "Mr. Right" came long.

And then what came along was the war.

Women and the War

What was it like to attend Augustana the four years that war lasted? I cannot see a train pull from a station nor hear its whistle keen without remembering farewells. "Lest We Forget" was the theme Charlotte Erickson [class of 1945] and I chose for the Rockety-I *Yearbook; the photo of Robert Bergstrom [Class of 1947] with sailor cap introduced each section of that pictorial record, providing the image for all Augustana students, past and present, in service. Char, the business manager and I, the editor, were the first Augustana women in those positions....*[sic]

Margaret Swanson Lacy, Class of 1944[29]

War work: Margaret Swanson Lacy (l), editor, and Charlotte Erickson (r), business manager, took over long male-dominated roles in producing the *Rockety-I* yearbook. (Actually Helen Searle was the first "girl elected editor." See p. 96.)

Robert Bergstrom

This mixture of poignance and pride in Dr. Margaret Lacy's recollections of her years at Augustana during the war catches the mixed experience it provided. While the war took friends and lovers, and the train whistle eternally keened for those gone, at the same time women assumed active roles in a depopulated college, and found themselves strengthened and stimulated by those roles.

"College in 1943–1944 will be different," Bergendoff wrote in his introduction to the Student Handbook of that year.

The shadow of war will lie over all the campus. Instead of merry laughter and care-free groups there will be the shouts of the drill sergeant and the marching of men to classes. [Extra-curricular] athletics will be at a minimum and many a student activity will be suspended. Boys who normally would be in college will be on every fighting front and their absence will sadden those who knew them as class-mates or school-mates....On the girls will fall the task of continuing the traditions of Augustana and keeping its spirit bright—the kind of a school to which our boys will want to come back.[30]

In fact, Bergendoff reflected later, the greatest change to be seen at Augustana as a result of the war was not only the absence of men, but "the record number of women, taxing the facilities of dormitories and the work of the Dean of women."[31] The dormitories weren't adequate. The Catalogue for 1945-1946 reports that "the large increase in women students has necessitated the use of three large homes [for resident women students]: the Woman's Building Annex, West Hall, and East Hall."[32] These quarters weren't always ideal, according to former dean Olive Johnson Schwiebert; in fact, some were old Victorian houses as close to dereliction as to campus. Most of the first-year women arriving with anxious parents in tow could overlook scratches, cracks, and leaks because the intimacy of the premises—most housed twenty or fewer—seemed less intimidating than multi-level dorms. But more than a few parents departed shaking their heads.[33]

As Bergendoff's introductory remarks to the Handbook noted, the campus took on a different look and feel, depleted of its male population. In the late thirties, according to Tredway, women had represented about 45% of the total enrollment;[34] 1941, degree recipients were nearly equally divided between genders: 33 women and 34 men. By the spring of 1944, although the proportion of graduating students held firm (41 women to

42 men), the roster of students for the following academic year showed a slump in the male population:

Seniors: 21 men and 30 women
Juniors: 11 men and 40 women
Sophomores: 17 men and 81 women
First-years: 58 men and 125 women[35]

By 1944 the ratio of women to men was 2.5:1.[36] The changing roles for women during these days were reflected officially in the college's curricular deliberations, and more personally, more internally, in the responses of the women themselves to a predominantly female student body. A conference at Northwestern University, attended by Dean Cervin, considered the role of women in the war effort. Dean Cervin reported that the conference stressed "the growing need for women in industry" and set up plans for "broader utilization of women in industry."[37] In response to this need, new courses were introduced. The Catalogue for 1942-1943 says that since women "are in increasing demand, in industry, in teaching, even in branches of the armed services…[s]ome of the courses listed below are planned especially for these demands."[38] And at a special faculty meeting designed to discuss the problems the college would face after the war, President Bergendoff listed three: the return of soldiers (males), *the return of women from industry and war services* (italics mine), and the question of what forms liberal education would assume in the post-war period.[39]

That Augustana would continue its strong liberal arts tradition was never in question. Echoing sentiments expressed during the First War, Bergendoff wrote that "amid the ruins of today the Christian college continues to stand as a conserver of the best things of the Past and as an Alma Mater nourishing the best graces of humanity."[40] Again, as in those days of 1918, the image of the college as nurturing mother is strongly invoked.

And Bergendoff saw women students specifically as "conservers" of those "best things": "We shall have to rely on the women to conserve the liberal arts tradition," he wrote, "since the men have had to turn principally to mathematics and the sciences."[41]

Dr. Charlotte Erickson, who spent her college years on the wartime campus, remembers the "male exodus" which "began in earnest" in 1942[42] with the chapel service, the walk to the Rock Island depot, the leave-taking, the long train whistles. To compensate for those who'd left, "a unit of the

Dr. Charlotte Erickson, with her
mother Lael Johnson Erickson,
Class of 1917

Army Air Corps [the 68th College Training Detachment] brought two hundred-fifty men to the campus" for officer training.[43] The men stayed for five months on campus while the college "had to house, feed, and instruct and care for these men,"[44] a somewhat daunting prospect as Bergendoff describes it.

But apparently the college did a good job. Cadet Albert Eddy recalled that the Corps were "treated like kings," with pleasant living quarters, good food, and a faculty that managed to make classes in physics, meteorology, trigonometry, navigation, and even English feel—if not exactly like play, then at least like work that could be enjoyed.[45] They also enjoyed evading the official prohibition against hanging around the women's dorm by meeting Augustana women students at the nearby College Drug on Seventh Avenue and Thirty-eighth Street (a legend of its own). Richard Powers, Class of 1950, Cadet Leader of Flight #8 housed in North Hall, conjectures that "persuasive advice from Dr. Bergendoff and his staff" caused the Army to rescind its "off-limits order."[46] All in all, as one member of the 68th put it, "Say, I like it a lot here. This is the kind of school I'd like to go to when the war is over."[47]

However happy a position for the Cadets, though, this incursion of vigorous young military males did create a different atmosphere on campus, one that not all students welcomed:

Cadets filled the halls and brought…songs, not in serenades late at night, but in marching music all day…[Reveille] every morning at five…Dress Parade on Saturday mornings…khaki and tweeds patterning our halls, classrooms, and walks….mob scenes at the Drug and College Inn between six and eight…mob scenes in front of the dorm at one on Saturday night.[48] The lingering smell of their presence in the library. Their silent scrutiny [because they were officially prohibited from speaking to the women] as you worked your way through the dinner line.[49]

Other students, though, enjoyed this exotic new presence on the campus. The silence barrier in many cases was effectively broken. Augustana women had been spotted at USO-sponsored dances in the college gymnasium, according to rumor. As we'll see, the first floor corner room of the Woman's Building provided convenient access for residents skirting curfew regulations. And—horror of horrors!—contraceptives were being handed out by Augustana medical staff, "just as at any other army post."[50]

But it wasn't all dances and defiance. With old friends and fellow students gone, women indeed took on the task of "continuing the traditions of Augustana and keeping its spirit bright." Those traditions included academic excellence and moral integrity. As Professor V. R. Pearson points out in his essay for the 1944 *Rockety-I*, "We need only look about us to see the earnestness and seriousness which fill every [woman student's] life. In unity of purpose, in performance of every duty, in preservation of high ideals Augustana's womanhood carried nobly her part in the war that is for Victory and Peace."[51] And that "earnestness and seriousness" permeated the way women looked at their own lives and aspirations. Charlotte Erickson conjectures that the lack of males may have helped make some Augustana women "more serious students than [they] might otherwise have been,"[52] partly because women "received attention," according to Erickson's classmate Betsey Brodahl. Certainly that's what Bergendoff wanted. "As a co-educational institution Augustana seeks to give equally as much attention to girl students as men," he stated in his 1942-43 President's Report. With a campus stripped of its men students, Augustana "has endeavored to give more rather than less care to the women."[53] In classes populated largely by women, Brodahl says, competition with men for both voice and, more pragmatically, for scholarship and fellowship support, was significantly reduced. Bright women discovered the rewards and challenges of scholarship, and pursued the options opened to them. As Brodahl says, "My opportunity to teach and work at Augustana came because of the war and its aftermath."[54]

Her story was repeated often. Erickson, for example, scaled academic heights then undreamed of for women in general, and certainly for Augustana women in particular. After a brilliant 27-year tenure at the London School of Economics, she became the first woman to teach at Corpus Christi College, Cambridge University, the college's first woman Fellow, and the first woman professor of history in any of the colleges of Cambridge. On the other side of the Atlantic—appropriately, since her speciality was immigration history—she garnered Guggenheim and Sherman Fairchild Distinguished Scholar awards. When she concluded her teaching career, she was designated a John T. and Catherine D. MacArthur Fellow. At her death July 9, 2008, colleagues and students eulogized her as "a superb historian, a marvelous person, a great teacher and a very influential exponent of American society, past and present, to a British audience"[55] and as a tutor who embodied the varied roles of "supportive parent, ... challenging friend and ... deep source of wisdom."[56] A serious student, indeed.

Fortunately, "there were no shortages of brilliant teachers at Augustana during that time," according to Margaret Swanson Lacy. One of them, as we've seen, was Henriette C. K. Naeseth. "Because of [her] marvelous teaching I wanted to pursue my own career in English," Lacy has said. That distinguished career included earning her doctorate from the University of Wisconsin, studying at Uppsala University in Sweden, and then teaching composition at Wisconsin; writing, and translating Swedish fiction and poetry.

Of course, not all women stayed on campus. Many elected to join branches of the service. "From air-flight nurses on the front lines to those in the lowest Freshman ranks the girls of our Alma Mater stand loyal and true," V. R. Pearson writes. "News and letters from those in the front lines tell of a work of sympathy and service much needed and well done."[57] Indeed, *Observer* "casualties" included 1943 editor Edith Reller, who was claimed by the WAVES for war service, the 1944 *Rockety-I* notes.

Life on Campus

Women students walked the campus in their saddle shoes and bobby sox, their pleated skirts and sweaters. They watched "winter...sunlight on Old Main's yellow stones"[58] as they arrived for classes. Each day they climbed the stairs to attend a chapel sprinkled sparsely with men, and listened somberly as President Bergendoff "brought 'a daily beauty' to our lives"[59] with his five-minute meditations on life and learning—in this case, life in wartime. Upperclass students on the first floor, and first-years in the balcony watched light fall from the large stained-glass window, watched Bergendoff's serious face and then-graying hair as he told them, in various ways, that "war destroys. But the stress of war also develops fine things in the human character....The year ahead will demonstrate if we are to succumb to pessimism and despair, or if we can rise above our difficulties and hold aloft faith in Christian manhood and womanhood."[60]

Reminders of the war were everywhere, not only in the decimated male population and in the vigorous rituals of the 68th, but in daily life. The rationing of gas, sugar, meat, and tires. The shoe coupons. The thin, brittle pages of textbooks. The yearbooks without the impressive and expensive padded covers. And reminders came from below the hill, in the world beyond the campus. Betsey Brodahl, a student in 1942, recalls:

> I lived in a dormitory room looking out over the Rock Island Arsenal, lighted and roaring with twenty-four-hour-a-day production. On the railroad yards just beyond the Woman's Building...there was constant movement of goods and services, men and women. Our window sill was covered every day with coal soot. We lived on a campus with no cars. City buses were packed with workers moving all hours of the day and night.[61]

Augustana's own Charlotte Erickson, destined for international scholarly acclaim, worked in a factory during those years.

The women on campus studied hard—or lightly, as energy and inclination took them. They sang in a choir "with a full, if somewhat inexperienced male section,"[62] a choir reduced from distant travel to "bucket" tours, but that ended up on Chicago's Orchestra Hall stage.[63] They played violin, piano, and sports. They chatted late into the night; lived with the drag of anxiety or the sharp edge of grief. They watched the mail for letters marked "free" or "censored" or "via air mail," "letters stamped...South Pacific, Italy, somewhere in nowhere."[64] They crowned a 1943 Vi-King with a dress-blue U. S. Navy sailor cap. Instead of late afternoon Coke dates they sat in groups at the College Drug reading, writing letters, or knitting socks.[65] They planned futures in some cases very different from the ones they'd envisioned when they thought about what college could give and be for them. They found that "religious activities had more meaning...activities like ten o'clock devotions every evening during Lent...St. John's and First Lutheran Church services...Julatto [*sic*—early morning Swedish Christmas service] in the Seminary Chapel...L.S.A. [Lutheran Student Association] meetings and suppers...Bach rehearsals...*Messiah*...campus devotions...the Bible classes...Woman's Missionary Society...not to mention, chapel... and Christianity classes."[66]

And as we've seen, women assumed leadership positions vacated by the men. They edited the *Observer* and the *Rockety-I*, sometimes as the first women to do so, often on short notice, when men who'd been assigned those positions received their call-ups. And they fulfilled their new responsibilities admirably; Charlotte Erickson, in fact, was the first (and last) business manager actually to make a profit for the yearbook. Women began to outnumber men in campus clubs and honorary organizations, even those such as geology's Sigma Gamma Episilon, formerly male-dominated. The Runic honor society, comprising the top five percent of senior students, went from three men and one woman in 1942 to two men and two women in 1943, two women in 1944, three women and one man in 1945, and two women and one man in 1946.[67] Publications of those years show a new seriousness of purpose. *Observers*, sent to "Augieites in service," "played an important and commendable part in building morale."[68] *Rockety-Is* tackled war themes—"Lest We Forget," "The Best of Things in the Worst of Times," and finally "The Victory Bell Has Rung." The texts of these yearbooks are rich, evocative, often deeply moving. The 1945 yearbook dedication, for instance, reads in part, "to all the Augie men and women in the armed forces who are fighting to preserve the best things, the Victory Song still in their hearts...to those who have died in the winning, we dedicate this book."[69] Lists of those "who are fighting" and "who have died in the winning" begin the books for each of the war years.

It wasn't only intellectual and artistic activity that claimed women's attention and honed their talents. In 1945 Lois M. Anderson, who also edited both the *Observer* and the *Rockety-I* and graduated at the top of her class, joined pre-seminarian Howard Johnson in heading the North Hall improvement committee.[70] What they did was to transform it into a student center, spearheading a cadre of fellow student workers, but doing much of the grunt work themselves. As the yearbook for 1946 says, "Unestimable planning and labor went into the Students' Union Building....Lois and Howie were co-chairmen of the project and stuck to it through paint and turpentine" and curtain sewing and ironing and furniture moving "to the finish. A mere statement of gratitude could never repay them for their untiring efforts."[71]

And women went off campus into the community, giving new forms to the missionary impetus that had shaped the Augustana Synod throughout its history. Dorothy Parkander and Catharine Nelson Edlen, Class of 1946, remember the Sunday night sessions at the then-Rock Island Rescue Mission that they and their fellow students initiated. They'd walk or bus down to meet with the children who came regularly to hear dramatic Bible stories ("I always ended on a cliff-hanger so they'd return the next week," Parkander reports), and to be given some discreet suggestions about personal hygiene as well.[72]

But the downside to these new choices and challenges was a limited social life. Cadets were all very well for some, but others had come to college at least in part to meet eligible men with backgrounds and values more like their own. It was disappointing to find so few of them.

And again, as we've seen in previous chapters, traditional images of "girl" students lingered. Expectations for behavior continued to differ according to gender. Olive Johnson Schwiebert, who served as Dean of Women from 1945 – 1948, remembers her irritation at the discrepancies in rules

Dean Olive Johnson: a bit dismayed that "girls had to behave, boys didn't"

for women and men, as laid down in the student handbook of the day. Interestingly, the college catalogue suggests pretty uniform expectations: "It is assumed that young men and women who enroll…at Augustana College are aware of the standards of Christian conduct and will govern themselves accordingly. Few specific rules are therefore considered necessary…."[73] In fact, the student handbook presents a rather different picture. Schwiebert puts it succinctly: "girls had to behave; boys didn't."[74]

During the forties the student handbook, which Schwiebert was charged to enforce, devoted three pages to rules for conduct in Women's Dormitories, as opposed to one page for Men's Dormitories. Women discovered that as first-years they were required to be in by 8:00 p.m. Monday through Thursday, by midnight on Friday and Saturday, and by 10:30 on Sunday. First-years who earned a B average the first semester were allowed upper-class privileges (10:00 Monday through Thursday) for their second semester. Curfews were strictly enforced, with dormitory doors locked at the specified "in" hours, lights turned out. If you wanted to study later, you took your books and papers to the still-lighted lounge—often an inconvenience. Male friends, who naturally were not allowed in private rooms, had to call during (decorously) designated time slots. Telephone calls were to be kept to five minutes. And of course, smoking was strictly taboo.

However, the war years—and the general social change they induced—did result in an easing of these strict rules. In 1941-1942 first-years were "required to remain in their rooms for study" Monday through Thursday nights during their first semester[75]; by 1944-1945 they were "advised" to do so.[76] By 1946-1947 each first-year woman, not just those with a satisfactory first-term grade-point, was allowed one late (*i.e.,* 10:00 p.m.) night a week. Perhaps by that time the necessity of housing women off-campus had shown "the girls" capable of conducting themselves under less stringently protected circumstances.

Still, the contrast between rules for women and men remained significant. Men were told that "lights are extinguished at 12:45 a.m." for each day of the week; no curfews or locked doors were mentioned. And though, like the women, they were expected to dress appropriately and sit in assigned places for dinner, few other rules were imposed. Those rules implied robust, "manly" offenses: they couldn't wrestle, drink alcohol (there was no specific prohibition against smoking), or have untidy rooms at morning inspection, and should they be out overnight (an option not offered women except in the case of an emergency), they had to register their destination. Their dormitories offered quiet hours but neither "required" nor "advised" rigid study schedules. They were told the importance of caring for their health and seeking medical attention when necessary, but with nothing like the almost hovering urgency that "requested [girls] to notify the nurse of every case of illness, no matter how slight it may seem."[77] The image of women that emerges from these handbooks is familiar and predictable: a weaker species, requiring instruction, guidance, and protection. An *Observer* writer from the 1930s described the cloistered atmosphere: "The girl's dormitory and the famous Sing Sing prison have one thing in common. Each has one guard per 25 inmates."[78] Things seem only slightly different a decade later.

"The idea seemed to be," Schwiebert speculates, "make the girls behave and the boys will have to." Possibly the strong family image Augustana projected, that nurturing, encouraging "Alma Mater" who formed an *in loco parentis*, might have reinforced the general notion, observed at other schools, of special responsibility to women. (One recruitment poster of the twenties read "Keep your Daughter Safe at Augustana.") Augustana certainly wasn't unique in keeping women students on such short leads, though. Schwiebert noted that similar hours for women were imposed at Syracuse University, where she earned her graduate degree in counseling.[79] And as late as the 1990s even a school as progressive as Mount Holyoke eschewed an "open dorm" policy.[80]

One explanation of how the women might be expected to spend their time outside class and inside the dorms is suggested in the breakdown of college costs for the 1945-46 school year: a $5 charge per semester for linen and laundry is imposed only on male students. Domestic expectations still surrounded women, and, as we've noted, career options for first-year women students in the early years of the 1940s remained limited.

Of course, as has been the case from student days immemorial, the Augustana handbook, as well as other "rules" for female behavior and aspiration, was sometimes circumvented. Residents of the Woman's Building on Seventh Avenue who could coerce an obliging friend into keeping the window of her first-floor room open and her eyes and mouth closed, could adjust the hour restrictions. And in a couple of cases known to Schwiebert, President Bergendoff himself, when personally appealed to, intervened to loosen other rules.

In a changing world with new possibilities, women faculty members made a particularly strong impression. No one at Augustana in the war years can forget Henriette C. K. Naeseth, one of the most powerful professors on campus (see Chapter V). Adda Bozeman (see below), whom the war brought, briefly, to teach history, presented a cosmopolitan sophistication and an academic background that caught bright minds. "A lady of foreign magic," she's called in the 1945 *Rockety-I*.[81] Women students caught that magic. They found in her an example of life-transforming possibilities; and she, in turn, encouraged their new aspirations.

The end of the war brought jubilation and reunion, ticker-tape parades, champagne and roses, and tears. But for women it brought also a regression. Now that the boys were back in charge, what was to become of those new roles, those carefully-nurtured aspirations?

A Lady of Foreign Magic: Adda Bruemmer Bozeman Barkhuus

She was exotically beautiful, her thick dark hair parted in the center and scooped into an elegant chignon. She dressed with a style not typically seen in the 1940s world of Augustana: svelte suits; a memorable veiled hat dotted with dancing butterflies. She sometimes brought her small daughter to class. And she brought credentials exceptional for women of her day.

Adda Bozeman: cosmopolitan influence

Born Adda von Bruemmer into a Baltic German family in Geistershof, Latvia, she graduated from L'Ecole Libre des Sciences Politiques, Paris, and the Academy of International Law, The Hague. She studied law in England, was admitted to the English Bar, and joined the Middle Temple (Inns of Court) in London—where she argued cases with the barrister's wig placed over her luxuriant hair, a detail she shared with fascinated American classes. Before her emigration in the 1930s, she had practiced with an international firm in Berlin, The Hague, and London.

In America she received a doctorate in law from Southern Methodist University and continued postgraduate studies at the Hoover Institute, Stanford University. She came to Augustana in 1943 as assistant professor of history, and taught here for four years. In 1947 she left to join the faculty of Sarah Lawrence College, where she remained until her retirement thirty years later.[82]

These international connections shaped her scholarly life. At Sarah Lawrence she taught history and international relations, preparing many students for careers in the Foreign Service. She published widely in the field of international studies. A "renowned scholar," according to the *Sarah Lawrence Magazine*, Bozeman "was avidly engaged in the study of the Middle East, Russia and Southeast Asia, among other critical areas, and wrote extensively about the interactions of cultures."[83] Her books include *Politics and Culture in International History: From Ancient Near East to the*

Opening of the Modern Age; Conflict in Africa: Concepts & Realities; Strategic Intelligence & Statecraft: Selected Essays, and *Regional Conflicts Around Geneva*, published collaboratively by Augustana Library Publications and Stanford University Press.[84] Sarah Lawrence commemorates her work in The Adda Bozeman Chair in International Relations, and in the Adda Bozeman lecture series.

Not surprisingly, at Augustana her teaching asked students to make connections: her history courses encouraged reflection on the larger significance of places, events, and eras, rather than rote memorization of data. And she supported the gifted women students in her classes. Nor, for all her cosmopolitan connections, did she forget her early days at Augustana. As late as the 1980s one of her former students, Betsey Brodahl, received a long, detailed letter from Bozeman recalling those years—and the students who were called to larger aspirations, by her.

The Moment I Was In: Betsey Brodahl

If you were an incoming student any time from the fifties through the early sixties, you'll have an indelible image of her sitting on a platform during the opening ceremonies to welcome and orient you. She is wand-straight and taller than any of the other dignitaries ranged beside her. Memory dresses her in something pastel and flowing. Her hands are folded, one over the other, in her lap; her feet, in elegant shoes we'd later gasp at the cost of, are placed side by side. Throughout the ceremony she looks attentively at whoever is speaking. She does not move, except to smile or laugh at what is said. Whoever is sitting next to her—dean or president or student—looks diminished in comparison. You notice round shoulders and restless hands. The light comes from above and shines directly on her, as if by her very presence she's summoned it.

She is Dean Betsey.

The host of a local radio program gives his guests a charming thank-you token; he opens a leather pouch and pours out on the table an array of colored glass orbs, like irregularly-sided marbles: deep amethyst, red, green, some swirled with strings of contrasting shades, some plain. When they're held up to the light, the small circles tilt and dance with color. The guest chooses which glass circle she wants, and carries away a tangible, living memory of the program.

Reflecting on her life, Betsey Brodahl once said, "I have always considered the place and the moment I'm in the best." Her life has consisted of many "best" moments, like those circles of colored glass dispensed by the radio host. She holds each up to the light, watches it live and dance,

Dean Betsey Brodahl: shining moments

each with its own color and character. For her the moments are gifts. But they also reflect the artistry of her own creating, the things she has cherished and given her life to make real and beautiful. And they range from watching Sand Hill Cranes return yearly to her home in Wahoo, Nebraska, to sailing the Nile and walking the streets of Florence, to exploring the diverse cultures of Sweden, Russia, and the Near East,[85] to making music and history and art live in her life and the lives of others.

Or, to change the metaphor, "she has worn many hats, each donned with ineffable elegance and panache. Generations of Augustana women and men will never hear the name 'Dean Betsey' without an evocation of her wit, charm, grace, and warmth."[86] So how does a girl from a small town in Nebraska come to experience and represent all of these world-ranging qualities?

Brodahl herself has given some of the best answers. She's written eloquently of the influence her Swedish-American family and her Nebraska home have exercised on her. Swedish on both sides of her family, Brodahl, born August 28, 1923, in Wahoo, grew up with stories about her grandparents who "worked on the railroad to get money for land available through the Homestead Act and through railroad sales; the women worked as domestics in the homes of earlier arrivals. Once established on the land they helped to build the community in which I was to live....What they were and what they had lived through in the development of the country loomed large in my mind."[87] They were stories she was never to forget: stories of Grandfather Brodahl, "a tall young Swede striding off the [30] miles on his way west from Lincoln to Malmo" for a Sunday visit to "his people" after he'd worked a full Saturday; of a grandmother delighted with the unending labor of keeping house in a sod dugout because it was *her* house where she could "nutur[e] her own American citizens."[88]

Brodahl's childhood was influenced by the values of these grandparents: the love for land earned by hard labor, because land represented independence; the interest in the shifting seasons, the beauty of rain and of wheat; the importance of extended family ("we were something of a tribe"[89]), and the ritualized activities associated with the Swedish heritage. Attending the Lutheran Church, hanging "Christmas curtains" made of Swedish "drapery material woven in bands of white with narrower bands of black, gold, blue, and deep red" which were, for the young child, "as important to Advent as [the hymn] 'Prepare the Way, O Zion!'"[90] And there were the small personal memories—of "sleigh bells, a pocket knife, and a wooden butter dish,…cherished remnants of my Grandfather Brodahl's immigrant trunk," prized in the family;[91] of her grandmother's housedresses, "made from the fabric her daughters had woven in Sweden…."

During my childhood we still had bolts of this material…, sky blue, pale grey, [or] striped.…I was comforted against this fabric many times and can still see its smooth threads magnified through…childish tears. I started college in a dress made from what was left of the gray and white stripe.[92]

She recalls also the solemn, almost sacred tradition of joining her grandparents in their home for *fira skymning*—the celebration of the sunset,

…a very special time and place for me. It was warm, there was food, I had their entire attention. The kitchen had a woodstove and cob box. My grandmother sat in her rocker, my grandfather in a high straight chair at the windows and I on the oven door, listening to them as they recited scripture, poetry, and sang—all this in Swedish. During the first years it didn't occur to me that I didn't understand the language. The sound, like everything else in that setting, was familiar and I knew what it meant. I listened, recited, spoke the language of the twilight and was rewarded with apple slices, sweetened as they dried in the afternoon sun.[93]

It was a heritage of strength and of certainty, of knowing your place and filling it with integrity. The Brodahl family commanded respect and position in the small ("about 3,000 population") Wahoo community, and that, for Betsey, was defining and empowering. Her father, Alfred Brodahl, who owned a Ford dealership in town, earned almost legendary status for fair trading in an occupation which could tempt to fraud. Denied the opportunity to attend college, he was, as Brodahl has said, "the best-read man I ever knew," and served in various leadership positions, including board presidency of Luther College in Wahoo.[94] Her mother, Ruth Erickson Brodahl, came from a family of wealth, intelligence, and artistic gifts. Her love for beauty in all offices of life, for clothes carefully selected and elegantly worn, for flowers on a beautifully-set dinner table and art work in the home, for civility and grace, all became part of Betsey's life and values. Encouraged, and in some ways indulged, by these parents, Betsey derived a clear sense of who she was. If not exactly a sense of entitlement, this view of herself gave her superb confidence that the things that mattered to her—family, integrity, responsibility, gentility—were the important things of life. She never lost this sense. Nor did she lose her love for land and the stability that land represents for families who gather on it, work it, revere its many faces. Her own family—her parents, her lovingly autocratic Aunt Clara, her adored older brother Don, her four nephews and their children—have remained a center of strength throughout her life.

A hometown like Wahoo, Nebraska, where roles are clearly defined and responsibly accepted, confers enormous security. Because the clearer and more certain a definition is, the more precisely it creates meaning. And if that meaning involves one's place in society, the place is correspondingly stable. You know your niche. Yet precision also involves limitation. And seeing limitations can invite exploration of them. This paradox seems to have operated in Brodahl's case. She has spent her life both celebrating and exploring the boundaries of traditional views.

This double perspective began in her childhood, as she grew up in the 1920s and 30s. Her church and family upheld traditional views of gender roles, among other things. Because of this influence, Brodahl says, when she was a child "it never occurred to me that I'd have a career. In my family women don't work outside the home."[95] Yet at the same time, she watched her family press against that reality. On her mother's side, the women were more highly educated than the men, though in traditionally "womanly" fields: nursing (Aunt Clara) and the arts (Aunt Nell and her mother Ruth Brodahl). Economic adversity or loss of male providers drove some of them into the workforce—again, in occupations traditionally assigned to women, such as teaching and nursing. Still, they presented an example of limits being pushed, or at least redefined. Brodahl has spoken often and admiringly of the "many strong women [in her family] who were tested,"[96] and of her belief that their testing tempered a special sort of strength. For Brodahl, one element of being a woman meant possessing that strength.

These women Brodahl admired seem, when one hears their stories, to be something like "closet rebels"—women who, loving their men and serving them in traditional ways, also seemed engaged in a covert conspiracy to undermine some of the perceived absolute authority of males. Such women may have encouraged Betsey's own testing of limits by providing simultaneously a stable base and permission to move beyond that base. Early on, Brodahl's mother, observing her gifts, suggested that Betsey "wouldn't have a 'normal' life." Both mother and daughter understood it not as a criticism but as a suggestion that Betsey would go beyond conventional expectations.

Her father, Alfred Brodahl, whom Betsey respected and adored, endorsed this idea of larger than normal possibilities for his talented daughter, and supported that idea in practical terms, once "trad[ing] a car for a fine violin when I was studying music" and later expressing some concern that his daughter had not been urged to "stay with music."[97] And despite his own lack of a college education, he "said he would send me to school as long as I was willing to go";[98] thus, according to Brodahl, "I never worried about finances for graduate school expenses; my assumption was that all would be provided, and it was. The family gave one hundred per cent support."[99]

It was a support amply rewarded. From her first arrival in an elementary school classroom Brodahl loved school. Self-confident and quick, she soon discovered the joy of excelling. Invariably she ended up at the top of her class. "I knew I was bright…I knew I'd be first…because I always was," she remembered. It wasn't arrogance; it was a simple statement of fact. She was doing well what she knew she was good at. "I have never been ambitious or goal-directed," she has said. Which probably explains why she ended up at a two-year college in Wahoo—Luther—and subsequently at Augustana, rather than at Bryn Mawr, where she'd been accepted.

She chose Luther in part because her father sat on its board of directors. But the choice turned out well for her, bringing her two lifelong friends and, because of them, her Augustana experience.

If going to Luther tended to reinforce her acceptance of the Brodahl niche, the young teachers she met there encouraged her pushing of limits. Both were to become long-time, much-beloved professors at Augustana, from which both had graduated. Each chaired his department: Dr. Ronald

Jesson music, and Dr. Iverne Dowie history. But in those Luther days, the mantle of professorial decorum sat lightly on them, and various escapades—including "beating the check" in a local restaurant—taught the young Betsey a delight in roguery that lasted as long as their friendship.

Augustana, where she enrolled in 1942, provided an opportunity for Brodahl to continue exploring definitions and limits. As we've seen, in part the school provided mixed signals for women. While investing them with the responsibility of upholding the liberal arts tradition in a war-torn world, at the same time it provided woman-exclusive occupational training. Brodahl found she could not only earn a teaching certificate, but also learn typing and dictation in college—and she did, at her father's request. "Women, then, were expected to teach, to be secretaries, or...nurses," Brodahl recalls, and to possess these skills provided women with job insurance, a back-up plan if other options failed. Augustana's courses in these fields "showed what the college felt it owed to women." And yet at the same time professors like Henriette Naeseth, and in Brodahl's field, history, O. Fritiof Ander and Adda Bozeman, were urging gifted women to attend graduate school and helping them secure financial assistance to do so. Brodahl, like Inez Rundstrom generations earlier, seemingly felt no tension between these two ways of regarding women. If you wanted to be an

Dean Betsey: helping students understand "what college was about—learning and studying"

efficient secretary, you could get the training; if you aspired to be a scholar, you had the opportunity.

Thanks to the influence of Ander and Bozeman, Brodahl earned degrees at two of the country's top universities: Syracuse (which, until Dr. Ander suggested it, "I'd never even heard of") and Stanford.

While excelling academically at Augustana (again, she graduated at the top of her class), she also cut a wide swathe socially. And she never lost the love of dealing playfully with too-rigid limits and proscriptions. Her continued success over a long tenure as Dean of Women, later Associate Dean of Students, arguably owes to this ability to both observe and to test limits. She's fond of saying that when she began her career as Dean, she was the youngest in the country; when she retired, she was the oldest. Considering the responsibilities of the Dean for understanding and dealing judiciously with issues of student behavior, and considering the seismic changes in student culture over the forty years of Brodahl's tenure, her ability to remain effective suggests both insight and flexibility. She began at a time when the Dean of Women instructed "girls" (as they were then designated) on issues of etiquette as well as monitoring their academic programs. She retired after the sexual revolution, after Viet Nam and "the Man" and the anti-Establishment protests (they were admittedly somewhat limited on the Augustana campus, though 1,200 students did march up the Slough Path to President Sorensen's house in support of the Student Bill of Rights, carefully urging one another to "stay off the grass"[100]), after torn jeans and long hair replaced suits and white gloves and sorority teas, after drugs, after the campus opened to international students with different cultural mores and different agendas—and she emerged with her reputation for fairness, discernment, and student support intact. It's a remarkable record. And it owes in part, surely, to the models of strong women she grew up with, women who could accommodate and even initiate change—certainly not fear it.

In part this trajectory may have been caused by the direction the college took after the retirement of Dr. Bergendoff (who remained her close friend to the end of his life). As she describes it, "In my early years as dean under Dr. Bergendoff I had considerably more power than in the later years. Dr. Bergendoff had an academic council and I was part of that; my ideas were sought, my opinions listened to. Later, the structure of the college was different....more like a business and less like a family..., so that my position on the ladder changed." More authority was delegated; templates were constructed for dealing with issues of student life. This approach proved uncongenial for Brodahl, who preferred "seeing students on an individual basis, not through a set of systems." She remembers cleaning her purse "during long discussions about systems" in staff meetings. The memory may be somewhat paradigmatic of her method for pushing limits. While attending the obligatory staff sessions, she made clear her disengagement from what she deemed inappropriate ways of approaching the job. It's tempting to note the classic gender split here: the male staff adopting a business model, the female preferring the familial model. (Which makes even more interesting the fact that what Brodahl did to demonstrate her disengagement was the very feminine task of cleaning her purse!) Brodahl's dissatisfaction with the "systems" approach increased as "I sensed a certain antagonism between faculty and administration, and I did not know how to confront or avert it; my friends were from the faculty, and I had always felt that our job [in the student services staff] was auxiliary—we tried to make things more comfortable and pleasant for the students so that they could do what college was about—learning and studying."[101]

It may, then, have been this discrepancy between what the authority figures mandated and what Brodahl's own perceptions recognized as valid, that explains her ability to understand a new generation of students also confronting "systems" they felt to be arbitrary and oppressive.

Another element in her success over a long span of student generations was a certain detachment. She sympathized with students, but could remain objective about them. This element was in large part a character trait. Brodahl calls herself a private person, wary of encouraging student confidences or intimacy. "There is a basic fierce selfishness that goes with privacy," she believes. While attending all the college events, especially in the early years (part of her understanding of her job), she maintained that privacy. Perhaps because she was able to do so, she could say at the end of her career, "I loved the school, I loved the students, and I was never afraid of them."[102]

If her collegiate years explored certain cultural and institutional limits, Brodahl's first years of teaching tested her own limits—of time, energy, and dedication. These were, she has said, some of the most difficult of her life.

She returned to Augustana to teach as part of the school's effort to serve the new, burgeoning student population created as a result of the G.I. Bill. The new faculty solicited included three outstanding women graduates, Brodahl, Dorothy Parkander, and Christena Lundborg (who had a brief tenure as physical education instructor before leaving to study and teach dance in California).

Parkander has left a vivid and amusing record of the conditions that faced these new, earnest, energetic young instructors (quoted elsewhere). But the cramped office space, offering neither silence nor privacy; the heavy teaching schedules; the jammed classes and the staggering amount of preparation needed—these became sources of comedy only in retrospect. Aflame with ideals of teaching, of serving not only the institution they'd loved but even more, the men who'd fought a war the country in general believed necessary, these young instructors got a stinging reality check. Short rations from frugal landladies. Sleep deprivation. And the always-guilty sense that their students deserved more than the overwhelming course loads enabled them to give. Brodahl recalls, "I had so many classes, I was teaching material in which I myself had never had courses, I liked to do my best, and I knew I wasn't doing it. I even felt that my best wouldn't be good enough for [the returning veterans]. I was just too tired to do the job I should have been doing." The normally optimistic Brodahl remembers that "sometimes I'd be crossing Seventh Avenue and think, if a car hit me, I wouldn't have to go on with this."[103] In part, the reason why she accepted the offer to become dean of women was to move into a job she felt she could handle with greater success.

She'd been trained for this work in her first graduate program at Syracuse University, a student dean training program offered by various schools. Brodahl enjoyed the balance Syracuse offered between studies in her own academic field, history, and the other requirements for counseling work.[104]

As dean, Brodahl emphasized the values she'd embraced throughout her life: the importance of academic excellence and of civility; the strength of place and of family (she never abandoned the metaphor of the "Augustana family"); the need for listening with intelligence and acuity to those whose experiences may differ from one's own; the centrality of personal integrity; and the love for the arts and the understanding that beauty can sustain.

For friends from college and community she was the consummate hostess. The tall wooden door to her apartment in House-on-the-Hill, where she lived amiably amid selected women students, would be hospitably open when guests arrived. A perfect fire danced in the fireplace. In the large bedroom, coats would be piled on the elegant antique settee surrounded by stacks of hatboxes. She never claimed great culinary skills, but she knew where to purchase the best food: the firm pink and white shrimp, the sweet smoked salmon, the specialty cheeses. Over pre-dinner drinks the conversation was lively, witty, informed. Her "kitchen" was a fold-back door that covered sink, stove, and refrigerator, so she wisely mastered a menu that always worked: parmesan chicken thighs, generous slices of French bread, broccoli, a crisp green salad, apple slices, and chocolates from Lagomarcino's confectionery, where she lunched nearly every day. As the coffee and chocolates went around the table, talk would often turn to her home and family. Photos of her four stalwart nephews, along with framed newspaper clippings of their academic and athletic exploits, hung on the walls. It wasn't so much that the evening wound down as that it eased into comfortable reflection. You left knowing you'd been in the presence of grace.

Brodahl's influence extended beyond the borders of Augustana—and in the same way as her admired elder colleague Henriette Naeseth, that influence also burnished Augustana's reputation. She entered activities in the Quad-Cities community, and in the national sphere, with the same graceful confidence that marked her presence on the Augustana campus. Profiles of her in local newspapers toward the end of her tenure devote entire columns to highlighting the many organizations she served, most of them concerned with education, historic preservation, the arts. Herself an accomplished violinist, she was particularly energetic in her support of the Quad-City Symphony Orchestra (a group she played in for many years). After her retirement, she maintained membership in two communities: Rock Island, where she was "in residence" in the elegant House-on-the-Hill, now supported by a fund established by friends and former students in honor of her mother, and in her own home in Wahoo, Nebraska. And, both during her time at Augustana, and after, she traveled the world. On campus she is recognized in a named building, the Brodahl Center for Communicative Disorders. And, bringing her life full circle, in 1976 she received the Vasa Medal from the King of Sweden for her work in promoting international relations.

The disabling stroke she suffered in 2003 brought her back home to Wahoo, again amid the family that has loved and supported her throughout her life. She continues to maintain extensive correspondence with friends and former students. And to reflect, from her chair by the window, on the moments of her life, vivid and luminous, fragile and enduring, as glass stones poured out on the hand.

Thinking About My Neighbors

"My world stopped and I got off," Betsey Brodahl has said about her stroke. Now, from the care center in Wahoo, Nebraska, where she spends her days, she has time to think, to look out the window at tree and sky, to look in, at the people she shares her space and life with. This is one of her reflections on those people.

I have been thinking about my neighbors here. When I sit under the [hair] dryer and check the faces looking out from other dryers, the unadorned or softened face carries its own congenital experiences of mother and grandmother, pioneer wives and mothers. Women whose faces show the mark of experiences of those who walked down the trail west with their men behind wagons and team that carried all that was left of home, knitting together the East and West to shape the farm and range with their step. No one asked, "Are we there yet?" They didn't even know if there was a *there* out there. But on they went, step by step, their eyes sweeping the horizon, these strong, cheering women, with their [immigrant] chests to create home, raise children, teach them to read and write, tell right from wrong, bury their dead. They were creating America and Americans. Their faces already were sculpted from granite. Theirs should be the faces on Mt. Rushmore.

As you can see, there is much time in this stroke, non-world to dream and imagine.

Betsey Brodahl

Wine-Dark Seas and New Dawns: Dorothy Parkander

She was younger than many of her students when she first began teaching in 1947. She taught classes jammed with returning World War II veterans. Enrollment in freshman writing classes numbered into the twenties and even thirties, and standing in Wallberg Hall's lecture room, with its gladiatorial arrangement of tiered seats, she must have offered an odd contrast to the drill sergeants her students were accustomed to. Those students were protective. When she once mentioned in class that "someone" had falsified his research,

Dorothy Parkander, Class of 1946, senior picture

a Marine Corps veteran rose from his seat, swiveled his bulk and his glare around the crowded classroom, and demanded: "All right, you guys—who did it?" It was the blush and the lurch of the Adam's apple up the 18-year-old throat of one of the few recent high school grads in the class that gave the kid away. The Marine turned back to his earnest young instructor and said gently, "All right, Miss Parkander. You can leave the room. I'll handle this." She doesn't know what went on as she waited half-nervous, half-amused, outside the closed door of the classroom. She does know that the red-faced boy turned in a scrupulously researched paper.

But she was no damsel in distress, the 22-year old beginning instructor, she was tough, and it was her toughness that prompted the class's respect. They'd looked into hell, some of them, and they'd come back with an eagerness for life that they met in the energy and enthusiasm of their writing professor. They respected discipline and rigor. And they knew "fair." Because of what she gave, they weren't about to let her get less than they deemed her due.

Though she has said, "Henriette was my model," she was very much her own person. She could be tough, but she was no formidable, gravel-voiced "Queen." She looks like a schoolgirl in her early faculty photos, round-cheeked and eager, and also vulnerable; the eyes ask approval. But, as the vets discovered, she was in fact unusually mature, wise to the nuances of human behavior. She was both idealist and ironist, and the balance meant she resisted the temptation to cynicism. Throughout her nearly half-century tenure at Augustana, her energy for life never flagged, the hope for and belief in a splendor that was sometimes realized, never left her.[105]

And it was perhaps just this unique combination of qualities that made her, almost against her will, a force on campus. In 1981, as she was completing thirty-four years at the college, an *Observer* article names her one of Augustana's "Twelve Most Powerful People," not because she held "positions" on important committees—in fact, she hated and avoided committee work—but because "when [people were] asked to name someone who helped form opinions at Augustana, her name was almost always mentioned."[106] For many students and some faculty in the fifties, sixties, and seventies, Dorothy Parkander *was* Augustana College.[107] And by the 1980s students would sign up for "a Parkander" course; it didn't really matter which. One student from that period asserted half-seriously that nobody should be allowed to graduate *without* taking "a Parkander" course.

Dorothy Parkander, the young instructor who "made students sit up...and pay attention"

Student assessment may or may not be on the mark. But in this case it seems to be supported by a number of high-profile institutional "firsts" accorded Parkander. She was the first woman to teach in the prestigious O. N. Olson lecture series for the Augustana Seminary, then still located in Rock Island. She was the first occupant of the first fully-endowed academic chair at the college, the Conrad Bergendoff Chair in the Humanities.[108] She was the first (and to date the only) faculty woman to be honored with the naming of an academic chair for her, the Dorothy J. Parkander Chair in Literature. She was the first faculty member at Augustana, male or female, to be selected Illinois Professor of the Year by the National Council for the Advancement and Support of Education (CASE). She was the first woman whose portrait was commissioned by the college.

The late Lutheran theologian Joseph Sittler described her this way: "Dorothy Parkander represents in herself and in her teaching all that we mean by the liberal arts." Few who knew her would dissent from this judgment.

Many contemporary feminists, of course, eschew mere "gender equity," insisting on recognition of women's unique capacities and contributions. They define "what we mean" in their own distinct and evolving ways. But Parkander's record stands as a powerful reshaping of perceptions and systems that then existed, more powerful, probably, than confrontational rhetoric would have been at the time. Certainly her "firsts," distributed throughout a career noted for both its intellectual commitment and its civility, supported the more intentional feminism that came to Augustana in the seventies and after.

She was born March 14, 1925, a child of the church and of the college. Her father graduated from the Augustana Seminary; he proposed to her mother during a church conference on campus; Dorothy grew up in an Augustana church parsonage; she and her sister attended Augustana College. Augustana's central values were a part of her inheritance.

She shared Naeseth's pride in family, not for its social stature but for the vision it gave her.

Her father, Joseph Parkander, was an oldest child and only son; her mother, Hazel Hamborg Parkander, was an only daughter amid six boys. Joseph Parkander was a country boy who knew the rigors of farm work in rural Minnesota; Hazel Hamborg grew up in Des Moines, Iowa. Both were children of Swedish immigrants. Both were gifted, he as minister, she as musician and teacher. Both were deeply religious. And neither feared the hard work of living out their beliefs. Where they did that longest, and perhaps most influentially, was in Gustavus Adolphus Church, 7426 Drexel Avenue, on Chicago's South Side.

The neighborhood has changed now. But in the 1920s and 30s when Dorothy was growing up, solid, red-brick "G.A." Church was the bustling center of a large Swedish-American population. The church itself listed over 1,000 members on its roll; the Sunday School, under Hazel Parkander's superintendence, numbered close to 300 children. Understandably the pastor's household was a busy one: phone and doorbell ringing at all hours, quick clip of running feet, music and meetings. This background taught Dorothy both the necessity of being available and the value of privacy.

During those years the church still functioned as it had in the earlier generation that Emmy Carlsson Evald remembered, offering advice on practical matters, legal and medical advocacy, help during hard economic times, and social activities, as well as worship services and instruction in moral behavior. And both Joseph and Hazel Parkander took these varied responsibilities seriously. On Depression Sundays, greeting parishioners after service, Pastor Parkander would slip a nickel or dime into the hand of a member he knew to be unusually hard-pressed. When itinerant beggars showed up at the parsonage door at dinnertime, they were invited to join the family around the table—all brothers in Christ. Dorothy never forgot this feeling of community; she also never forgot how the brothers in Christ sometimes smelled.

Joseph Parkander was constantly on the run, chronically short on sleep. But he was no gloomy, duty-driven moralist. During a period when pietism tended to lean toward the lugubrious, he accented the joy of faith. That certainty, anchored in practical reality, conveyed with the warmth of his personality, the meticulous preparation of his sermons, the firmness of his handshake, and the energy of his smile, attracted people hungry for just such a vision. He was no career pastor. His ministry was about service to something larger than self. The Work, he called it. In capital letters.

Dorothy Josephine Parkander carried not just the feminine counterpart of her father's name, she carried his view of life as well. She quickly absorbed the personal qualities she observed in him and her mother: hard work, strong self-discipline, high aspiration, patience and tact and decorum and an almost inexhaustible capacity for delight. The Parkanders' example in the hungry thirties showed her what a working model of social justice looked like. And, in more personal terms, her father's attitude toward women demonstrated an egalitarianism that she accepted as normal. "I suppose the most important thing [as an influence] was that my dad wanted careers for both his daughters" and that he never regretted not having sons, Parkander reflected. "It was just expected that we would achieve in school. He didn't really hold up a domestic model at all."[109] His support went beyond the ideological. When Dorothy needed money for graduate school tuition at the University of Chicago, he sold his car to provide her with funds. And a visit to her class after she'd returned to Augustana to teach remained one of the high points of his life.

She entered Augustana College in the fall of 1942. Though she'd graduated from high school as valedictorian, no great deliberation went into her choice of college. She enrolled at Augustana because it was the expected place for her, because her sister was completing her education there, and because as a pastor's daughter she got special tuition consideration.

As we've seen, the war, in reducing the male population, provided opportunities for gifted young women. Both male and female professors encouraged their academic aspirations. For Dorothy Parkander they opened doors to more cosmopolitan worlds and ideas. The brilliant, internationally-credentialled scholar Adda Bruemmer Bozeman, for example, who'd come from a war-torn Europe to Rock Island as the wife of a local attorney, represented possibilities for intellectual achievement not usually seen in the homes of most Augustana women.

Without question, however, the defining experience of Parkander's college years—"a thrilling academic experience"—was the English curriculum, particularly the classes she took from then departmental giants Drs. Traugott Richter and Henriette C. K. Naeseth. The English majors of those years, Parkander recalled, were among the best students at the school, and they were predominantly women. High-powered, demanding classes offered brisk yet friendly competition. She was challenged by those classes. And by the liberalism of thought and the rigor of intellect she saw especially in Naeseth.

The encounter with Naeseth seemed to Parkander, if not quite like launching onto the wine-dark seas she was to lecture on so eloquently, at least like glimpses of vistas she hadn't imagined back home in her Swedish Chicago neighborhood. When she'd arrived on campus, she had brought with her ways of thinking and of expressing herself that reflected the community she'd been raised in. "My rhetoric was influenced by the last-century syntax and dramatic preaching style I heard from the pulpit each Sunday," she has said. (In fact, one of her childhood escapades was preaching to the canisters in the Parkander pantry—much to the amusement of the Swedish maid Betty, who declared her "as good as Pastor!") And that rhetoric carried its own weight of moral absolutism. Naeseth helped her to see beyond those modes of thought in ways that brought illumination. Undoubtedly the example of her father's respect for the life of the mind and the encouragement he provided for her to pursue it, made jettisoning some received certainties less painful and more fruitful than it would otherwise have been. She could retain the joy and possibility of his vision while exploring new ways of interpreting it. "When I discovered writers of clear, lucid prose who raised central questions of Christian belief, I found it a liberating experience," she says. "Writers like Dorothy L. Sayers [a favorite of Naeseth's] and C. S. Lewis showed me models of style that helped me frame and explore important philosophical and theological questions."

Still, she understood the real anguish of leaving behind secure and comforting answers. This understanding was to give her particular sympathy with students encountering concepts such as existentialism or Nihilism for the first time. As a young faculty member she'd listen long into the night when students made their way to her apartment and wrestled through troubling new ideas. To them, she would quote playwright George Bernard Shaw's famous observation, "When you first learn something, it feels as if you've lost something." The solution? Learn more.

It was Naeseth's influence that brought Parkander back to Augustana to teach after her graduation—at the top of her class—in 1946. "[She] showed a destiny possible for me [as a college professor]," Parkander said. And Naeseth provided her with support both practical and psychological as Parkander undertook the rigorous master's and doctoral program in English at Naeseth's own graduate school, The University of Chicago. Throughout Parkander's graduate career, which spanned two decades, given her heavy teaching load, Naeseth encouraged her, writing often when she was in residence at Chicago, introducing her to her own faculty friends there, and always offering a model of the future in store for the woman scholar.

So at the age of 22, a new-minted Chicago M.A. out of college just one year, Dorothy Parkander returned to Augustana to launch her teaching career. Like her colleague Betsey Brodahl, Parkander faced the daunting challenges of the post-war academy: classes swollen with the influx of veterans, course loads to stagger even the most enthusiastic novice, inadequate preparation time. In the next chapter we'll look more fully at that situation.

For Parkander, as for Brodahl, it meant long hours, little sleep, and less social life. But in that hectic era Parkander built the foundations of her professional reputation. By the time she retired in 1996, she could list an eclectic array of course creations ranging from the obligatory freshman composition to Homer and Dante in the Readings in World Literature class she designed and called "my baby." She taught the dead white males with an élan that made them her own: Chaucer, Milton, and Jacobean playwrights. She taught the Victorian novel, contemporary drama—and tucked in a few independent studies in classical Greek plays for variety. She was the campus authority on detective fiction. And for relaxation, she read books on archeology.

Dr. Dorothy Parkander, Illinois Professor of the year 1992

The intellectual liberation that had first exhilarated her in classrooms with Richter, Bozeman, and Naeseth continued to create its own excitement and make its own demands. In her first years of teaching she openly challenged the pronouncements of her beloved mentor President Conrad Bergendoff on the "immorality" of contemporary literature during the fifties, teaching plays from the post-war absurdist tradition, guiding her students to look carefully at those writers who probed the darkness of the human condition, and insisting always on the freedom of the artist to create the world as his or her vision presented it. A 1956 speech, for example, warns students that "the yardstick of morality is a dangerous one if misunderstood and improperly used."[110] She adopted the metaphor of the journey before it entered popular culture. The meaning is in the questions rather than in the answers, she would tell students.

And it wasn't only her views on literature that made her something of an anomaly during those early years. On a campus of largely conservative Republicans she was a staunch Democrat. On a campus slow to shake off the restraints of pietism she fought for a theater where sophisticated dramatic techniques could be taught and practiced. (Unfortunately, as actors and directors from the sixties can attest, she was roundly defeated; the original Potter Hall was built on the model of a church social hall, complete with tile floor, folding chairs, and kitchen facilities!) On a campus where a feared "intermarriage" could mean Catholic and Lutheran, she advocated "inclusivity"—before the term existed.

Parkander earned her doctorate with honors in 1962. Interestingly, given her background, she chose to study the rhetoric of seventeenth century Puritan sermons, and with characteristic scholarly thoroughness read ten thousand of them. Meanwhile, she was handling the teaching loads Naeseth had called "inhuman," as well as devoting much time to student activities. *Observer* articles that span her association with the college note speeches, panel discussions, book reviews, and other presentations to student groups. And since her first years of teaching offered little social life for young instructors (most of the faculty consisted of senior professors with their own established patterns of socializing), Parkander often entertained student groups. Her cooking, a gift which continues to amaze, as well as the opportunity for good conversation, remains a happy memory for many former students.

Like Naeseth, Parkander soon achieved iconic status at Augustana. Assessing her life, she has said, "The only thing I ever wanted to do was teach," and that teaching garnered recognition both serious and whimsical. Festschrifts from students on her 25th and 40th anniversaries of teaching attest to her influence on individuals; institutional honors signal her importance to the college as a whole. More than a decade after her retirement, alumni requested that Augustana's newest Transitional Living residence hall be named for her. And since 2004 she's been the honored guest at fiftieth anniversary class reunion dinners.

Parkander legends abound, of course, as they do for iconic figures. And most of them are true. The Chaucer parties, with lavish spreads of food, excellent punch, and no one to ask who was underage. World Lit in the fifties and sixties that got students out of bed at 4 a.m. to line up for registration so that they could be assured of a seat in one of the fastest-closing classes on campus. The famous mystery of the missing professor, when Parkander went into Chicago to take her Ph. D. qualifying exams and students planned a surprise welcome back—complete with red roses—at the Rock Island train Depot. Several of the daily Chicago trains chugged in, students dutifully presented themselves on the platform, but Miss Parkander failed to appear. The *Observer* carried a front page story about the incident, headlined: "NOT HERE...NOT HERE...Where Is Miss Parkander?" and showing a bewildered train porter scratching his head.[111] (She had taken an earlier train.)

•

Books fill the shelves, lecturers fill the air with prescriptions for great teaching. Certainly one element is awakening mind and heart. Parkander's students felt that awakening. And they knew, as students do know, that it was an invitation given with love.

She was no pedagogical innovator. She followed the then-accepted mode of instruction, lecturing. But she did it with an artistry and passion that were unforgettable. And she allowed herself no duplication from year to year; no yellowed notes from dog-eared files. Each class was a new experience, each work approached from a different angle. Yet the same themes sounded throughout the many texts and classes, and the many speeches to college and community groups: insistence on intellectual integrity, and its concomitant excellence in intellectual achievement; respect for the mysteries of mind, heart, and spirit; emphasis on the importance of the search to discover what can illuminate and heal; reverence before the act of creation, both divine and human, and a faith that mandates not only social justice in the abstract, but an immediate recognition that, as she has said, "every personality is sacred." One student noted her practical approach to forgiveness: "she believes second chances are everyone's birthright."[112] Her enactment of these values, the fact that her scholarly interests and personal beliefs interweave, suggest reasons for the influence students and colleagues have remarked. And, as many have noted, her sense of the comic, the astonishing smile that made crescents of her eyes, and the laugh that her colleague Roald Tweet calls "deep and irreverent," was pretty compelling also.

Parkander speaks often and passionately about vocation, about finding, in her father's words, The Work. Today's Center for Community Engagement at the college embodies that same understanding. "I could do only one thing and I was allowed to do that thing," she has said. The first part of her statement may be disputed, but no one can deny that she was in the right place at the right time, that indeed her joy matched the world's need.

For women students in the fifties and sixties, emerging from the "co-ed" model to define themselves against new opportunities and new social mores, Parkander was proof that a woman could be intellectually serious without sacrificing traditional "feminine" attributes. And in those years, that balance mattered. Like her colleague Betsey Brodahl, Parkander embodied grace. And she demonstrated that a person who happened to be a woman could have fun being scholarly, domestic, tactful, and witty, as occasion demanded. A student during her last years of teaching, for example, when asked about his course with the academically daunting Dr. Parkander, replied: "Oh, she's a riot!"

The seas might be dark, but the rosy-fingered dawn lay just ahead. You looked at Dorothy Parkander and knew it.

What I'd Like To Tell Dorothy

if I could
is that she made me sit up
and pay attention, stretch
my spine and open my mind

as if I were riding on the crest
of an extended simile, battered
by allusions and ideas I rarely
understood but determined

to hang on until washed ashore
by wave upon wave of words
meted out like lifesaving veil
and rugged rafts to a traveler

who in that damp Old Main
classroom began to witness
a rosy-fingered dawn unlike any
either she—or Homer—had ever seen.

Janice Bowman Swanson (1940-2009)
Class of 1962
Poet, Professor of English and Women's Studies Emerita,
California Lutheran College

A Calm and Compassionate Dean: Dora Carlson Cervin

"It's Hard to Believe...

"...that it is possible for one woman to fill a responsible position at Augie, keep a large house going, meet innumerable social obligations and yet be as calm and collected as Mrs. Cervin...."[113]

She was impeccably elegant and unshakably dignified. Early photos show her with neatly waved hair and an expression of serene confidence; later, the hair whitened and gathered in soft discipline atop her head, her trim figure neatly suited or dressed, her ankles decorously crossed, she projects the same calm confidence, the same demeanor that says "lady." Twice, during particularly significant eras in Augustana's history, she was dean of women.

Dean Dora Carlson Cervin: knitting women's abilities with opportunities

She first came to Augustana in 1928, just after the new Woman's Building had been completed and women were settling in. Whether Dora Carlson knew about the conflict between the Woman's Missionary Society and the College over the location of the dormitory when she "assume[d] complete charge" of it isn't, of course, part of the record. She belonged to a Lutheran congregation in Iowa; she may have. Certainly if any sparks of outrage made their way to her office, her cool, civilized command of awkward situations would have quenched them.

Dora Carlson succeeded Iva Carrie Pearce as Dean of Women. Unlike Miss Pearce, who'd been recruited from faculty ranks to assume the newly-created position, Carlson had been selected because "she is specially qualified..., both by experience and by ...university work," according to the *Observer*. A graduate of Morningside College in Sioux City, Iowa, Carlson took a year's graduate study at the University of Chicago before enrolling at Columbia University where she ultimately earned her master's degree in what the *Observer* calls "modern methods in special work for girls and women," presumably counseling. She had taught high school, served as dean of girls in a Sioux City junior high, and immediately before joining Augustana, as dean of women at Nebraska State Teachers' College.[114]

Augustana's choice of Dora Carlson made an important statement. It declared that women students had specific needs and concerns, and that the college had elected to invest in someone trained to address those needs, as her major responsibility. (Like a later successor, Betsey Brodahl, Carlson taught some classes, but spent most of her time as dean.)

She arrived on campus at a decisive time for Augustana's women. The new dormitory was to be more than a finely furnished place to house the increasing numbers of women students. It was also to provide those women with some experience in self-governance through a house council advised by the new dean.

And that was just the beginning. Much of Dean Carlson's activity centered on preparing women to assume control, in various ways, of the lives they would enter after graduation. She set up vocational conferences for women students, one of them extending over three days and involving both plenary and individual sessions. She also instructed them in domestic arts—in the way to set a table, pour at a tea, furnish a room. Under her sponsorship the Woman's Club (whose history we deal with elsewhere) grew and flourished, ultimately becoming the organization she'd hoped for, "foremost among [groups for] girls on campus," coordinating women's service and social activities.

In 1931 she resigned, marrying the local architect O. Z. Cervin. Five years later she was persuaded to return.

Her second session as dean lasted from 1937 until 1946—another critical time in the college's history, and in the experience of its women. As we've noted, those years saw the erosion of male enrollment as the war claimed men's services, and the arrival of more and more women students. The campus was, in fact, bursting with female undergraduates. The President's Report for 1942-43 recorded "overflowing" women's dorms, more than a hundred women housed in the infirmary, and crowded dining quarters—121 women using facilities "adequate for 80." The report stresses the need for more staff—a full-time nurse, housekeeping help, assistance for overstretched housemothers.

President Bergendoff goes to some lengths to make it clear that Augustana's women students aren't the default plan for keeping the college going until the men return. Instead, women were to be given full attention, "more rather than less care,"[115] because it would fall to women to "conserve the liberal arts tradition" so important to Bergendoff as a way of healing a world gone sick and mad, while the men studied mathematics and sciences to keep abreast of military technology. And yet "at the same time we have not been unaware of the many calls to women to fill positions left vacant by men, or offered through new war demands. We have sought to counsel women regarding these opportunities."[116]

Obviously much of the onus for fulfilling these varied responsibilities to women students, seeking their way in a changed and changing world, fell on the dean of women. Cervin encouraged her advisees to try these new roles. As she prepared for retirement in 1946, she told the *Observer* that she'd been "interested in seeing the girls successfully take over the work and activities on campus which had formerly been shared by both men and women before the war years,"[117] and had "particularly enjoyed" academic and vocational counseling, "bringing to [women's] attention the various opportunities in vocations."[118]

But Dean Cervin's job involved more than advising women on classes and careers during those critical years. She spent much time listening to women students as they shared anxieties and grief. As Bergendoff told the college constituency in his President's Report, the year 1943-44 "has not been an easy [one] for the Dean of Women. Not a girl but has a brother or friend in the armed services. Both the absence and the presence of news have put her under tension."[119] And added to that, the Air Crew trainees who came to campus, filling the empty men's dormitories, enacting their early and noisy training rituals, and tempting the weak-willed to those threatening U.S.O. dances, posed disciplinary challenges—though Bergendoff assures his readers that "the number of disciplinary cases is no larger than in more normal years."[120] Undoubtedly both the high quality of female students ("a capable group, having much ability and high standards," according to Cervin[121]) and the dean's vigilance accounted for this relative decorum.

Dean Cervin's position on the role of women in a changing world challenged few existing assumptions. Instead, she presented her advisees with a reasonable middle course between the traditional and the emergent. While counseling women students on new occupations they might be asked to take on, she assumed *de facto* that they would need "womanly" skills, and to that end worked with President Bergendoff to explore the possibility of adding courses in domestic science after the war.

The middle course she represented is reflected in her retirement observations. She was honored at a "dessert party" arranged by "faculty members and women employed on campus" and (mostly) faculty wives. And her parting gift, presented before a group of 75 guests, was a silver coffee service, expressing the elegance that made her an impeccable wife and hostess. Yet throughout her career she encouraged women to explore vocations outside the home, and she herself led and celebrated life in the academy. In addition to her work as dean, she taught courses in history and religion, and clearly did it well: President Bergendoff's Report following her retirement glowingly commends her as "one of the finest educators among Lutheran women in America."[122] To underline her support for women in higher education, she cited as a "highlight" of her years at Augustana seeing the college achieve accreditation from the American Association of University Women.

And she advocated for women's professional and educational development in other, more private ways as well. Though her dignity and reserve could be intimidating, students in need "had an unique view into her inner caring self." Bergendoff may have glimpsed this "inner self" in stories that weren't part of the public record; he praises her not just for her pedagogical skill, but for having "done more for our women students than any other one person."[123] In one especially moving case, an eager, bright student who'd gone to college supported by scholarships and her own hard summer work, couldn't come up with the $200 tuition to complete her senior year. As she recalled, "my parents were unable to fund my tuition," and in any case they considered "a high school education…entirely sufficient for life's challenges. I was crushed…." The young woman then

…made an appointment to see Dean Cervin to tell her that I would not be completing my degree. I was probably on the verge of tears as this was very important to me. I so much wanted to finish….After listening to my story she said something like, I do not remember her exact words, "I'll take care of it." I couldn't even think what this meant, it was so unreal….I mentioned that I could not see how I could repay her and she indicated that was not necessary. I left her office on a cloud of unreality. I could not imagine how this bit of fantastic luck had come my way. It was an outright gift and to this day I consider it a miracle. I completed my undergraduate degree....

The young woman justified Dean Cervin's investment. That senior year she considered an "outright gift" brought her election to both Runic academic honor society and Aglaia, scholarship and service honorary. She went on to win a scholarship to the Illinois Institute of Technology and earn her M.A. in bacteriology. And she saved money to repay Cervin.

She repaid her in a fuller way as well. Virginia Penniston Wheeler, Class of 1943, established a scholarship honoring the woman who had given her the "miracle" of an education.[124]

The Zesty Spirit: Zilpha Colee

The droop of the eyes was the giveaway.

She dressed conservatively, even, toward the end of her tenure, almost dowdily: mid-calf skirts, long sweaters, sensible shoes. But in the droop of the eyes that looked sidelong at life with comic, often outrageous irony, Zilpha Colee defined herself. She questioned, challenged, punctured unexamined certainties. If something had "always been," she wanted to know why. She had little tolerance for the pretentious, the rigid, the self-satisfied and self-serving.

But to the vulnerable and marginalized, to those struggling with classes, relationships, social injustice, and their own perceived lack of worth, she was a staunch friend. Always pragmatic, she shored up not only their aspirations but their health, feeding them substantial meals as well as insights gained from varied teaching and life experiences. And she never, never forgot to give them the gift of laughter.

Zilpha Colee came to Augustana in 1947 as part of the post-war additions to the faculty. She was something of a maverick even in those days of cautiously emerging diversity: she wasn't Scandinavian, Lutheran, or Republican. She'd earned her B. A. from Simpson College in Iowa—a school founded by Methodists, not Lutherans; then completed her A.M. and done additional graduate study at the University of Iowa. She'd taught in both high school and junior college. She'd seen a fair amount of life when she arrived on the campus that fall.

She soon took on the important responsibility of preparing English majors for teaching, many of them, at that time, women. It was a demanding assignment. But it fit her insistence on combining the theoretical with the practical. She could introduce students to what the educational gurus thought, and then show them how that might actually work in the classroom. Twenty-five years and piles of notes and handouts later, Augustana English teachers across the country could say they owed much to her instruction.

And to her vision. She was an impassioned advocate for social justice. And, again, it wasn't just an ideological commitment. In an era

Zilpha Colee: education for social justice

when faculty housing tended to cluster around the college, she deliberately sought a home in Rock Island's west end, not only to give tangible form to her political views, but more immediately to get to know people whose lives and backgrounds differed from her own. That active curiosity about people, that love for discovering other stories and other lives, was what fueled her zeal for travel, as well as her keen interest in the performing arts. Like several of her English department colleagues, her notion of the ideal weekend was a run into Chicago to see a play, film, or ballet. And when the weekend had to be spent at home grading papers, there was the current dog or cat colleague to share space, love, and, of course, food.

She retired in 1972. A graduate student from the University of Chicago assumed both her course responsibilities and her insistence on social justice—specifically, on gender equity. Her name was Nancy Lyman Huse, and her story is one that another generation of writers and researchers will tell. Nancy Lyman, as she then was, tall and statuesque, and Colee, stooping a little from age and past surgeries, spent an entire day in Colee's home, talking about the English major. The living room was stacked with materials Colee had assembled during her professional life. "She gave me brochures about the social justice issues involved in teaching English," Huse remembers. "She gave me advice, books, names of helpful people in the high schools, a hot and hearty lunch, and a dose of confidence as I embarked on my life at Augie."

She did one more thing for her successor: she introduced her to a dear friend in the English department, Dale Huse. Nancy Lyman and Dale Huse were married the following June.

Colee spent her years after retirement in Loveland, Colorado, tutoring, entertaining friends with her substantial meals, living well into her nineties—witty, "a little cantankerous," outrageous and generous to the end.[125]

BALANCING ON THE THRESHOLD:
POST-WAR AND THE FIFTIES

Jean loves research. She is a tall slender pixie of a woman, with a cap of short auburn hair and an unexpectedly mature voice. She's managed to fit in an astonishingly large number and variety of courses in both English and history during her time at Augustana. One Christmas she gives her professors small flat pens inscribed with a quotation from John Adams: "Let us dare to read, think, speak, and write." The accompanying card she signs "Jean, a student." It's a fitting description; she knows herself that well. She will, of course, go on to graduate school.

When she's not in classes or at work in the library, Jean spends time at the round tables in Special Collections, looking up information about the earliest of the Augustana women. She's not angling for extra academic credit; she's maxed out her course allowances in English and history. She wants to get to know them as people, she says, these women separated from her by several generations. She wants to know, and to do them the justice of telling their stories, restoring their living identities. She creates a presentation on her findings, and offers it to the Alumni Board. People are impressed with her polish, her confidence, her deep interest.

Jean the student is also Jean the teacher. She's fascinated by the concept of *liminality*, of the between-spaces in experience when reality is neither absolutely one thing nor absolutely its opposite, but a blend of the two: dawn that is both night and morning, dusk that is both day and night. Progress and regress—the thresholds of our individual and communal lives. I think this is why women's history fascinates her: we have lived so long on thresholds.

CHAPTER 7

Balancing on the Threshold:
Post-War and the Fifties

Educate a woman!
Educate a woman?
Educate a woman.
Educate a woman!

In this witty manipulation of punctuation marks, sure to please any English teacher, Mildred Helen McAfee encapsulates the history of women in the academy.

Preposterous!
Maybe—but how?
Just do it.
We must do it!

But what McAfee fears, writing in 1942, is that the final exclamation's imperative may be lost as soon as the war ends and men return expecting to take up their pre-war positions. And she warns that to unseat skilled and dedicated women from work they're doing well would be folly.

McAfee knew what she was talking about. As Lieutenant-Commander, Women's Reserve of the United States Naval Reserve, and also as president of Wellesley College, she had observed what women could do on both academic and non-academic fronts. She was profoundly aware of the ways in which educated and trained women could help reconstruct the post-war world. The case she makes, then, is pragmatically based. But it's also ideological: we're fighting in part to "attack a social philosophy which treats individuals as nothing but representatives of their group," she asserts, so we'd be both hypocritical and immoral if we apply that same philosophy to women, assuming that gender alone determines what an individual can do and be.[1]

Not everyone shared McAffee's view. And there were certainly reasons for restoring to the veterans jobs they'd held before the war. After all, they'd risked their lives to wrest peace and stability from a world that had veered into chaos. How were they to lead their post-war lives if women continued to do the work they'd left behind?

The problem, as McAffee set it out, was, again, ideological as well as practical. Withdrawal of women from the work force in order to restore employment to men seemed also to mean resuming or reinforcing stereotypical assumptions about gender. And that inevitably affected ideas about women's education. The exclamation point of urgency slid back to the question mark of conjecture. Should we? How? Was it necessary for women to pursue higher education? Should they be educated separately, in programs designed to serve their more specified employment options? Did they need places in graduate school and fellowships to support advanced study?

Many women wrestled with such questions, which were essentially questions of identity. Posters and magazine ads with curly-haired children stretching out chubby hands to plead with working mothers to "come back"; silhouettes of slumping servicemen denied their "rightful" jobs because women were now doing them—these images were meant to, and did, induce doubt and guilt in the minds of women who'd found work they did well and enjoyed. And so post war time was in many ways a liminal time, a threshold time, looking forward and backward. Yes, we're glad to have the men safely home, but what about the progress we've made? While some studies emphasize the contentment women felt in returning to "normal" gender roles, other research challenges this perception. Susan M. Hartmann, for instance, has looked at polls conducted among women workers between 1943 and 1945. Those polls showed that 61 to 85 percent of all women workers, and 47 to 68 percent of married women workers, wanted to keep their jobs after the war.[2] So the comfortable, comforting "Father Knows Best" scene of the fifties, with its precisely delineated gender roles and expectations, often covered deep tensions. In Barbara Miller Solomon's phrase, "unfulfilled aspirations haunted" many women. Where did their true selves lie? Who were they?

At Augustana similar questions of identity were being posed, on a variety of levels. The college was engaging in self-studies, reviewing and tweaking the curriculum, adding faculty of a somewhat more diverse cast—more women, fewer Lutherans—to handle the influx of ex-servicemen taking advantage of the G.I. Bill. That phenomenon in itself wrought dramatic changes to the previously rather homogeneous Scandinavian-American campus.

The G.I. Bill

The Augustana I returned to in 1947 was not at all the college I had graduated from in 1946.

Dorothy Parkander

"[The vets] came in flight jackets, pea jackets, army fatigues, carrying duffel bags, limping, strutting, smoking, cussing." Some were boys, most were men.

Betsey Brodahl

Betsey Brodahl, one of the new young faculty recruited to handle the enlarged student body, describes the phenomenon and its effect on Augustana. The so-called "Servicemen's Readjustment Act of 1944," quickly shortened to the "G.I. Bill of Rights," provided a variety of benefits for returning servicemen, most notably opportunities for higher education. The motives for this legislation weren't altogether patriotic. According to a study by Syracuse University (the graduate school Brodahl attended), some "hard-headed" economic reasons operated to support returning veterans: the influx of new civilians to the work force would, it was feared, choke a job market artificially inflated by the increased production needs of the war effort.[3] This circumstance, of course, provided yet another compelling reason for the propaganda aimed at persuading women to return to their homes.

But if Rosie was urged to exchange her riveting gun for a Mixmaster, women of the war generation who had been encouraged to pursue academic aspirations fared somewhat better. G.I.s taking advantage of the Bill swelled college and university enrollments. More than a million ex-service personnel arrived on American campuses the first year the legislation went into effect; five years later that number had shot up to an unanticipated 2,232,000. "Shocked college administration and faculty watched their facilities strain to accommodate the influx," Brodahl notes.[4] Part of that accommodation involved hiring more faculty. And some of them were women.

Augustana's growth reflected this national trend. Liberal arts students in the spring of 1946 numbered about 600; by 1947 that number had more than doubled (1,304 in the College, more in the School of Music). Brodahl remembers "cramming sixty and seventy people in classrooms designed for perhaps half that number."[5] Brodahl's "fellow newcomer," Dorothy Parkander, recalls teaching freshman composition literally from attic to basement in Wallberg Hall of Science during her first year. "Freshman English for me since then has always worn a chemical perfume," she observes wryly.[6] And it wasn't just crowded classrooms that faculty had to contend with. The difficulties were pedagogical as well as practical. Parkander gives a vivid picture of those daunting days:

[When I graduated in 1946] the English Department numbered three faculty; now it numbered eight….[So] [t]here was first the question: where could the college find us office space? [Senior English Department members] Henriette Naeseth had her own office in the basement of the [Denkmann] library; Traugott Richter shared with philosophy professor Hjalmar Johnson a cheerful room on the south-west corner of Old Main's first floor. The rest of us landed on the top floor of Old Main in a closet which, up to then, had housed band and orchestra instruments. Our location had problems other than lack of space, too. The center room of the top floor, just above Cable Hall, featured the orchestra rehearsals. The east wing, part of the Chapel, held two organs, both in constant use [for practice]. The west wing held the Speech Department who daily and conscientiously shaped their orators and debaters, and, at times, in the open hall, created a stage where budding actors could be eloquent. From 4 p.m. to 6 p.m. daily, Old Main's top floor was bedlam.[7]

Most serious and most disheartening to earnest young faculty members, though, were the staggering course loads. The number of classes instructors were expected to handle "paralyzed," according to Parkander. "An instructor's load could be 4 three-credit courses a semester, sometimes five. Three of my courses were usually composition, each class numbering between 25 and 30 and each student submitting a 500-800-word essay a week….If you got behind on just one week's theme grading, you could be engulfed forever."[8] Even the seemingly indefatigable Henriette Naeseth understood. In 1948 she wrote to Dr. Bergendoff that teaching loads were "inhumanly exhausting…preclud[ing] the best teaching."[9] Parkander and

Brodahl both remember long months of sleep deprivation (Brodahl would walk down to the Rock Island Depot for bacon and eggs at three in the morning). Parkander once actually dozed off in the middle of her own lecture. Given these calls on time and energy the few opportunities for social life, especially among young unmarried women instructors, became non-issues. You didn't even have time to cash your modest paycheck, much less gallivant around to parties. Brodahl has commented that her first year of teaching "was the only time life didn't seem good" to her, so overwhelmed was she with the impossible course loads and her urgent sense of responsibility for giving her best to the returning veterans who had given so much for their country.[10]

The college did take steps to address these issues. More new faculty were hired. A fund drive to "repair, restore, and build facilities to accommodate the numbers" was mounted.[11] To assist veterans making their way through the maze of college requirements, a special advisor, Harley Rhom, was appointed.

But perhaps the most lasting result of the G.I. Bill—one both obvious and subtle—was its effect on the perception of higher education and on the ethos of colleges and universities nation-wide. In the previous half of the century, college had been viewed as an "elitist" experience, according to Brodahl. After the war "a new era in American education" began, President Conrad Bergendoff writes in his introductory essay to the 1947 yearbook. The "new thing" that year "was the breaking down of barriers which formerly had surrounded the American campus. Within a year there was a crashing of the gates of colleges and universities by a whole portion of the population which before had not had financial means." To Bergendoff this signals that American young men and women believe a college education can enable them "to train themselves for better jobs and fuller living...."

How exactly that belief translated into action was a force that reshaped the college. The new generation of college students, in particular the returning vets, didn't necessarily share the heritage and ethos of Augustana. "[They] were more ethnically, religiously, and culturally diverse," Brodahl notes. "Their educational goals were different. They didn't all aspire to teach or minister." For example, of the 323 graduates in the class of 1950, business, education, music, and accounting were the most frequently chosen majors.[12]

In 1947 Bergendoff posed the question "Can...college education..give what these youth are seeking?" That question raised others. How much should a college like Augustana accommodate its programs to "what these youth are seeking"? Bergendoff's answer was that Augustana "did not propose to educate everybody. It did hope to influence leaders in every profession."[13] But reflecting on the issue in 1995 Brodahl discerned change and, perhaps, compromise: although "we attempted to balance consideration for returning vets with the maintenance of our academic standards and the character of the institution,"[14] still, "American education [and Augustana were] never the same again."[15]

The Curriculum: Questions of Identity

As a microcosm of the larger culture, then, Augustana also stood at a liminal moment as the post-war forties turned into the fifties. Minutes from faculty meetings especially during the first half of the 1950s show the college assessing itself in a variety of terms, both theoretical and practical, asking itself questions ranging from what it means to be a Christian college in the present culture, to what salary and benefits it's necessary to offer in order to attract and retain competent faculty. These kinds of questions reflected the interest of Augustana's accrediting body, the North Central Colleges Association, as well. Various national testing standards were invoked to determine teaching effectiveness—for example, the "Purdue rating scale"—and to measure what are now called "outcomes"—for example, the Junior English Exam.[16] The college committee structure was reorganized. The tightly-centered Swedish Lutheran identity gave way to a more diverse, more cosmopolitan faculty: Magda Glatter from Hungary; Ed Hamming from the Netherlands; John Sirevaag from Norway; Theodore Celms from Latvia, for example; the Covenant and Canterbury Clubs (the latter for students of Episcopalian background) were endorsed after some discussion about ecumenical issues on campus.[17] There was guarded conversation over issues of discrimination—presumably racial—both at the College and in the community.[18] As the homogeneity dissolved, priorities seemed to shift. President Bergendoff felt it necessary to urge faculty attendance at chapel,[19] but found no such exhortation necessary when it came to faculty meetings. "Room 27 was crowded," the Minutes from September of 1957 read… "—in fact there were not enough chairs for several members to sit on."[20]

As we've seen, curricular deliberations had begun as early as 1942, when it was evident that colleges would face the changed and changing world of the next decade. The result was the "Augustana Plan" of 1944. Bergendoff described it in his 1995 retrospective as "the faculty's thorough revision of the curriculum after two years' study under the direction of Dean Arthur Wald and the Educational Policies Committee."[21] As Bergendoff saw it, the Plan "was an expression of the faculty as to what should be a graduate's preparation for the difficult years of peace, not less difficult than war years. It clarified the purpose of a Christian liberal arts college in a confused secular age."[22]   We've noted in the previous chapter that this "new" plan in fact reworked the curriculum Bergendoff had inherited, emphasizing the liberal arts, and carefully negotiating between liberal and practical studies. Student interest in the so-called "Functional" majors, designed to prepare for specific careers, showed in the significant percentage who chose fields such as business administration, accounting, Christian service, music ministry, and speech rehabilitation.[23] Many of those students were women.

When he was 99, Dr. Bergendoff watched Augustana students process across snow-covered fields to the Jenny Lind Chapel in nearby Andover, Illinois, site of L. P. Esbjorn's first American parish. As Bergendoff recalled, the sight of those young people bundled in winter coats, walking in a long line and carrying tapers to light their way to the candlelit chapel where communion was being served, was "an inspiration in itself." What he saw was to him paradigmatic of Augustana's mission: sending young people out into a dark world, holding candles steady against the night.[24] As he said in his inaugural address in 1936 and persistently believed, "as we break up the atom or weigh the stars or discover the secrets of organisms, let us also be trained to spiritual discernment of Him Who put the atoms together and upholds the stars and awakens the life of each day and night."[25]

But this certainty that the college functioned as a beacon in a confused secular world eroded, according to religion professor emeritus Arnold Levin, who observed from the dual perspective of an outsider and a member of the community. Levin had graduated from the University of Oregon before coming to Augustana Seminary "in my 1948 Chevy" and later earned his Ph. D. from Harvard Divinity School. Subsequently he taught at the college from 1966 till 1998. Reflecting on his long and varied association with Augustana, he discerns a movement from the parochial to the more secular, from the insular to the global. Whereas an early conversation with President Bergendoff indicated "that the college intended to go it alone in isolation from the rest of the country" by choosing to "remain independent from federal and state money and its requirements,"[26] by the mid-sixties, President C. W. Sorensen believed that "Augustana had to take advantage of the funds that the government offered to institutions that were receptive to the new government guidelines."[27] Other "new perspectives" represented by the college under Sorensen included a widening of the cultural and geographical arenas for study, and a lessening of the emphasis on Western traditions. And inevitably, that led to interest in feminist scholarship.

In part, perhaps, this intentional and intensive focus on the changing identity of the college, begun in the fifties, resulted from the 1948 break between College and Seminary. Though Bergendoff deplored the separation, the college benefited from his exclusive attention. And of course, it was the college, not the Seminary, that invited women to study.

Thresholds: Backward and Forward

So the fifties were a threshold. In the immediate post-war years they looked, with that pull of nostalgia that is often pain, toward the past, toward getting back to normal. Men were welcomed home. The 1946 *Rockety-I* chose as its theme "The Victory Bell Has Rung." "The war is over," its copy declared triumphantly. "Men whom we had seen leave for service are back on campus"—at least, some of them. And that, as we've noted, implicitly assumed getting back to "normal" understanding about gender roles and expectations.

Male students from those years, while recognizing their bright female colleagues, often assumed that their goals basically centered on getting married, after a few years of teaching, nursing, or secretarial work. And women either agreed or didn't speak up to correct them. A pair of photos from the 1952 yearbook suggests just this perception about women's interest and expectations. Both photos deal with out-of-class settings. In the first, women circle around one of their number who holds her left hand triumphantly outstretched. The rest ecstatically gush over the size of her diamond, which, the text tells us, often provides the topic for "gab-fests." The other photo shows men grouped casually for conversation. The cutline explains that they're in a "bull session," which might cover anything from "'phrigs' [campus pranks] to philosophy."[28] As if to emphasize the discrepancy between male and female roles, in that same yearbook, a double-page photo[29] introducing the faculty section shows another group gathering: professors seated around a long table. They are all men.

In this resumed "normality" that Mildred McAfee had feared, leadership roles assumed by women in the war years now were, for the most part, reclaimed by men.[30] Men edited the newspaper and the yearbook; served as business managers of publications; were, inevitably, elected to the top offices in classes and organizations, while the women, with a wearying predictability, served as secretaries or secretary-treasurers; sometimes as historians, sometimes as program chairs, even in groups in which the numbers of male and female were equal, or in which women predominated. (An honorary organization for future secretaries assumed all-female membership, stating that it was open to "any girl" who maintained the requisite grade-point average.) Female membership in honorary science fraternities shrank from majorities to small minorities; the exception was Beta Beta Beta, the biology honorary, probably because of women enrolled in the nursing program, then a separate-but-equal entity.

The Korean War

And in the early years of the fifties, another force pulled backward, toward a nostalgic "normality." That was the Korean War, and the threat it posed then of a third World War "and the possibility of the destruction of Western culture."[31] While some students remained detached from the escalating conflict over the fate of South Korea "in this little, tightly enclosed world," others enlisted or waited tensely for draft notices. Still others devoted thought and study to the world situation, attending an on-campus meeting of the Quad-City Institute of World Affairs, forming the Students for Political Education and Action, and considering the war situation in poetry and essays. Six hundred students signed the Freedom Scroll and collected $54.80 in donations for the Crusade for Freedom, an organization formed to fight "propaganda and oppression" by underwriting broadcasting facilities to carry messages of freedom to Iron Curtain countries. Chapel talks by President Bergendoff and others called for a steady faith in a time of instability. An advertisement placed by the Augustana Book Concern shows a smiling serviceman with his "heart-shield New Testament" tucked in front left pocket. The special edition featured a "gold-plated steel front cover to protect the heart" physically as well as metaphorically (available for "Your Hero" from $1.95 to $3.95). Institutionally, Augustana sought involvement by applying for an R.O.T.C. Unit on campus (the application was denied). Reminders of the war, and of what it meant for the Western world, then, weren't far to seek.

As is the case in times of tension and the edge of change, looking backward to perceived happier days appealed strongly. In an extraordinarily mature and thoughtful essay of 1950, student Charles Rushing reprises songs, styles, and shapes of thought from the twenties to the fifties, describing the twenties as "our Happy Time" when today's pessimism was merely "embryonic." "The college student of 25 years ago," Rushing claims, "looked forward to a graduation into a world of eternal peace, of unlimited prosperity, of bigger bathtubs in which to make more gin" while today's student, beset with anxiety, "look[s] backward to 'The Happy Years' with increasing fondness."[32]

And doesn't talk much about his feelings. Fifties students were called "the silent generation," and at least one Augustana student, *Observer* columnist Clarence Wittenstrom, accepts the label. Fifties students believe, he writes, that "if only we can hurry fast enough, maybe the all-pervading gloom of impending disaster will blow away in the breeze of our haste—But...to no avail, so we clam up, become more practical, more realistic; and more cynical; in short, we become silent. Silent in what we think or what we hope."[33] "It wasn't that you didn't care," though, the late Richard Collins, Class of 1956, has said. "It was that you could find nothing to say."[34]

In the end, of course, the Korean conflict produced no joyful catharsis. The War, abandoned rather than won in July of 1953, wasn't a popular one, and returning veterans, like their children a generation later in Viet Nam, came home to no ticker-tape parades, came home to a country chagrined and disgruntled by the whole thing. Notoriously, Korea was "the forgotten war," and the traumas of those who had fought and suffered in it were largely ignored. For example, after reflecting thoughtfully and often poignantly on the anxiety produced by the Korean conflict, the *Observer* briefly notes in a column devoted to tidbits of college gossip that "It's Hard to Believe" there are 57 Korean vets at Augie.[35] Dorothy Parkander, Class of 1946, a young faculty member during the war, remembers veterans coming to her apartment to talk through the bewilderment, anger, and depression this inattention produced. You can't go home again, they found, however deeply you longed to.

Looking Forward

Yet as the college considered its identity, as students wrestled with their collective and personal identities, you could turn and look across the threshold to the new era for American education described by President Bergendoff and Dean Brodahl. Diversity, to use the terminology of our day, appears not only in the faculty hires of the fifties, but in new clubs and interest organizations formed during those years. The "interracial" club of the late 40s changed to the "Cosmopolitan" Club (which originally published the campus phone book and supplied the name "Cosmo" to this periodical). Admittedly, the sea of white Anglo-Saxon faces in yearbook photos pretty much engulfs students of color and non-Caucasian origin. But the impulse to recognize, rather than ignore or assimilate, students of different racial and ethnic backgrounds, anticipates later developments.

Women who were what's now termed "non-traditional"—*i.e.*, older—students formed the "3 x 7 Club." Organized in November of 1946, the club invited women students over twenty-one years of age, and included sixteen members that first year. Many of them were public school teachers who'd begun their careers before the B.A. was required and were now finishing up college work amid family and job responsibilities. In addition to socializing and supporting one another, they conducted service projects such as sponsoring parties for the Iowa Soldiers' Orphans Home and for some inmates of the East Moline State Hospital. Clearly these women affected the campus. Their presence could enrich class discussions, bringing a dimension of experience that younger students lacked. Their group activities solidified college and community ties. And the fact that they often earned honors[36] offered models of encouragement to other women, especially fellow "non-trads."

On the other end of the age scale, in 1950 a new sorority, Chi Delta, was formed, the first in twenty-five years. Friendship Fair, launched as an "international carnival" in 1945 to aid the World Student Service Fund, grew to elaborate proportions in the next twenty-odd years, bringing students from abroad to Augustana and supporting Augustana students in a year's study overseas. And to emphasize the movement toward "diversity," the 1955 *Rockety-I* provides an interesting contrast to that all-male faculty picture in the yearbook of three years earlier: a full-page picture of one professor marks the beginning of the Faculty section, and that professor is female.

Amid these new forces and shifting constituencies another element was working to move the college away from its past: student pressure for greater autonomy and involvement in decisions that affected them. Inevitably tensions erupted when the church-driven *in loco parentis* model of appropriate student-college relationships clashed with the new needs and goals of the postwar generation. And inevitably, the church's influence weakened. Hot-button issues included Greek affiliation and student governance, as well as more localized concerns such as mandatory chapel attendance and the ever-present conflict over dancing.[37]

As is still the case, membership in Greek groups was regarded as a serious and important commitment by students—even students who were high achievers in other arenas. In 1935, for example, about 45% belonged to a Greek group, though by 1960 the percentage had declined to 36%.[38] Greek groups sponsored much of the social and service activity on campus; commuter students especially were urged to join a sorority or fraternity in order to become fully integrated into campus life. Efforts by the administration to direct the activities of these groups—in particular to abolish hell week (in line with practices at other colleges, it was briefly called "help" week)—met with determined, and successful, student resistance.[39]

But perhaps most representative—almost paradigmatic—of the increasing opposition between the church's position and student behavior can be seen in the dancing issue. The church disapproved of dancing as a potentially immoral activity, and specifically prohibited it on the campuses of its colleges. This position was eroded by student practices. So, as Tredway has put it, despite official synodical refusal to countenance such dubious activity, "the dance went on."[40]

These pushes toward some degree of self-determination can be seen in a request by the Student Union for answers to central questions: "Is student government legitimate? Why? Why was student Government at Augustana sanctioned? What is the attitude of the present faculty toward student government? What does the faculty think is the relationship between the student body and the faculty?"[41] The questions are significant, and, one might imagine, loaded. It's interesting to note that they're referred to the Student Affairs committee for study, and don't come up in subsequent minutes. But four years later, the Board of Directors approved a new Student Union Constitution emphasizing "academic freedom and student rights," as well as students' obligations as responsible citizens. And in 1959 students requested and received permission to attend the Educational Policies Committee meetings.[42]

What seems to emerge from these cross-currents is the idea of forces pushing for change beneath a fairly placid surface.

The Fifties: A Golden Poise?

And still. Whatever the tensions of adjustment in this time of transition, it's clear that the college emerged from the fifties a stronger institution than it had been when it entered the decade. If 1949 produced the embarrassing panty raid as an expression of thoughtless student hi-jinks, it also brought the college a signal recognition of its academic reputation: a chapter of Phi Beta Kappa, the sixth to be awarded in Illinois. Other honors followed. The American Chemical Society accredited Augustana in 1955, the Augustana Choir under Dr. Henry Veld appeared on national television in 1952 and marked the quarter-century anniversary of its first appearance in Chicago's Orchestra Hall with a gala reception at the Congress Hotel following a 1956 concert there. Victories accumulated for the oratory and debate programs, with individuals and teams—many of them women—placing high in state and national contests. Augustana was the only school that had qualified for the West Point Invitational Debate Tournament every year since the contest had been established. A consultant in higher education hired by the Augustana Lutheran Church to evaluate its five colleges praised Augustana as "one of the outstanding liberal arts and church colleges....The [Lutheran Church has] been significantly influenced through leaders from the alumni of Augustana College." Galesburg poet Carl Sandburg, honorary alumnus, put it more informally in a 1957 letter to Bergendoff: "Admiring your report for the academic year '56-'57 I had to say, 'Good and beneficent Lord, what would that grand old Pioneer Hasselquist say of the seed sown long ago?'"[43]

Fulbrights, Guggenheims, and National Science Foundation awards supported faculty research, and Bergendoff noted with satisfaction that a small turnover, despite more lucrative offers elsewhere, demonstrated that this faculty was committed to the idea of education Augustana stood for. Students came with strong records, scored above average on national tests, and left with fellowships and grants to attend graduate schools nationwide. College and community relationships broadened and deepened with the expansion of the Foundation for Crippled Children and Adults (later the Easter Seals Foundation), and with opportunities provided by the Handel Oratorio Society, and the many campus cultural events open to the public.[44]

In part this energy, optimism, and achievement could be attributed to the college's increasingly selective admission policies; in part to the new, more highly qualified faculty; in part to President Bergendoff's leadership. Tredway believes that one of the most important aspects of that leadership "was to personify in his own life and work high academic and scholarly ideals."[45] His wise, irenic presence, often tested, was to inspire the college for many years beyond his own term of office.

People like myself who were raised in the fifties look back on that decade as a good time. True, over our heads hung the shadow of the Communist sickle with its threat of world domination and nuclear war, and if you didn't eat your vegetables you were reminded of the starving Korean orphans; but generally, for us life offered peace and prosperity. We had a strong economy, a "likeable" president who'd brought us through the war, now a genially-grinning grandfather figure. We had root beer stands, sock hops, and poodle skirts. And at Augustana, as you turn the pages of the *Observer*s and yearbooks and look at the students with their scrubbed and smiling faces, neat suits, sweater sets and saddle shoes, you see a similar glow of confidence and security—"healthy, hopeful, earnest, and eager," according to Dean Betsey Brodahl.[46] If they worried on the pages of the *Observer*, their days seemingly were ordered by secure and predictable rhythms. They scuffed through leaves to class in the early days of first semester. They went to daily Chapel, its speeches duly reprised in the *Observer;* they participated in a variety of extra-curricular activities; they studied in the "lib" and walked back up campus in the chill of a fall evening to hang out with friends and share late-night popcorn in the dorms. They built Homecoming floats, formed Bible study groups, worshiped, gave blood, and mounted various service projects. On the way to class they greeted friends with "Going down?"—which meant a sometimes "muddy walk to the big brick building" on the north side of campus known as Stu-U, "the nerve center of campus." Student-managed and run, it provided a "general headquarters" for Tri-City students and a hangout for dorm dwellers. You could conduct meetings in the upper lounge, knock off a fast game of ping-pong, swill the ever present (if sometimes less than excellent) coffee, and even get up a game of bridge.[47]

Saturday afternoons meant cheering in the football stands, energized by cheerleaders of both genders; Saturday nights meant movie dates with carefully regulated curfews for women. Sexual exploration/experimentation was usually limited to the cramped back seats of cars, as memoirist Mary Clearman Blew has wryly described, or contained within early marriages.

At Christmas students published special "literary supplements" to the *Observer*; elected a Sankta Lucia to wear the crown of light; sang or played in or attended annual performances of Handel's *Messiah*. They learned to regard the Rock Island depot as a second home: "a chug, a whistle, and the sound of steel wheels turning on iron tracks" would mean " 'Grab your luggage, we're off again,' for Christmas or summer vacation and a gala homecoming with the folks"[48] in families where mother, father, and siblings lived in the same house. And they stored "lingering images" of "the way the birches shivered during the ice storms…the sound of the organ filtering through the Chapel windows in early evening…the boy who bought you coffee one spring afternoon…the girl who held your hand the night of the [fraternity] steak fry…."[49]

"I don't know where a finer group of a thousand young people would be found," Dr. Bergendoff told the Augustana constituency in his 1952 President's Report. "Cynics and pessimists might change their attitude if they associated more with them."[50]

So perhaps, in that threshold time, there was a kind of golden poise.

And If You Were a Woman….

They kept coming to college—in larger and larger numbers. Though, as Tredway notes, the balance between men and women "evened out after the war," as the decade progressed the college began to receive more applications from women than they felt they could accommodate.[51] To address this situation Bergendoff envisioned a "women's campus" on the Davis property (now House-on-the-Hill), which was given to the college in 1954 and created a 26-acre upper campus for Augustana. The complex would consist of a series of dormitories housing 75 women each, with a common dining area. Later, perhaps, a women's gymnasium with pool could be added, as well as facilities for arts and crafts.[52] Such a plan, Bergendoff felt, would have several advantages: it would combine the co-educational experience with "something of the privacy of a girls' school," allowing women to share recreation and socializing (in somewhat the same way as they had back in the "Ladies Hall" days), and it would provide a venue where "womanly" subjects such as domestic science and nursing could be offered.[53] (Tredway also conjectures that a special woman's campus on the hill would keep panty-raiding men at bay!) Interestingly, though, at the same time that Bergendoff was exploring a form of segregated experience for women students, the college was setting up a counseling program "especially aimed at" the many more "career-minded women" who, since the war, now saw traditionally "male" occupations in business and the professions as options.[54]

So for women students the "liminality" of this time was particularly intense. On campus they participated actively, in both academic and extracurricular venues. They sang in the choir; they wrote for the *Observer;* they edited *Saga*, the literary magazine; they acted in plays; they competed in intramural sports; they participated in and won debate and oratory contests in Augustana's tough, competitive program. Dorothy Ann Koch, Class of 1950, became the first woman to reach the final round of the National Debate Tournament (then held each year at West Point) in 1950. Along the way she and her partner Charlie Lindberg bested Yale—whose team included William Buckley.[55] Women of the fifties were elected to Phi Beta Kappa and graduated with high honors. At the same time they also competed for various "queen" or "princess" positions, determined by popular vote (and good looks certainly didn't hurt in those full-page yearbook photos). Star debater Koch, for instance, reigned as 1950 Vi-Queen.

These accomplishments could raise questions, though. As we've noted, expectations were confused, sometimes conflicting: should women dream/imagine/plan for lives of demanding, encompassing, fulfilling vocations? Or should they be content to hone skills that could serve to support themselves, and later potential spouses and families, in temporary situations? Would husbands assent to wives pursuing full-time careers? Often women felt they must choose, or, in some cases, were forced by outside circumstances to choose. As late as 1958, for example, the state of Massachusetts did not hire married women as teachers.[56] Girls who did well in high school often came away uncertain what use to make of their academic abilities. As one mid-fifties student put it, "I knew I'd always gotten good grades, but what did my good grades mean in the scheme of things?"[57]

Seemingly, secretarial work, nursing, or teaching in primary or secondary school. Gloria Ellison Levin, for instance, a bright student encouraged by high school counselors to aspire to work as secretary or nurse, enrolled in secretarial courses in her Chicago high school—courses in which she excelled—but courses which meant missing the college prep classes she'd need for admission to college. Fortunately Augustana recognized her intellectual gifts and accepted her without the usual high school prerequisites.[58]

That kind of recognition and support didn't operate in all cases throughout the country, though. For example, a collegian studying in Switzerland sent a letter to 48 college newspapers, urging student involvement in world affairs. One answer she received from a Maine editor read in part, "stop worrying your pretty little head over European matters—we have quite enough problems of our own in the U.S.A."[59]

But as the fifties moved toward the next decade, women moved forward as well. Many who came to Augustana not knowing what their academic gifts meant "in the scheme of things" ended their college careers with answers, often because of the women they encountered on campus—women who taught them, women students who shared and shaped their ambitions. Certainly the marriage/career conflict lingered as an issue. Some women chose the life of the single professional. Others, roughly two-thirds, according to the latest Alumni Survey, fit comfortably into traditional patterns, finding their vocation on the domestic scene, in support roles, in teaching, nursing, secretarial or clerical work, and in various forms of volunteerism. Still others could rejoice in their pins and rings, and yet make plans not only for weddings but for graduate school or career path—and find ways to succeed in both.

Educate a woman! (And see where she goes.)

Life in a Green World: Florence Neely

Her apartment was full of plants. A fishtail palm arched graceful fronds over the end of the sofa. On the opposite wall, when she'd look up from reading or writing, she could see a water color of the Mississippi River from Credit Island. It was a venue that celebrated the green world she explored, analyzed, and appreciated.

In her quiet way Florence Neely, who came to Augustana in 1960, made college history. She was the second tenured woman professor to have earned a doctorate, the first woman tenured in the sciences, a three-time

Dr. Florence Neely, cultivating plants, talents, connections

National Science Foundation grant recipient, a low-key feminist whose form of advocacy was the professional excellence she modeled.[60]

She was born September 13, 1920, in Bushnell, Iowa. Her interest in plants developed early, absorbed from her mother (a "nontraditional" Augustana graduate, Class of 1959, and later a junior high school teacher in Moline, Illinois) and fostered by growing up in different venues where she could see first-hand various terrains and the growth they produced. The quiet, observant child easily found wonder in what she called the "abundant sizes and kinds" of plants that covered the earth outside her homes—from Iowa towns to a Montana ranch.

Though she was raised during a time when advanced study in the sciences was less common for women than it is today, Neely said she had "no fear" of tackling plant science seriously, partly because she received warm encouragement to do so from public school teachers. After two years at Ellsworth Junior College, she finished her undergraduate degree in general science at the University of Iowa. She earned her Master's in botany from Iowa, and her Ph. D. in paleobotany from the University of Illinois.

She was a reserved, self-contained woman, who, just six months before her death, talked about her life in phrases as elegant as her tall, graceful person. It was a good life, she said, despite, or even because of, the issues that accompanied her choice of academic discipline. Unintimidated by the study itself, still she knew the professional and personal challenges that faced women in a predominantly men's field, and the sometime-difficulty of finding the right "home." Those challenges she tackled in ways that reflected both her character and her scientific training: calmly, efficiently, honestly, and with a dry, sometimes unpredictable, wit. And before she was sixty, she knew the daunting reality of terminal cancer. None of it shook her civility, her irenic decorum, or her sense of humor. ("Do I renew this magazine subscription? Well, maybe not for six years, but possibly for one.")

She brought to the college a view that balanced Augustana's ethos with values from the different academic venues where she'd taught—university, small church-affiliated and single-gender colleges in various parts of the country—the University of Kansas City, Salem College in North Carolina, Grays Harbor College in Washington State, Vassar College. And she brought a strong belief in the value of travel and global study. Her own sabbaticals in South America, Australia and New Zealand broadened both her botanical and her cultural knowledge.

In the old Wallberg Hall classrooms, permeated with chemical smells and inhabited mostly by men during her tenure, she created the anomaly of female elegance, dignity, and brains. Students remember her as a precise, exact, and formidably knowledgeable lecturer on fields ranging from general botany to microbiology to paleobotany; but they also appreciate her commitment to "hands-on" learning. Patient in explaining general procedures, generous in offering suggestions, she was convinced that students ultimately learn more effectively when allowed the freedom to do things their way. It was a principle she applied to more than general botany classes. For her it defined gender equity, "the opportunity [for women and men] to try out various interests, to develop as people, to mature." A small college environment best fostered that opportunity, she felt. "It even gives [students] the chance to be squirrelly for awhile, and still be understood and accepted." And while it's hard to imagine the dignified Dr. Neely ever being squirrelly—she'd stand before her large classes in sweater sets, pearls, and later in stylish pants suits—still, in her exploration of various teaching experiences she clearly knew and valued the freedom to find her own way "home."

She called herself a "middle-ground" feminist: "on a scale of one to ten, I'd rank my feminism at about six or seven," she once said with a smile. She didn't make waves. But she also saw, clearly and keenly, the need for progress in gender equity, especially in her field. Teaching at Vassar, she'd watched women with a freedom of spirit, as she put it, tackling and succeeding in leadership positions that might not have been available to them at co-educational institutions. (Something like what happened at Augustana during the years of the Second World War.) The challenge for them after school, as she saw it in the 1960s and 70s, was to retain that freedom and maintain that confidence in the face of professional situations that granted women nominal equality but actually excluded them from decision-making. Careers often turn and rise over cocktails in the local off-campus bar, Neely discovered, and for her, "there's no great future in trying to tail your male colleagues down there." Augustana wasn't exempt from this kind of practice; it reflected a culture that still "permitted" rather than actively welcoming women into certain professional ranks. As a single woman especially Neely knew the need for personal strength and resilience: you're "dependent upon [yourself] for certain important things: financial support, social life, and a sense of worth."

Like Margaret Olmsted before her, she was neither Scandinavian nor Lutheran. But some of what Olmsted admired at Augustana—"high standards, good character, morality, and goodness of life"—were congenial to the English/German Methodist from Iowa as well. And preeminently, Augustana offered the same strong sense of community Neely had discovered in her previous experience of the church-related college. That mattered to her. And in the end it sustained her. When bone cancer mandated early retirement, colleagues and students provided the support of notes, calls, visits, dinner invitations, and outings. "I've been amazed at the sensitivity of my students," she observed. For students, the attention paid to Neely was simply a response to what they'd been given; as one put it, "We keep in touch with her because of the love and concern she has shown for us."[61]

She died only a few months after her retirement, at the age of 60. During her last days in a local hospital, a young colleague read aloud to her from James Herriot's *All Creatures Great and Small*, the comic and poignant chronicles of a veterinarian in a small Yorkshire community. The book seemed fitting final company for Neely. Like Herriot, she cared for her world with a profound commitment, celebrating its beauty and smiling in gentle irony at its follies.

And One Last Word....

Because she often had it—although she knew when to relinquish it. Mostly. As one student of college history, Roald Tweet, has pointed out, the story of Augustana's women wouldn't really be complete without her. Even though her role falls outside the boundaries set for this book, she filled that role so faithfully, so ebulliently, and so memorably, that she stamped the college ethos with her personality for more than two decades.

Most people who were around during the forties and fifties have a Gertrude Bergendoff story—everyone from visiting celebrities like Carl Sandburg, who shared a fried egg with her at three in the morning, to students whose performances and pinnings, elections and engagements, she followed almost as closely as their families, to staff members whose joys and sorrows she made her own.

What all the stories are about, ultimately, is a woman who took the college into her heart. The campus was her home, its denizens her fam-ily. Hospitality came to her as natu-

Conrad and Gertrude Bergendoff: last word in love

rally as song (when arthritis prevented her from standing up long enough to participate in the Handel Oratorio Society choruses, she would join in from the audience). People who may have forgotten the date of the Glorious Revolution or the meaning of a quadratic equation remember the warmth of her welcome, the beauty of her garden, and the savor of her cooking, whether a full-scale dinner or toasted cheese sandwiches on a Sunday night.

And no one can forget the loveable eccentricities, the wide-eyed straightforward look at life that saw beyond machination to essentials, the honesty that cut through politics and posing, sometimes to the embar-rassment of the poseur. She was Gertrude: outgoing, unintimidated, irrepressible.

But of all the Gertrude stories, perhaps the best one is her love story. As a young woman singing in a church choir, she caught the ear and eye of the young pastor Conrad Bergendoff. She kept them all her life. And that relationship centered her life. "Isn't Dr. B. *wonderful?*" she used to say after every speech he made. In more formal terms he returned the compliment. "She has carried more than her share of the responsibility in the president's home," he wrote in his valedictory President's Report (1962), "and few are aware of the extent of her willing service."

Dr. Bergendoff lived nearly two decades after Gertrude's death in 1979, but never, for a moment, without her.

CHAPTER 8

Forging Bonds:
Women's Groups

They were girls, women, dames, ladies. They "met, mingled, and munched," they presented petitions and staged debates, they sang, read, and sewed curtains, they sponsored war orphans and raised money for college necessities. They were the women's groups: The Endowment Society, the Woman's Club, the Augustana Dames. They existed side-by-side with curricular concerns; they included students, faculty, faculty wives, and alumnae. In many ways and places, they have shaped and served Augustana. And in the process, they've served and shaped Augustana women.

Endowment Society

They came to the first meetings in neck-choking collars, upswept hair, and hats that looked as if they would fly away.

But there was nothing flighty about these women. They were some of the most determined, astute, and loyal supporters Augustana had in the 1890s and early nineteen-hundreds. And if they didn't actually save the college, they built some pretty impressive lifeboats during stormy financial episodes.

They were the Augustana Endowment Society.[1]

And they're still going strong.

They came into being in 1894. The times were tense and finances precarious for Augustana. "Development campaigns" often consisted of a few tireless individuals traveling from church to church in the Augustana Synod, or appealing to local philanthropists for funds. By these means gifts did come. But operating expenses quickly devoured income. And as the Augustana Synod grew and spread geographically, new colleges were established in other areas—colleges which also needed, and received, church support.

That Augustana had a future, none of its friends doubted. A splendid new building—today's Old Main—had just been finished after a decade

Endowment Society. Margaret Shuey Foss is second from left.

of money-related delays. The student body numbered five hundred. The only problem was scraping together enough cash to pay for things like food and coal. While the philosophical implications of creating an endowment fund were being thrashed out in high synodical circles—some church leaders claimed Augustana would "fall away from the faith" if it became financially independent—students were occasionally reduced to bread and molasses for dinner, and faculty and administration alike were wondering how on earth the college could afford to heat its classrooms in the long Rock Island winters.[2]

So the women took matters in hand.

As private individuals, they were perfectly free to form any sort of society, for whatever purpose, they wished.[3] Accordingly, Mrs. Johannes Jesperson, whose husband was business manager of the college, and who presumably watched the unpaid bills pile up on his desk and administered tea and sympathy to his midnight anxiety attacks, gathered "a few devoted friends of the college and seminary,"[4] and formed the nucleus of a society to address the problem. They had one purpose: to build an endowment for Augustana. Modest dues—fifteen cents to begin with, then a quarter, with occasional ten-dollar life memberships—were so carefully invested that by 1942 the Society had accumulated a principal of $40,000 which it turned over to the college. (Interest from the principal had been used throughout this time to ease immediate financial strains.) President Conrad Bergendoff commented, "[This] amount is a remarkable example of what persistency and faithfulness to purpose can accomplish."[5]

They weren't, as Endowment Society historian Lillian Nelson puts it, "tea party matrons."[6] They were practical visionaries, working hard to fulfill their purpose. They sponsored bazaars and concerts, mounted entertainments, sold homemade food, aprons, slippers, and handkerchiefs, and vigorously promoted "honorary memberships" among local dignitaries. In 1929 President Gustav Andreen cited "the gifts [the Society] has given" and "the time it has helped in emergencies…[It] has not only created a large fund for the support of the college," he continued, "it has brought hundreds of Tri-City women into close contact with the college and has earned for it their friendship."[7] And to give their organization a certain cachet, they produced elaborate "resolutions of respect" on the death of leading citizens—as if, Nelson says, "they believed that the community was waiting to hear from them."[8]

All this was, of course, a group effort. But one member who particularly exemplified "persistency and faithfulness" in the early years was Sarah Margaret[9] Shuey Foss, a charter member and president of the group at various times, for a total of twenty years (1898-1904; 1905-1914, and

Mrs. Foss presents the fruits of Endowment Society investments to Augustana representatives.

1915-1920). She was by all accounts remarkable. A "Virginia gentlewoman," she's remembered as gracious and cultured. But she didn't lack spunk. As we've seen earlier, she came to Rock Island to teach Latin, Rhetoric, and Calisthenics in Fairview Academy, Anna Reck's school for young women, "because I wanted to see the wild and woolly west," and later, with her husband history professor C. W. Foss, served as principal of Ladies Hall. And however determined and earnest she might have been, she clearly enjoyed a strong sense of humor. In one anecdote she recalls that the Academy presented "quite a few plays," and when one of these productions caricatured an Augustana commencement,

[s]ome of the longbeards on the college faculty thought we were engaging in too much levity, so we turned extra pious and put on a play in which I was climbing the golden stairs, with Christmas tree icicles and frosting in my hair, pointing the little kids heavenward. I was keeping company with Mr. Foss of the college faculty, but when others came up to congratulate me, he looked very solemn. All he would say was that it was "very beautiful," but he told me later that he had a premonition that my role meant that I was going to heaven too soon.[10]

Fortunately Dr. Foss turned out to be better at history than at prophecy. Sarah Margaret Shuey did not die prematurely; she married Dr. Foss and lived until 1949, surviving her husband by fourteen years.

The energy and courage that led her to dare the "wild and woolly west" she poured into the many legal and social ramifications of creating an Endowment Society. And she thought big. A letter written during her first term as president urges Mrs. William McKinley—with resounding eloquence—to head a list of subscribers supporting Augustana, "the educational center of the large Swedish Lutheran population in this country," which "with its sound orthodox Christian principles as a foundation and its teachings of morality and practical true law-abiding patriotism…does and must ever exert a powerful influence for good upon the large number of students who are annually gathered within its walls."[11] Mrs. McKinley, alas, wasn't moved to subscribe. But others were, including many leaders in the Quad-Cities community. (Men could be, and were, honorary members.) To Mrs. Foss, also, can probably be credited the quality of programs presented at each Endowment Society meeting. By the early 1940s, according to Bergendoff, "the Endowment Society had become a real force in the community....No women's organization of the city maintained higher standards in its cultural offerings."[12] And few groups on campus have contributed so much to the aesthetic and cultural experience that students, especially resident women students, can enjoy. As Endowment president Lael Erickson put it after the Society had purchased a grand piano for the newly-built Westerlin Lounge and moved its meetings there, "If we are to be a vital factor in [the college's expansion] we must expand too....Let us be ready....Enjoy not only our Endowment Society meetings but also the many concerts, recitals, lectures, art exhibits and classes offered."[13]

They did enjoy, and they made it possible for others to enjoy. They helped to furnish Westerlin Hall and to purchase a grand piano for the Erickson Hall men; they supported renovations of House-on-the-Hill, and contributed to music, theatre, art, and science programs, among other philanthropies.[14]

In the early days Mrs. Foss had rallied the energies of her group by telling them, "The best endowment any institution can have is a host of loyal friends and intelligent supporters." Her words became motto and mantra for the Augustana College Endowment Society.

The Woman's Club/League

A March afternoon in 1917. At tables patriotically decked in national colors, and sporting small flags for favors, sixty Augustana women gathered for a "light luncheon." They included students, faculty members and faculty wives. They'd been brought together by student Florence Anderson to "support school spirit among the women" and to "assist in all undertakings of the school as a whole, and further the interest of" Augustana, as their Constitution was to read.

The talk that first day must have been animated and intense, full of creative brainstorming as well as of laughter. Because the "school spirit among women" became woman spirit, inciting attention to various issues and concerns that affected women specifically.

That first March meeting jump-started the group by electing Anderson president, Sarah Margaret Shuey Foss vice-president, student Esthena Randolph, whose satiric essay on early antifeminist attitudes we've quoted, as secretary, and Esther Andreen, daughter of the president, treasurer. The energy and engagement that made these women leaders in their day they transmitted to subsequent members.

They didn't abandon expected gender roles while nudging the college to expand opportunities for women. They hosted the kinds of social events women traditionally enjoyed—parties, coffees, and an annual "coed banquet." They raised money to furnish and refurbish campus buildings. During the two World Wars, they provided the kind of home front support so essential for morale-boosting. In World War I they voted enthusiastically to "mend the uniforms and do all other necessary sewing for the boys in the S.A.T.C. [Students' Army Training Corps, briefly on campus]," collected money for the local Red Cross, and packed up a box of "eats" for "the boys at the camp in Houston, Texas." In World War II they sponsored a tea to benefit refugees in Sweden, and participated in the "Kits for Europe's Children" in conjunction with the Save the Children Federation in New York, assembling necessities unavailable for children in war-torn Europe.

Yet because their concerns encompassed a range of women's experiences, addressing, sometimes redressing, these concerns occasionally required a hint or two to college authorities. The women were skillful, adroit in tactics. When they decided to take action, they discussed the prospect thoroughly and then carefully appointed a committee or representative to approach the appropriate authorities, through appropriate channels. A good example is their work on behalf of women's health.

As early as their initial meetings they were considering measures to enhance women's physical activity and general health. At their second meeting they agreed to present a request that the "girls" be given the use of gym facilities on the afternoons of Monday and Tuesday. A third meeting that same month, November 1917, resolved to ask that the "ladies' entrance" of the new gym be opened from 8 in the morning to six at night. And they went further than simply requesting use of facilities. In 1919 they successfully petitioned the college to hire a "girls' gymnastic teacher," resulting in the arrival at Augustana of Northwestern University graduate Alice McNulty. That same year they conferred with the Athletic Director about extending swimming hours for women. And in 1928 they joined with the Augustana Girls' Athletic Association to install a Kotex machine on campus. The good news here was that college officials permitted the installation, certainly a signal that women's specific needs were to be accommodated. The bad news was that the women themselves had to foot

The Women's League serves tea

the bill for what arguably should have come out of the college's operating budget. (The machine cost $20.[15])

Other activities explored other interests. Exhorted, inspired, and bolstered by the older women—Dean Dora Carlson, for instance, "expressed the idea that the Woman's Club should be the foremost organization among girls on campus"[16]—they ushered for the Missionary Conference on campus; visited local hospitals and raised money from tag days to support hospital programs; made dolls and beanbags as Christmas presents for the orphaned children at Bethany Home, and donated to the Rock Island Welfare Association for Thanksgiving baskets. They served tea to the League of Women Voters and considered "forming a new voters league among the girls." No follow-up to this suggestion is recorded in the Minutes, although later, during the forties and fifties, when "Women's Week" became a popular campus series of events—for the Women's League,[17] the "biggest event of the year"—they organized symposia on national and international events, and staged mock political conventions.

As early as 1919 they sent delegates to the National Federation of College Women in Chicago, subsequently (1939) were invited to join the National Organization of Women's Clubs, and attended state conferences of the Illinois Association of Women's Leagues. Ultimately, in 1940, the group became what Dean Carlson (now Cervin) had envisioned for it in 1928, recasting its constitution to specify new responsibilities as coordinator for all the women's groups at Augustana.

The Club explored vocational paths as well. Assisted by the seemingly indefatigable Dean Cervin, they invited a variety of professional women from the community to serve as guest speakers. The Club heard, for example, "Mrs. Galley, Moline lawyer"; Barbara Garst, Augustana Class of 1922, Moline High School English teacher[18]; Rock Island Welfare Association representative Ada Barker; Dr. Betty Nelson, missionary doctor trained and supported by the Woman's Missionary Society, the early Augustana protofeminist Mrs. K. T. Anderson, and Dr. Mabel Otis, Augustana's own physician for women. The 1937 week-long vocational conference featuring both group and individual sessions drew so many participants that "we could have used twice as much time for individual conferences," Cervin reported.

Determined to create solidarity among Augustana women, as well as to "back the boys in bringing about a greater and better Augustana," they organized a support system for newly arrived women students. Fresh[wo]men, timid, boisterous, curious, or bewildered, were shepherded by upperclass mentors through the challenges of finding accommodation and generally adjusting to college life. Parties and get-acquainted fall receptions helped ease the transition from home to campus. The orientation program expanded, and ultimately became part of the "Big Sister Movement" initiated on other campuses in the late 1920s. It was a rousing success; by 1934, despite Depression austerities, 200 attended the fall Big Sister/Little Sister Tea.

But the Woman's Club/Woman's League saw itself as a feminine more than a feminist presence on campus. Its contributions, as we've noted, were "womanly": furnishing and feeding at home and abroad. They purchased curtains and table cloths. They learned to knit for the boys in service during World War II. After the war, calling themselves "Orphan Aunties," they sponsored young Irene Fabellini through the Foster Parents Association and urged the campus to join in supporting the little Italian girl. They invited charm school counselors to speak. The 1937 vocational conference was likely gender specific, if other vocational activities sponsored by the Woman's Club are any indication. In 1940, for example, mock job interviews were conducted by two community leaders: one by Rock Island Superintendent of Schools Earl Hanson, the other by the head of the Employment Department at International Harvester, for women "planning to work in a business office." In other words, the two obvious employment roles for women—teacher and secretary. Neither the Minutes nor

WOMEN'S GROUPS *Chapter 8*

Dean Cervin's report specifies the kinds of careers presented as appropriate for women at the 1937 conference, but what's said about the leader, "Mrs. Robnett, former dean of women at Northwestern," provides a clue. She was "able to talk on every representative field in the vocational sphere," according to the Minutes.[19] Either she was exceptionally well rounded, or she discussed a limited number of jobs.

And much is made, in a way that may seem puzzling on the contemporary dating scene, of role reversals perpetrated by Women's Week. As early as 1937, for a Mardi Gras party, "it was decided to again elect a Mardi Gras queen from the male Augustana enrollment."[20] (Obviously, in that more innocent age, the term hardly bore the connotations it does today.) For the "Spinster Spree" in 1940—the name indicative of the focus—the "Leap Year Sweetheart" was "one of Augie's handsomest males." In the fifties, along with female professors and journalists who urged women to participate in global affairs, most of the activities (and publicity) of Women's Week concerned women assuming then-traditional male behaviors: asking men out, paying for dinners and movies, carrying books, holding coats and doors, etc.[21]

So despite the extended role and activities of the Woman's Club as it matured, it seems to lose some of its edge over the decades. That may be a good development, signaling that what it was formed to do and be was accomplished. Women achieved their place, distinctively as women, in the college culture.

As we've seen, the fifties brought a return to gender "normality" in occupations and aspirations. The descendents of those Woman's Club founders articulated where women had been and where they understood themselves to be now. "Women's League is counting on you to take responsibility," president Eleanor Larson writes to returning upperclass women in 1951, "responsibility in yourself to make the most of what you are and of what your school offers you, and responsibility to Augie women to cooperate and participate in all that they do." An unsigned editorial in *The Augie Argus*, a publication of the Women's League, defines a little more precisely "making the most of what you are":

In today's world …[women's] accomplishments in the fields of science, religion, music, art, education, and entertainment are such that we have just reason to be proud that we are women.

Women today have the opportunity to contribute to virtually every field of endeavor. We should recognize and avail ourselves of that opportunity. We should assume responsibility for contributing our time and talents to community and national welfare, *but we should also accept the very important challenge which belongs first and foremost to women—that of 'setting the type' [theme of the Women's League banquet] in our homes so that future generations may in turn make their contributions to society"* [italics mine].[22]

What, finally, can be said about the Woman's Club/League is that it was, for its time, a remarkable group. It was student-inspired. It was campus-wide, including women from various constituencies: it welcomed all female students—no rush or requirements to get in—as well as faculty women and wives. The Deans, Mrs. Foss, and Mrs. Andreen figure prominently in the proceedings. It sponsored an extraordinarily varied series of activities, everything from sports events to concerts and lectures, to service opportunities, to the simple fun of pig-tail days (always possible in the years before short haircuts). It acquired an almost professional degree of sophisticated organization, undoubtedly helped by the older women who understood the nuanced politics of committee culture. It summoned a faithful, enthusiastic, and growing membership. It influenced the curriculum. In the midst of a Depression so severe that college officials sometimes feared for Augustana's survival, it managed to raise money for its various service and social projects. And because of all this, it brought women's presence, women's concerns, and women's abilities to the attention of the entire college.

Augustana Dames Club

No one who was there will forget Lorian Sundelius Swanson processing gracefully down the improvised catwalk to model her newly-made coat. It was a unique style show, designed to highlight the talents of women who, with some instruction from Margaret Tweet, had created the outfits themselves. And those outfits were impressive. But none quite so impressive as Lorian's—when she swished her coat open to reveal its unfinished lining.

And that was in a way paradigmatic of the challenges this group faced, and the wit they brought to those challenges. They were the young faculty wives dealing with settling into a new community, managing homes and growing families, seeking friends. As Lorian's example showed, there wasn't always time to get everything done. But for many, Dames Club was a priority.

> *Once a month they gathered to share food thoughtfully prepared and beautifully served, programs of interest to them, and an afternoon of leisure and fellowship. And of laughter.*

The narrative of Dames Club presents a microcosmic pattern of women's stories as they unfolded after the war and into the fifties and sixties. Formed in 1946, it assumed the postwar model of many women's lives: stay-at-home wives and mothers for whom afternoon meetings were both possible and desireable. A baby-sitting service staffed by women students was provided; in the early sixties Dames paid fifty cents for the first child and a quarter for siblings. (Reservations were necessary.)[23]

Programs addressed the interests and concerns of the constituency: they included style shows—from local stores as well as from members' own hands; luncheons, talks, slide lectures, scenes from college and community theatrical productions, and skits and songs wittily commenting on the kind of experiences their members shared. As late as 1970, for instance, a musical/comedy revue addressed the "chores, duties, routines, etc. of women and wives," with the emphasis on the latter ("Wedded Bliss," "Exciting Relations with Husbands," "The Baby Bulge," "Woes of the Housewife"). During at least part of the fifties most women are designated by their marital names, *i.e.,* Mrs. John Smith.[24] And in 1962, underlining their activities and interests, the president, Patricia Hasselmo, missed a meeting because she was hospitalized with her new baby boy. Faculty women appeared on the membership list and were welcomed—Hasselmo invited them to become "full-time" members if their schedules allowed them to attend afternoon sessions—but except for evening meetings, at which they were "special guests," they rarely came. Only one, speech pathology professor Margaret Hatton, served as president.

As social patterns changed through the years, membership in Dames Club eroded. Economic necessities, professional training, or church and community activism took more women out of the home, focused their energies on the demands of the workplace as well as on domestic responsibilities, and provided them colleagues with common interests. But in its heyday, boasting a roster of ninety, Dames served well the purpose of integrating women into the "Augustana family." As one former member, Margaret Tweet, put it, Dames was "an important network for me until I got onto my own ground."[25]

CHAPTER 9

The Challenge for a Chance:
Women's Athletics

"The honor which the co-eds have brot [sic] *has, perhaps, not been so great as that which the boys have brot, nor have they triumphantly borne home any shield. But who knows what they might do if given a chance?"*[1]

Blanche Carpenter, '18

Blanche Carpenter, a.k.a. the aggressive and indefatigable "Carp" of women's basketball, wrote this in 1917, when her team had played and won four games. Her comments summarize the feelings of many collegiate women across the country in the early years of the twentieth century. Making vigorous physical activity (often in abbreviated attire) legitimate for women was the first battle. And when the idea of women participating in competitive sports was accepted, the practical realities of providing coaching support and allocating practice facilities touched off fresh contests. Title IX, the 1972 statute that prevented academic institutions from discriminating on the basis of gender, provided equal opportunities for women in athletic competition. But it didn't, of course, assure compliance.[2] The challenge for "a chance" continued.

Competing athletically had significant implications for women. Obviously, sports provided an arena for gifted athletes. But beyond that, putting women's athletic competition on equal footing with men's defined a shift in the culture. Long-held stereotypes about what women could and couldn't (and should and shouldn't) do and be, had to be revised. Although the idea of female fragility persists well into mid-century (it took Title IX to assure that women were allowed equality of consideration when they sought to study traditionally male fields as the sciences and engineering), still, as early as the nineteen-teens colleges began to promote physical fitness as a goal for "the womanly woman" as well as "the manly man," according to Barbara Miller Solomon. "Athletics fulfilled the educators' commitment to make college women stronger and healthier and thus disprove the warnings of opponents of higher education for women," Solomon writes.[3]

In her presentation to a 1915 conference on "The Relation of Health to the Woman Movement" Stanford physician Dr. Clelia Mosher concludes rather lyrically that "the day of the type of woman who is all spirit, a burning flame consuming her misused body, is passing. What we need are women no less fine and womanly, but with beautiful perfect bodies, a suitable receptacle for their equally beautiful souls, who look sanely out on life with steady nerves and clear vision."[4] The ubiquitous image of the tall, vigorous Gibson Girl, swinging her tennis racquet and knocking croquet balls, gave strong popular support for the woman who could be attractive despite—or rather, because of—health and athletic prowess. And as the new century moved into the twenties, the inescapable photos of a tall, slender, daring young woman with a gap-toothed smile that publicists advised her to conceal in official photos, came to command national attention. Amelia Earhart caught the imagination of the twenties and thirties with her many aviation "firsts."[5] Clearly, then, a woman could be both elegant and "womanly" (Earhart's entrepreuneral enterprises included a line of clothing) and also challenge traditional gender categories.

Augustana reflected these views of the larger culture. In the 1890s, according to Netta Bartholomew Anderson, class of 1894, "the College Board decreed" that "the first [women's] gym class should be started." This, to Anderson and her cohorts, "was a thrilling innovation." Margaret Shuey Foss, who had come to Augustana to teach Latin, rhetoric, and calisthenics in the short-lived Fairview Hall preparatory school, served as the first instructor. And, says Anderson, "the first question to be settled was that of dress."

After long and careful consideration of the matter, we finally agreed on a suitable uniform which consisted of a hunter's green sateen blouse with a sailor collar of gold sateen, the V of the neck modestly closed with a dicky and to avert any possibility of losing a button while doing our exercises, the front of the blouse was laced up with a gold cord instead of buttoned up. We had long sleeves with cuffs securely buttoned around the wrist, a full gathered skirt which after much measuring and debate we agreed should be a daring eight inches from the floor and no more. Underneath we wore voluminous bloomers of sateen, long black cotton stockings, white gym shoes and we were instructed to leave off our bustles and stays which, being the rigid armor they were, might interfere with our free movement. Thus arrayed in the height of athletic suitability we would make our way by devious, if possible concealed, paths to the gym, fearful of being seen by some of the boys in our what we thought very unconventional outfits and yet secretly wishing we would be caught on the way so they could see how fetching were our uniforms.[6]

By 1897 a "ladies physical culture class" was introduced into the Conservatory curriculum to complement students' elocution training. We've described elsewhere the discipline termed "Elocution and Physical culture" which Mary Searles Penrose initiated two years later, a discipline that made "every effort...to cultivate the grace of body, that it may act in perfect harmony with the mind" in interpreting texts for public readings.[7] Activities the ladies physical culture class engaged in seem modest and decorous, as they're described in the Catalogue: "proper exercises, movements, marches, etc."

The first decade of the twentieth century ushered in more robust activities: basketball, tennis, cycling. "Even women students played basketball," reports Conrad Bergendoff, "engaging Macomb, Normal and Monmouth."[8] In the spring of 1904 the newly organized tennis club distributed awards to nine women and four men; by 1908 the Athletic Society, organized in 1899 at student request, includes both genders.[9] The oldest women's social sorority, Sigma Pi Delta, organized in 1909, began as a tennis club. And in 1916, after years of student petitions and fund-raising appeals, the New Gym arose on the central quad.

The amenities of the one-story (with balcony and basement) brick and steel building, 90 by 140 feet, were rhapsodically described in the College catalogue. The main assembly hall and balcony could seat 2,300. Above the balcony was a "first-class running track," cork-carpeted, where you could complete a mile in 14 2/3 laps. The basement included a 60 by 25 foot swimming pool as well as dressing rooms "with ample locker facilities." And throughout "new and ample paraphernalia" offered a variety of athletic opportunities. According to Glen Brolander, "until 1930" the gym "was considered the finest...in the Quad-Cities area."[10] And in addition to these facilities for workouts, classes, and sports, the assembly hall boasted a "first class pipe organ" for exercise of a more cultural stamp. Concerts were held here. In part, then, this new facility, which replaced a small and less-than-adequate gym (located south and west of Old Main on what's now the Quad[11]) was responsible for the growth in athletics during the decade of the twenties and early thirties.

Not surprisingly, that growth occurred more significantly in men's than in women's athletics. While as early as 1912 "the athletic board had asked for [and got] a college or university-trained man to place athletics on a higher level,"[12] it wasn't until 1919 that Northwestern University graduate Alice McNulty joined the faculty to "have charge of the young ladies' gymnastics."[13] She's listed as Director of Women's Athletics in the 1921 yearbook, and praised for her "untiring efforts" in generating enthusiasm for physical education classes. Unfortunately illness forced her to resign close to the end of spring term. A substitute, "Miss Grafhorn," finished out the academic year.[14] Despite this interruption, student Martha Martinson claims great advancement for girls' athletics during 1921-1922—it was "a glorious" year: "At no other time in the school's history has such excellent progress been made toward our sought goal—gymnasium work as a vital part of girls' school life at Augustana." And with higher enrollment of women students, women's athletics must and will achieve greater importance, Martinson insists. "We want a more complete and well-rounded [physical education] curriculum," with seasonal sports such as hockey and tennis, as well as basketball, "each culminating in a lively tournament. This is the beginning of a movement toward a Girls' Physical Education Program, in which every girl will have a part. We need the whole-hearted support of every student. Boost Augustana Girls' Athletics."[15]

Yet despite the energetic confidence of this article, with its cheerleading finish, after McNulty's departure women's athletics through the mid-twenties were managed by students: Dorothy Rogers (1921-1923), listed as a "graduate instructor" who lived at the Rock Island Y.W.C.A.; Luceia Acuff, class of 1924 (1923-1924), and Anne Catherine Greve, class of 1926 (1923-1934). They may have provided "inspiring leadership"—we know Rogers and Greve did—but compared with the Director of Athletics (meaning men's), 1917 alumnus, war hero, and University of Iowa M.A. recipient Major Arthur Swedberg, these enthusiastic, untried women come off more as stop-gaps than as carefully selected professionals. Not until the 1922-1923 school year does the catalogue officially list a "Department of Physical Education," and that includes two men (both with full academic accreditation) and one woman (student/teacher Luceia Acuff). The Board of Control of Athletics for that year includes eleven men and one woman, student Tyra Mauritzson.[16]

On the other side of the record, physicians of both genders served as "medical examiners." And, love it or loathe it, the college instituted a

Ladies' Physical Culture Class, circa 1897

requirement in "physical training" for "all students of the Freshmen *[sic]* and Sophomore Classes."[17] (This broadened somewhat the earlier requirement for two hours per week of gymnastics.[18]) Physical training as a part of the curriculum led to interest in athletics. The yearbook for 1923 reports that 85 women were enrolled in the Physical Education department and 125 came out for various sports, including hockey, tennis, hiking, rhythmic gymnastics, swimming (required of the two underclasses), and the Red Cross Lifesaving class, Swedish gymnastics, and basketball. Women's teams from the various classes and sometimes from community organizations faced off in competitive sports.

The physical education staff was small. Still, the men's program received more attention, time, and highly trained instructors than did the women's. And, though similar discrepancies existed in schools throughout the country, in the minds of Augustana's students, at least, the college lagged behind even those uneven standards. In the 1923 yearbook section titled "Our Girls' Athletics" the writer claims that "one of the greatest aims of the girls at Augustana is to place Girls' Athletics on a par with that of the larger colleges and universities of the country" and that "excellent progress" in doing so is to be attributed to "the instructress, Miss Dorothy

Rogers, who has given her best efforts and inspirations to the department."[19] In addition to interesting the numbers of women in the activities noted above, Rogers helped students organize the Augustana Girls' Athletic Association (A.G.A.A.), thus, according to the yearbook writer, meeting a long-felt need.[20]

By the following year Maude Adams, class of 1924, is able to report that "Augustana has at last become interested in girls' athletics and realizes that it is a vital point in a girl's life. Women's athletics," she maintains, "have been held down until a few energetic workers have given their attention to that fact and have now made it possible for women's athletics to bloom forth."[21] The A.G.A.A. has been largely responsible for this growth, that has put "Augie on a par with other schools," and initiated inter-collegiate competition. "Augustana's being represented at the Millikin University inter-scholastic tennis tournament was a direct result of the A.G.A.A.," Adams concludes. "It promises to become the central organization for athletic activities of the girls at Augustana."[22] And in the large accompanying photo, at least fifty women smile into the camera as happy members of the A.G.A.A.

But the real growth surge in women's athletics came during the decade of 1923-1934, when Anne Catherine Greve taught physical education and coached a variety of sports. Her story is interwoven with that of women's athletics, and to a certain degree, of women's position at Augustana.

Pushing Boundaries: Anne Catherine Greve

She was young and fit. She was pretty, with short curly hair and an engaging grin that crinkled her eyes and stopped just short of roguish. Later, her height and the warmth of her smile were to make her elegant. But in these first years at Augustana, little older than the students she taught, she charmed with a radiance that even the posed yearbook pictures couldn't obscure.

In the conflicting terminology of catalogue and yearbook, Anne Catherine Greve is alternately referred to as "Instructor in Women's Gymnastics and Swimming" and "Director of Women's Athletics." To be one, in those less sophisticated times, was, it seems, to be the other. But as yearbook copy and photos suggest, Anne Greve did a lot more than gymnastics and swimming during her ten years at the college.

She had received a "G.G." degree, and a "B.P.E" from Normal College of Physical Education in Indianapolis, affiliated with Indiana University, one of the country's oldest colleges for the preparation of physical education teachers,[23] and, according to the yearbook, one of the best.[24] By the end of 1925, majoring in English (never a walk in the park and certainly not under the formidable, mutton-chopped Dr. Bartholomew), she had yet managed, through hard work, to spark enthusiasm for athletics among Augustana women, according to the 1925 yearbook. She was active in extra-curricular pursuits as well: during her junior year she edited the "classes" section in the yearbook; as a senior she served as treasurer of her sorority, Sigma Pi Delta, in addition to sitting on the

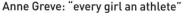

Anne Greve: "every girl an athlete"

Athletic Board, and participating in the Woman's Club and (of course) the A.G. A.A.—all the while listed among the faculty.

That she was both effective and beloved is clear from the record. In those days of lavish yearbook prose she's praised for her "fine work," (1928),[25] for her "capable and efficient direction" (1932),[26] for her "splendid and untiring efforts in the interest of girls' athletics" (1928).[27] She "won...a warm place in the hearts of Augie girls," the 1932 yearbook notes.[28] The "Augie Girls" section of the 1928 yearbook is dedicated to her. A brief profile of her and her teaching aims makes clear that, in the buzz-word of today, she was "passionate" about her commitment to women's athletics. When she came to Augustana, "Anne immediately set to work arousing interest in athletics for girls, using as her slogan, 'Every girl an athlete participating in at least one sport'"[29]—that goal first defined almost a decade earlier by Martha Martinson. And what Greve accomplished seems little short of astonishing, especially considering other aspects of her life during that time.

Essentially, she realized the hopes of her predecessors, students and instructors, from the early 1920s. Recalling the struggles of those years for a women's athletic program that could simply equal what other colleges and universities offered, the 1929 yearbook triumphantly proclaims:

Augustana may justly and proudly boast that she has one of the most highly developed girls' athletic departments of any college in the state. The credit for this wonderful system goes to Miss Anne Greve, director of girls' athletics, and to Miss Linnea Sandholm [Greve's student assistant], assistant director of swimming.

When Anne, as the girls affectionately call her, came to Augie six years ago, the athletic department had nothing to offer the girls except two hours of gym a week.... [N]ow Augie has two girls' varsity basketball teams, a baseball team, a volleyball team, a tennis team, and a Red Cross Life Saving Corps.[30]

Under Greve's direction Augustana also offered archery, horseback riding, and, briefly, riflery.

The yearbook notice concludes, "Surely Anne's dream of having every Augie girl active in athletics is nearer realization through the untiring efforts of two of Augie girls' best pals—Anne and 'Sandy' [Linnea Sandholm]."[31] By 1933, the year before Greve resigned, the yearbook could declare that "Augie may now boast of one of the largest, most inclusive athletics departments of any college in the state....The department now offers so broad a program that each girl in college can find at least one sport in which she can excel."[32] "From practically nothing at the beginning," the 1934 yearbook states, "Miss Greve has developed for the girls at Augustana a program of athletics which is far superior to that of other colleges of a similar size."[33]

She achieved this transformation, apparently, through a judicious combination of charm and challenge. The unsparing efforts, the "wholehearted understanding," and the enthusiastic commitment—as well as the elegance and what must have been great capacity for fun—fired the women she mentored to participate in and push for a wider program of athletics. They were obviously proud of the program as it unfolded. But Anne's winsome grin could contract into severity. A determined jaw suggests that when sterner approaches were called for, she didn't flinch. Even if "putting girls' athletics on a practical par with boys'"—a goal stated in 1926—awaited Title IX and beyond for full realization, still progress was being made. Women athletes were awarded letter sweaters for the first time that year. And some of the issues that plagued women's athletic programs through the seventies and beyond were addressed: "Gym requirements, lockable dressing rooms, and practice hours have all been gained through the steady effort of Miss Greve and some few interested girls. Progress has been made against all the odds of conservative thought, sarcastic word, and common practice."[34] (Unfortunately the sarcastic word wasn't silenced in the 1920s; in the 1970s such words were still being spoken by persons in authority.)

Besides expanding the sports opportunities for women, Anne Greve presided over extracurricular activities. Under her direction the Valkyries were organized. This elite group of women athletes who accumulated points through participation in a variety of sports, was limited to 24 members. (To get in you had to earn 150; to stay in, 75 per semester.) The fact that so high a number was assigned for the membership limit indicates how many women participated in athletics. The first "Play Days" also came into being while Greve presided over women's athletics—day-long events to which other schools were invited, and which featured various athletic activities, usually concluding with a banquet. As the *Observer* for March 12, 1931, notes, the "big athletic event" of the spring is Play Day, in which 8 schools will participate.[35] And in her spare time, the energetic Miss Greve organized a weekly swimming class for faculty wives. Clearly she devoted to this outside activity the same rigor and energy she gave to her curricular duties, as the *Observer* records that when professorial husbands occasionally joined their spouses in the pool, "their better halves, due to the excellent training of the teacher, far outshine their mates in all departments of the sport."[36]

Anne Greve's protofeminism, suggested in these descriptions, may have had another dimension, at least for the Augustana of the twenties and thirties. And this part of her story explains, perhaps, the reason why it's difficult to find appropriate recognition for her achievements.

In 1928 Anne Greve married; she's listed as "Anne Greve Byrd" and her marriage noted in the 1931 yearbook. Sometime between that year and 1933 we can infer that she divorced her husband and in the last year of her tenure at Augustana is once again listed as "Anne Greve." The following year she married Dr. Wendell Lund, a fellow English major who had graduated the year after herself and had returned in 1931 to teach, chair the English Department, and serve as Alumni Secretary at Augustana. It's fairly easy to fill in the gaps of this story. The Augustana of those years—indeed, the culture of the time—frowned on divorce. And the likely circumstances of this one made it particularly unacceptable to church-related Augustana. Yet in later years Wendell Lund, who went on to become a key player in President Franklin D. Roosevelt's War Production Board and later a successful attorney in Washington, D. C., maintained cordial relationships with the college, and Anne Greve Lund (breathtakingly elegant in the latest fashions) served on the Alumni Board. The reason may not be far to seek. In his autobiography, published when he was 90, Lund said: "Of all Augustana's gifts, the greatest was my wife, Anne. Augustana brought us together, and we shared 45 years of happiness and love."[37]

Of greater interest than the ashes of old scandal is what it may suggest about the women of Augustana. Did Greve's students, who regarded her with such respect and affection, know or hear rumors of the situation? One college historian conjectures that it's not impossible. The college was small, and the women who participated in athletics formed a close-knit community, especially since Greve was assisted in her teaching by a student (who received tuition credit for that work). So the heartfelt tribute to Miss Greve as she left Augustana may suggest that students judged her on her professional, rather than her personal, activities; that, in their eyes, a woman could be successful and beloved even when she pushed boundaries. At any rate, the section "Girls' Athletics" in the 1934 yearbook is dedicated to Anne C. Greve, "who this year finishes her last term at Augustana"—"in appreciation of the splendid work she has done in organizing and developing her department during her ten years as Director of Women's Athletics."[38] And the annual A.G.A.A. banquet, conducted at no less a glamour spot than the Blackhawk Hotel in Davenport, honored her, the Valkyries presenting her "with a gift in token of their appreciation for her work with the organization."[39] Whatever the background story, the affirmation is solid.

Anne Greve Lund died in 1979—ironically, over two decades before the husband whose sometimes-precarious health she had cared for with attentive love.[40]

After Anne Greve's departure her former student assistant Hildegarde Kummer, now graduated, assumed the responsibility for women's physical education instruction. The stocky, bespectacled Kummer contrasted physically with Greve, but according to the yearbook for 1936 shared Greve's commitment to athletics for every girl, and "successfully maintained the high standards of the physical education department of Augustana."[41]

To that end "she is planning several changes in the set-up of her department"—what changes aren't clear, since she left at the end of that year. Kummer was followed in 1936 by Margaret Jane Sweet (later Brissman), who compiled the longest tenure as a member of the women's physical education faculty—31 years altogether (she took a break from teaching in 1943 to attend to her family, returning to the faculty in 1950 and retiring in 1974), and the highest rank—she concluded her tenure as associate professor. Her predecessors had been ranked as instructors until Anne Greve, and subsequently Christena May Lindborg, reached the level of assistant professor. In Brissman's absence several able teachers, including Augustana graduates Lindborg and Doris Charlet, carried on the program of women's athletics.

Sweet and Savvy: Margaret Jane Sweet Brissman

Unlike the statuesque Anne Greve, Jane Sweet was petite. A certain reported billet-doux rhymed "fragile" with "agile" in describing her. Early yearbook pictures show her smaller than many of her students, with bright brown eyes and a perky, frankly impudent smile. To the end of her long life she remained small and fit, enjoying physical exercise, in particular swimming and dancing, at an age when many of her contemporaries were coddling rheumatic joints or tricky hearts. As a teacher she was brisk, direct, brooking no squeamishness; if you couldn't swim when

Jane Sweet Brissman: carrying on the "splendid" ride

you enrolled in her beginning class, you could by the end of the semester, and you passed the proficiency test in swimming—as of 1944, required of all students for graduation—with insouciant ease. That aquatic confidence, and the health benefits it provided, continued lifelong for some of Brissman's grateful students.

She continued the "splendid" work of her predecessor Anne Greve. But what Greve seems to have accomplished largely through personal arrangements, Brissman was able to build into a curriculum. Several factors account for this success. First, she came with experience. A 1932 graduate of Purdue University, she earned a master's degree in Education from Northwestern. She'd taught in both high school (New Trier) and college (Bethany) before coming to Augustana. She knew how to organize, and she did it effectively. Besides activity electives, Brissman initiated courses dealing with theory and practice in physical education training, useful for students aiming to teach. Outside the classroom she added ping-pong and dance to the extracurricular choices offered by Greve and her predecessors. A second element in Brissman's success was the larger culture itself. The war helped strengthen the image of physically-fit women, capable of undertaking jobs formerly handled only by men. Rosie may have abandoned the rivet-gun and returned to the kitchen, but the poster-picture of her bared muscular arm, with all it implied of female strength and assertiveness, remained.

And finally, Jane Sweet's marriage in 1938 to Augustana Director of Athletics Leroy Brissman created a fortunate professional as well as personal collaboration: Leroy Brissman joined her in promoting expanded athletic opportunities for women.

Under Jane Brissman's leadership the Women's Athletic Association, the new incarnation of the A.A.G.A. originally formed under Dorothy Rogers in 1923, grew to include every woman in the school—even those blatantly nonathletic. A much-anticipated annual event in its early years was the all-woman Kat Banquet. Students and staff alike found wildly amusing the chance to roast each other in satiric prose, song, and verse (an interesting form of sisterly bonding). More seriously, the banquet honored women who'd earned the requisite number of points for participation in sports—the highest award was the coveted letter sweater. And, "as the climax of the evening, The Kat presented the Black Kat Award" "to the faculty or staff woman who has done the most for the Augustana coeds during the past year."[42] The awardees spanned the range of collegiate

Jane Brissman (far right), honorary member, Tribe of Vikings Hall of Fame

offices, each "being a real and sincere friend to all the girls at Augie."[43] Dr. Henriette C. K. Naeseth, English Department chair, was succeeded the following year by one of the dieticians. The next year, appropriately, Miss Jane Sweet took the Black Kat.[44]

But Brissman didn't confine her activities on behalf of women's physical education to Augustana. Four years after her arrival she and two students represented Augustana at the North Central district Convention of the Atlantic Federation of College Women. That same year, September of 1940, Brissman was one of three presenters in the Physical Education Committee meetings—the only woman—at the Sixth Annual Conference of Lutheran College Faculties, held at Wartburg College.[45]

As a tribute to her contributions, she was inducted as an honorary member of Augustana's Tribe of Vikings Hall of Fame in 2002. She died in 2006.

Afterword: The Sixties....

...And so, in that moment of precarious poise between tradition and possibility, the fifties ended.

And things became very different.

Civil rights pressures...national television coverage of an increasingly unpopular war...seismic shifts in traditional views of authority. By women, as by African-Americans, increasingly aggressive challenges to entrenched white male power structures. New music, new voices, new ways to heighten experience, to love, to die. Flowers and blood. The dawning of the age of Aquarius, a dawn that broke in vivid and violent colors.

And at Augustana, a new regime, a new president who broke the traditional pastoral mold and brought keen business savvy to the role. Restructuring of administrative patterns. New courses, a shifting emphasis toward global venues and cultures. Draft anxiety, and varied responses to it.

And yet for many of us who spent our time on campus during the early to late sixties, life went on much as it had in the fifties. The big changes, the ground swells upsetting traditional patterns elsewhere, were only small tremors here in the Midwest. Most of us found the authorities who presided over our lives benignant; some of us idolized them. Most of us still sat in front-facing rows of desks and took notes on class lectures; we wrote our exams longhand in blue books, which our patient professors deciphered. We went, if not always enthusiastically, at least compliantly, to required chapel, signing our attendance cards lest we lose quality points for absences; some of us found the brief worship service with the whole college gathered in one place an instructive and uplifting experience. As women, we had curfews and dress codes (no pants unless the temperature fell below a certain point, or you were traveling home for vacation); and except for sorority formals, most of us waited for the men to ask us out. Many of us were very happy, excited about what we were learning, thrilled when hard work was rewarded, honors bestowed, and opportunities we wouldn't have dreamed of extended to us—extended by the faculty women we saw as models, and by the practical assistance for graduate studies they and their male colleagues procured for us.

The sixties saw more women joining the faculty, some of whom still occupy key positions. They have taught, challenged, and wrought with high energy, with brilliance, with courage. Their story remains to be told, their contributions to be fully assessed with that true seeing which is the daughter of time. That they have made Augustana a stronger, more enlightened place for women and men no one who has watched them, worked with them, been energized by their vision, can question.

Theirs is the next chapter of the Augustana story.

Conclusion

Oh! that the happy school days would return!...[N]o one knows how very hard it is for me to give up my studies altogether....Give up!—I cannot do that!
Anna Olsson

If you will continue what I have tried to do all these many years, and if you stay as long as I did, our college will not have to worry about the mathematics department for almost a century!
A girl needs Christ for home building. God has given each girl a desire to have a real home of her own, and she must have Christ in order that that desire may be fulfilled according to his will, and the home be a true home....
Inez Rundstrom

I can read and study all day long without the former consequences [becoming ill]. That I am happy over the fact, you can easily imagine.
Anna Westman

We were frankly told that while they [male students] loved us as girls, they did not care for us a students....I very much resented this male assumption of superiority, and this accounts for some of the willful forwardness that made me somewhat of a 'problem child' and involved me in some...'firsts.'...
Netta Bartholomew Anderson

Well, really!
Henriette C. K. Naeseth

The only thing I ever wanted to do was teach, and I was allowed to do that.
Dorothy Parkander

I have always believed I can do what I want to do.
Betsey Brodahl

As a single woman you're dependent upon yourself for certain important things: financial support, social life, and a sense of worth.
Florence Neely

What I have enjoyed most is just plain teaching.
Margaret Olmsted

*The first work…to be done is to free the student from self-consciousness…
so that [she] may express what [she] already knows….*
Iva Carrie Pearce

These are some of the voices that have echoed down the long corridors of the past, from lecture room and podium, across coffee tables, in the deep and sometimes lonely places of the heart. They have moved, amused, and inspired me, and I hope you also.

What, in the end, have they said?

That Augustana women, like their counterparts in other schools and venues across the country, fought, believed in, and ultimately found self and work and worth in those classrooms, dorms, stages, and playing fields. Was it harder for them here? Maybe. A strong church connection reinforced cultural patterns of gender expectation with its "gospel" authority. Or was it easier for them? Maybe. For the church, and in particular the Augustana Synod, saw itself as an instrument of social justice, and at least some of its thinkers wrestled with the question of what exactly that meant. Giving "girls" gender-specific education so that they could be the "homebuilders" their very nature mandated? Or offering them an education that would instead fit their specific, individual talents and dreams? Permitting or urging? Tolerating or encouraging?

And what about the women? Did their essentially conservative upbringing restrict or enable? Did it breed content with the way things had always been, or did it give them the flexibility to maneuver within systems that, though clearly imperfect, seemed to be the best going?

This year, at All Saint's Day in my church, we lit candles for those who had gone before and shaped our lives. I looked up at the young, serenely determined face of our pastor, an Augustana woman I've known since her student days, and I thought of those other women whose voices speak over the generations, whose light shines in my life, whose light has *given* me my life. I touched my small votive candle to the larger flame. From them, for them.

A Selected Bibliography

Books and articles

Ander, Oscar Fritiof. *T. N. Hasselquist: The Career and Influence of a Swedish-American Clergyman, Journalist and Educator.* Rock Island: Augustana Historical Society, 1931.

Barry, John. *The Great Influenza: The Epic Story of the Deadliest Plague in History.* New York: Viking, 2004.

Bergendoff, Conrad. *Augustana...A Profession of Faith.* Rock Island: Augustana Library Publications, 1960.

Bergendoff, Conrad. "The College and the War." *Augustana College Magazine.* Summer 1995.

Boaden, Ann. "Weighing the Stars and Hearing the Word: Conrad Bergendoff's Idea of Christian Higher Education at Augustana College and Theological Seminary." *Aspects of Augustana and Swedish America: Essays in Honor of Dr. Conrad Bergendoff on His 100th Year.* Rock Island: Augustana Historical Society, 1995.

Boardman, Barrington. *Flappers, Bootleggers, "Typhoid Mary," & The Bomb: An Anecdotal History of the United States from 1923-1945.* New York: Harper & Row, 1988.

Brodahl, Betsey. "A Revolution in American Education." *Augustana College Magazine.* Summer 1995.

Brodahl, Betsey. "Nebraska." *Augustana Swedish Institute Yearbook 1966-1967.*

Brolander, Glen. *An Historical Survey of the Augustana Campus.* Revised edition. Rock Island: Augustana Historical Society, 1992.

Erickson, Charlotte. "Some Reminiscences about Life at Augustana, 1941-1945." *Augustana College Magazine.* Summer 1995.

Jones, Alan. "A Brief History of Grinnell College." *Grinnell College Alumni Directory.* White Plains, New York: Bernard C. Harris Publishing Company, Inc., 1997.

Koren, Elisabeth. *The Diary of Elisabeth Koren 1853-1855.* Trans. David Nelson. St. Paul, Minnesota: Norwegian-American Historical Society, 1955.

McAfee, Mildred Helen. "Educate a Woman." *Association of American Colleges Bulletin.* December 1942.

Naeseth, Henriette C. Koren, and Napier Wilt. "Two Early Norwegian Dramatic Societies in Chicago." *Norwegian-American Studies and Records* X. Northfield: Minnesota: Norwegian-American Historical Association, 1958.

Naeseth, Henriette. "Drama in Early Deadwood." *American Literature.* November 1938.

Naeseth, Henriette C. K. "Drama in Swedish Chicago." *Journal of the Illinois State Historical Society* XLI (June, 1948).

Naeseth, Henriette C. K. *The Swedish Theater of Chicago.* Rock Island: Augustana Historical Society and Augustana Library, 1951.

Nelson, Lillian. *The Augustana College Endowment Society.* Esbjorn Bicentennial Newsletter of the Augustana Historical Society. Fall 2008.

Olson, E. and M. Engberg. *History of the Swedes in Illinois* Part III.

Olsson, Anna. *A Child of the Prairie.* Trans. Martha Winblad. Ed. Elizabeth Jaderborg. Lindsborg, Kansas: Bethany College, 1978. Originally published in Swedish as *En prärieunges funderingar.* Rock Island: Augustana Book Concern, 1917.

Parkander, Dorothy J. "Exalted Manna: the Psalms as Literature." *Word and World*. St. Paul, Minnesota: Luther Seminary, 1985.

Parkander, Dorothy J. *Poetry*. Santa Ana, California: Pioneer Press, 1967.

"Prof. Kling's Best Student." *Augustana Bulletin*. Summer 1967.

Ronnegard, Sam. *Prairie Shepherd: a Biography of Lars Paul Esbjorn*. Trans. G. Everett Arden. Rock Island: Augustana Book Concern, 1952.

Sebelius, S. J. *Master Builders of Augustana*. Rock Island: Augustana Book Concern, 1949.

Seusy, Kathleen, Diann Moore, Curtis C. Roseman, and Regena Schantz, ed. *Echoes from Riverside Cemetery, Moline, Illinois*. Moline, Illinois: Heritage Documentaries, Inc., 2009.

Solomon, Barbara Miller. *In the Company of Educated Women*. New Haven: Yale University Press, 1985.

Telleen, Jane. "Yours in the Master's Service: Emmy Evald and the Woman's Missionary Society of the American Lutheran Church, 1892-1942." *Swedish Pioneer Historical Quarterly* 30 (July 1979).

Tredway, Thomas. *Coming of Age: A History of Augustana College, 1935-1975*. Rock Island: Augustana College, 2010.

Undset, Sigrid. *Return to the Future*. Trans. Henriette C. K. Naeseth. New York: A. A. Knopf, 1942.

Walton, Clyde C. *Illinois Lives: The Prairie State Biographical Record*. Hopkinsville, Kentucky: Historical Record Association, 1969.

Manuscript sources, located in Augustana College Special Collections

Presidential Papers
Olof Olsson Papers
Gustav Andreen Papers
Conrad Bergendoff Papers

Faculty Papers
Netta Bartholomew Anderson Papers
Jane Brissman Papers
Henriette C. K. Naeseth Papers
Margaret Olmsted Papers

Minutes
Minutes of the Board of Directors, Augustana College
Minutes of the Faculty, Augustana College
Minutes of the Augustana Woman's Club
Minutes of the Augustana Dames Club

Organizational Records
Augustana Endowment Society Papers

Yearbooks and College newspapers

College Catalogues

Collections from other colleges
Inez Rundstrom Papers: Gustavus Adolphus College, St. Peter, Minnesota
Emmy Carlsson Evald Papers: Rockford (Illinois) College

End notes

Chapter 1
The Early Years: Promise and Progress

1 B," '15, "Memories and Visions," *Augustana Observer*, April 1920.

2 Indeed, it could be argued that a woman influenced the very creation of Augustana. When Esbjorn arrived in America, so the story goes, the solidly-entrenched Methodists offered financial support—Esjborn was at the end of his resources—in exchange for allegiance. Esbjorn asked for a day to consider the offer. But Mrs. Esbjorn countenanced no such waffling. She's said to have declared that she'd "rather seek employment as a washer woman than renounce my Lutheran faith." Her husband listened to her, stood firm—and the rest is history (Sam Ronnegard, *Prairie Shepherd: A Biography of Lars Paul Esbjorn*, tr. G. Everett Arden [Rock Island: Augustana Book Concern, 1952], 98).

3 *Hemlandet* November 28, 1860 qtd. in Oscar Fritiof Ander, *T. N. Hasselquist: The Career and Influence of a Swedish-American Clergyman, Journalist and Educator* (Rock Island: Augustana Historical Society, 1931).

4 Ander, 65.

5 Barbara Miller Solomon, *In the Company of Educated Women: A History of Women and Higher Education in America* (New Haven: Yale University Press, 1985), 50.

6 Ander, 70-71.

7 Conrad Bergendoff, *Augustana—A Profession of Faith* (Rock Island: Augustana Library Publications, 1960), 72.

8 Ander, 71.

9 Ander, 77.

10 Ander, 70.

11 Solomon, 50.

12 Stephen Jay Gould, "Women's Brains," *The Panda's Thumb* (New York: W. W. Norton & Company, 1980), 152-159.

13 Edward Clarke, *Sex in Education* [1873] qtd. in Solomon, 56. As we'll see, the idea of women's physical and mental fragility persisted into the 1940s.

14 Stephen Jay Gould, for instance, explores (and explodes) the "logic" of the study measuring women's brains.

15 *Gustavian Weekly*, February 17, 1925.

16 Ander, 70.

17 Qtd. in Solomon, 44.

18 Qtd. in Ann Boaden, "Vikings and Visionaries," *Augustana College Magazine*, Spring 1985, 18.

19 Ander, 71.

20 Unpublished Journal, October 7, 1890, Olof Olsson Papers.

21 Anton Peterson, "Dr. John Rundstrom Another Interesting Pioneer Here," *The Lindsborg News-Record*, July 14, 1960, 6.

22 Peterson, 6.

23 The Maria Charlotta Rundstrom Scholarship Fund was "to be used to aid that lady student in the college whom the faculty, considering character, scholarship, and needs, shall recommend" (*Gustavian Weekly* December 13, 1921).

24 *En prärieunges funderingar* (Rock Island, Illinois: Augustana Book Concern, 1917).

25 Irene Bengtson, personal conversation, June 2008, Lindsborg, Kansas. Ms. Bengtson and her husband lived in the former Rundstrom house from 1949 until 1986.

26 Irene Bengtson.

27 Irene Bengtson.

28 See *En prärieunges funderingar.*

29 *Gustavian Weekly,* February 17, 1925.

30 *Gustavian Weekly,* February 18, 1930.

31 Qtd. in Peterson.

32 It's interesting that around 1883, when Inez was making her big move to Rock Island, Dr. Rundstrom seems to have been seized with a fever for the grandiose, building a large farmhouse with "lumber [soft pine], windows, and doors shipped from Chicago, gothic windows with shutters and a lookout tower…with a view over much of the Smoky Valley," a vineyard, and a grove of trees (Peterson, "Dr. John Rundstrom Another Interesting Pioneer Here"). This might represent a proto-empty nest syndrome, or simply the restless energy of a man whose major project—the education of his daughter—was completed and who needed a new interest for his non-professional hours. Whichever it was, the end result was the "most stylish house" in the region (Irene Bengtson).

33 Netta Bartholomew Anderson, "Augustana Fifty Years Ago through a Co-ed's Eyes," unpublished paper, 1944, Netta Bartholomew Anderson Papers; Esthena Randolph, "The Women of Augustana," *Rockety-I* 1921, 160.

34 Swedish-Finnish poet Johan Ludvig Runeberg (1804-1877) wrote the "enormously popular *Fanrik Stals sagner* (Tales of Ensign Stal)—once published in the U.S.A. by the Augustana Book Concern" (Lars Scott, e-mail to the writer).

35 Philip Dowell, unpublished Journal.

36 Olof Olsson, "A Brief Visit in the lecture rooms of Augustana College and Theological Seminary," *Augustana,* qtd. in Bergendoff, 86.

37 Dowell.

38 Harry E. Nelson, "Mathematics and Astronomy at Augustana," unpublished Lily Foundation Paper, 1.

39 Aina Abrahamson, personal letter to the writer, July 2008.

40 Aina Abrahamson, personal interview.

41 John Kindschuh, class of 1948.

42 Funeral eulogy, Inez Rundstrom Papers.

43 *Gustavian Weekly,* October 1, 1940.

44 Anna Olsson, unpublished Journal, September 25, 1890.

45 Anna Olsson, *A Child of the Prairie,* trans. Martha Winblad, ed. Elizabeth Jaderborg (Lindsborg, Kansas: Bethany College, 1978). Originally published in Swedish as *En prärieunges funderingar* in 1917. All quotations are from the 1978 translation.

46 For a clear overview of this controversy, see Vance Eckstrom, "Lutherans in the Smoky Valley," *The Heritage of Augustana: Essays on the Life and Legacy of the Augustana Lutheran Church,* ed. Harland H. Gifford and Arland J. Hultgren (Minneapolis: Kirk House Publishers, 2004), 110-127.

47 *A Child of the Prairie,* 69.

48 *A Child of the Prairie,* Chapter 25.

49 *A Child of the Prairie,* 69.

50 *A Child of the Prairie,* 69.

51 *A Child of the Prairie,* Chapter 14.

52 Eckstrom, 121.

53 In fact, she titles her own translation of *En prärieunges funderingar* "I'm Scairt."

54 *A Child of the Prairie,* Chapter 1.

55 *A Child of the Prairie*, Chapter 22.

56 *A Child of the Prairie*, 99.

57 Olsson, Journal, December 1883; see also September 25, 1890.

58 Olsson, Journal, December 2, 1889.

59 Olsson, recollections, trans. Conrad Bergendoff, Olof Olsson Papers.

60 She had attended a similar kind of school, Bethany Academy, for a year in Lindsborg.

61 Olsson, "Complete Schedule, Augustana College," September 1883.

62 Catalogue, 59.

63 Anderson, "Augustana Fifty Years Ago through a Co-ed's Eyes."

64 Olsson, Journal, January 14, 1891.

65 Olsson, Journal, October 31, 1889.

66 Olsson, Journal, December 2, 1889.

67 Olsson, Journal, May 5, 1891 and December 4, 1890.

68 Olsson, Journal, August 18, 1890.

69 Olsson, Journal, September 25, 1890.

70 Olsson, Journal, October 7, 1898.

71 Olsson, Journal, July 26, 1890.

72 Olsson, Journal, August 19, 1890.

73 See, *i.e.*, January 30, 1893.

74 Olsson, Journal, July 26, 1890.

75 Olsson, Journal, July 26, 1890.

76 A rather extravagant claim on the Rock Island website featuring the "Anna Olsson House" asserts that Olsson "is as well known as Mark Twain and Harriet Beecher Stowe for her children's books" (website). According to Swedish historian and Augustana graduate Dag Blanck, however, this estimation is a bit generous. Reviewing the Swedish publishing history of *En prärieunges funderingar* (her best-known work) Blanck notes that it has appeared in several editions, though today it's included mainly in academic libraries. A search of LIBRIS, the national Swedish online bibliography, indicates that the 1917 Augustana Book Concern edition can be found in the Royal Library in Stockholm and the Uppsala University Library; two libraries carry a 1919 reprint from a leading Swedish publisher, Bonniers forlag i Stockholm, and two libraries also house the 1927 edition published in Stockholm by Diakonistyrelsens forlag, a publishing house with strong ties to the Church of Sweden. The revised edition of 1984, under the imprimis Natur & Kultur, another major Swedish publisher (edited by Joan Sandin under the title *Prärieungen: Anna Olssons barndomsminnen* [The Prairie Child: The Childhood Memories of Anna Olsson]), appears in 15 libraries. Finally, in 1988 a facsimile version of the 1927 edition appeared in Karlstad as part of a series devoted to literature about the province of Värmland (the Olsson family Swedish home), where it was noted as a "minor classic." Seven libraries house this edition. Blanck concludes that this distribution suggests more of an historical/cultural than a popular interest in Olsson's work. The number of editions does, he feels, suggest "some popularity," but the estimate of her reputation as equaling that of Twain or Stowe seems to him "very clearly exaggerated."

77 Dag Blanck, e-mail to the writer, June 28, 2005. See also Dorothy Burton Skarsdal, "The Scandinavian Immigrant Writer in America" (Norwegian American Historic Association, *Norwegian-American Studies* 21 [1962], 14-53).

78 Unpublished letter, August 14, 1940.

79 A sampling of titles gives a clue to their character: "The Angels' Gift," "The Lend-a-Hand Club," "The Jolly Picnickers," and "Ethel's Repentance," Olof Olsson Papers.

80 Olsson, Journal, October 18, 1890.

81 See *A Child of the Prairie* and Journals.

82 Betsey Brodahl, personal interview; Doris Quist Anderson, Class of 1941, telephone interview.

83 Qtd. in Alice Johnson, "Anna Olsson: Experiences and Expression," *Saga* 1939.

84 An example of her devotion to the interests of the college occurs when, in 1895, she was offered the job of "Lady Principal" of Ladies Hall. She requested that her monthly salary be reduced by one-third to help ease financial strains (Board Minutes, November 1, 1895).

85 Doris Quist Anderson.

86 Catalogue, 1884-1885.

87 "Sad and Terrible," *The Rock Island Argus*, November 25, 1889.

88 Bergendoff, 52; 80.

89 S. J. Sebelius, "Andrew Woods Williamson: Good and Faithful Servant," *Master Builders of Augustana* (Rock Island: Augustana Book Concern, 1949), 97-104.

90 "Particulars Elicited at the Coroner's Inquest," *Rock Island Daily Union*, November 26, 1889.

91 *Rock Island Daily Union*, November 30, 1889.

92 Board Minutes, 1891.

93 See, *i.e.*, December 30, 1892; January 30, March 21, and December 26, 1893.

94 See, *i.e.*, Lydia Olsson, unpublished Journal, November 1, 1896, Olof Olsson Papers.

95 Lydia Olsson, Journal, October 23, 1896.

96 Lydia Olsson, Journal, October 20, 1896.

97 Board Minutes, August 3, 1894.

98 August 10, 1894.

99 Unpublished letter, March 28, 1895.

100 Board Minutes, 1895.

101 1910 Census, Cuyahoga County, Cleveland.

102 1910 Census.

103 http://sdre.lib.uiowa.edu/traveling-culture/chaul/img/adamsalmeda/l/l.gif.

104 http://www.thecmss.org.

105 Death notice, *The Plain Dealer*, August 3, 1910.

106 An *Observer* article for March 1911 gives a different source for this scholarship, stating that Westman herself "expressed the desire that the sum of $50 be set aside from her estate each year to be given to some worthy lady student" (March 1911). But the tribute quoted year by year in the Catalogue suggests rather a donor who knew and admired Westman; it would hardly have been written by Westman herself.

107 Bergendoff, 51.

108 S. Marguerite Shuey Foss, "Fairview Academy," unpublished paper, February 10, 1943. Mrs. Foss spells her name alternately "Marguerite" and "Margaret" in her various documents.

109 George Wickstrom, "Purchase of Double Stucco House by College Recalls Old Fairview Academy," *The Town Crier, Rock Island Argus*, January 12, 1946.

110 Bergendoff, 69.

111 Foss, qtd. in Wickstrom.

112 *Annual Catalogue of Fairview Academy, Rock Island*, 1885-1886 (Rock Island: Augustana Book Concern), 10. Hereafter cited as *Fairview Academy Catalogue*.

113 "Course of Study and Text-Books," *Fairview Academy Catalogue*, 6-8.

114 "Course of Study and Text-Books," 8.

115 *Fairview Academy Catalogue*, 11-12.

116 "Daily Routine," *Fairview Academy Catalogue*, 12-13.

117 "Expenses," *Fairview Academy Catalogue*, 13.

118 Foss, qtd. in Wickstrom.

119 "Register of Pupils," *Fairview Academy Catalogue*, 4.
120 Foss, qtd. in Wickstrom.
121 Bergendoff, 52.
122 Catalogue 1890-1891, 59.
123 Catalogue 1890-1891, 59.
124 Unpublished letter to Emmy Evald, January 25, 1926, qtd. in Board Minutes, February 11, 1926.
125 Bergendoff, 52. The building persisted, in various incarnations, until 1978 when it was razed to make way for the College Center. Students from the teens and early twenties knew it as "Hashamyam" (allegedly "Home of the Angels") because of its female denizens; later it became the music building, and, in its final days, East Hall, home of English and languages.
126 Catalogue 1890-1891, 59.
127 Qtd. in Bergendoff, 77.
128 "Life at Ladies' Hall," *Observer*, December 1915, 19-20.
129 *Observer*, January 1911.

Chapter 2
After the Pioneers

1 Solomon, especially 45.
2 Catalogue, 1890-1891.
3 Catalogue, 1907-1909.
4 "The Women of Augustana," *Rockety I* 1921, 160.
5 *In the Company of Educated Women*, 90.
6 August 1903.
7 May 1903.
8 Qtd. in Solomon, 90.
9 Catalogues.
10 Conrad Bergendoff, *Augustana...A Profession of Faith*, 100.
11 Records from Grand Mount (Rochester) Cemetery, near Olympia, Washington.
12 E. Olson and M. Engberg, *History of the Swedes in Illinois Part III*, 110.
13 Olson and Engberg.
14 Bergendoff, 59.
15 Bergendoff, 69.
16 He composed, for instance, the "Jubilee" cantata for Augustana's 1893 celebration commemorating "the Council of Uppsala of 1593 when Sweden decisively rejected the efforts of the Counter Reformation" (Bergendoff, 88).
17 Bergendoff, 126; 76.
18 Olson and Engberg, 110.
19 Olson and Engberg, 110.
20 Bergendoff, 127.
21 Olson and Engberg, 110.
22 Catalogue, 1899-1900.
23 Qtd. in Bergendoff, 127.
24 *Observer*, October 1910, 237.
25 Lydia Olsson, unpublished Journal, October 9, 1896, Olof Olsson Papers.
26 Bergendoff, 94.
27 Bergendoff, 147-148.
28 Board Minutes, June 1911.

29 Board Minutes, April 1912.

30 Bergendoff, 144.

31 Esthena Randolph, "The Women of Augustana," *Rockety-I*, 160.

32 Catalogue, 1902-1903.

33 Catalogue, 1899-1900.

34 "The Augustana School of Expression," Augustana College and Theological Seminary, n.d.

35 "The Augustana School of Expression."

36 "The Augustana School of Expression."

37 "The Teacher."

38 Paula Youngberg Arnell, personal interview.

39 During the 1925 or 26 spring term Pearce took a leave of absence and Arnell assumed responsibility for her duties, teaching classes and supervising student assistants. According to the 1927 yearbook, "Miss Arnell has done some exceptionally fine work in the Children's department, and here, also [as well as in the School of Oral Expression as a whole], the enrollment has been increased" ("The Augustana School of Oral Expression," *Rockety-I* 1927, 101).

40 President's Report, 1936-1937, 5.

41 Glen Brolander, *An Historical Survey of the Augustana Campus*, Revised edition (Rock Island: Augustana Historical Society, 1992), 66.

42 Bergendoff, 80.

43 Netta Bartholomew Anderson, "Augustana Fifty Years Ago through a Co-ed's Eyes."

44 Anderson.

45 Netta Bartholomew Anderson Papers.

46 Anderson Papers.

47 Betsey Brodahl, personal interview.

48 Solomon, 116. This tension, as we'll see, continues to plague women collegians throughout much of the history this study covers.

Chapter 3
The First World War: Vivid Rhetoric, Modest Moves

1 "History of the Class of 1920," *Observer*, May 1920.

2 "For a Greater Augustana," *Rockety-I* 1912, n. p.

3 Qtd. in *Observer*, April 1917.

4 "The Minute Men of '17," *Observer*, April 1917.

5 *Observer*, April 1917.

6 *Observer*, November 1917.

7 *Observer*, November 1917.

8 Fritiof Fryxell, Class of 1922, personal interview.

9 "History of the Class of 1920."

10 John M. Barry, *The Great Influenza: The Epic Story of the Deadliest Plague in History* (New York: Viking, 2004), 4.

11 Tim Lainhart, "The Killer in the Shadow of the Great War: Spanish Influenza Outbreak in the Quad-Cities," unpublished paper, 2010, 4.

12 "The Influenza Pandemic of 1918" (http://virus.stanford.edu/uda/index.html).

13 Qtd. in Billings.

14 Qtd. in Lainhart, 7.

15 Barry, 145.

16 Barry, 119.
17 Barry; see also Lainhart.
18 "General News."
19 Qtd. in Barry, 311.
20 *Observer*, 291.
21 October 4, 1918.
22 "General News," November 1, 1918.
23 "General News."
24 *Observer*, December 1918.
25 Conrad Bergendoff, *Augustana...A Profession of Faith*, 152.
26 See Barbara Miller Solomon, *In the Company of Educated Women*, 139-140.
27 Bergendoff, 151.
28 Bergendoff, 148.
29 Bergendoff, 150.
30 Qtd. in Bergendoff, 152.
31 Carol Marquardsen, unpublished paper, 2003.
32 Qtd. in "Prof. Kling's Best Student," *Augustana Bulletin* Summer 1967, 10.
33 "Judge Robert Olmsted, 90, Dies; Funeral Wednesday," *Rock Island Argus*, August 18, 1958.
34 Olmsted Papers.
35 Qtd. in "Prof. Kling's Best Student," 9.
36 "Judge Olmsted, 90, Dies...."
37 According to the website of Iowa State University, formerly (as of 1898) Iowa State College of Agricultural and Mechanical Sciences, the school admitted women as early as 1869, so this would have been an option for Margaret.
38 Olmsted Papers.
39 Qtd. in "Prof. Kling's Best Student," 9.
40 "Olmsted, Deaths," *Reynolds Press*, May 5, 1911.
41 "Olmsted, Deaths."
42 Olmsted Papers.
43 "John's Battle," *Observer*, March 1913.
44 Qtd. in "Prof. Kling's Best Student," 10.
45 *Observer*, April 1913.
46 Thorsten Sellin "went on to such a stellar career in sociology that the University of Pennsylvania—where he taught from 1922 to 1967—named a major research center in his honor" (Kai Swanson, manuscript note).
47 "Valedictorian Announced," January 1915.
48 *Observer*, May 1915.
49 Qtd. in "Prof. Kling's Best Student," 10.
50 Dora Cervin, Margaret Olmsted, Ethel Anderson, "Tribute to Alma Johnson from Rock Island, Moline Branch of the American Association of University Women, February, 1959," unpublished paper.
51 Qtd. in "In Memoriam: Margaret Olmsted," *Augustana College Magazine*, Winter 1995, 25.
52 "Judge Robert Olmsted, 90, Dies...."
53 Evelyn Boaden, personal interview.
54 Many years later, from 1987-1989, Kai Swanson lived in the Olmsted Apartments. He recalls the aged Miss Olmstead taking walks with a helper in pleasant weather.
55 Qtd. in "Prof. Kling's Best Student," 10.
56 Qtd. in "Prof. Kling's Best Student," 10.

Chapter 4
The Twenties: Polls and Prohibition, Flappers and—Feminists?

1 Conrad Bergendoff, *Augustana...A Profession of Faith*, 161.

2 Qtd. in Bergendoff, 161.

3 Qtd. in Bergendoff, 161.

4 The name preferred by Frances Willard for young people's temperance organizations ("The Cold Water Army," *The Daily Union*, March 21, 1879).

5 George H. Ryan, "Illinois Was First State East of the Mississippi to Grant Suffrage," pamphlet 1996.

6 "Report of the Proceedings of the Woman's Total Abstinence League, of Moline," *Moline Review*, July 22, 1874.

7 Among other objections to equal rights was the charge that by exploring their own abilities and going out to work, women would break up homes and families.

8 "A Street Riot," *Moline Review*, June 5, 1874.

9 Kathleen Seusy, "Mary Elenora Kerr Steward, 1832-1920," dramatic monologue, *Echoes From Riverside Cemetery, Moline, Illinois* (Moline: Heritage Documentaries, Inc., 2009), 204-205.

10 Taught by the amazingly eclectic Dr. Edward Fry Bartholomew.

11 Bergendoff, 149.

12 February 1913, 16.

13 *Observer*, February 1913.

14 Barrington Boardman, *Flappers, Bootleggers, "Typhoid Mary," & The Bomb: An Anecdotal History of the United States from 1923-1945* (New York: Harper & Row, 1988), 11.

15 Boardman, 11.

16 Paraphrased in "The Cold Water Army."

17 "The Cold Water Army."

18 Ryan.

19 Olof B. Hanson, '12, "The Divorce Problem," *Observer*, February 1912.

20 T. H., "Higher Motives," *Observer*, April and May 1912.

21 "Higher Motives."

22 "On the Way," *Observer*, November 1912.

23 "Augustana Suffragets *[sic]*," *Observer*, April 1911.

24 "Illinois Women: 75 Years of the Right to Vote", pamphlet, 17.

25 "Augustana now has a co-ed debating club," *Observer*, October 1913.

26 March 13, 1919.

27 Seusy; see also "Female Suffrage Society," *The Daily Union*, May 11, 1877. Elizabeth Cady Stanton, in fact, who visited Moline, inspired the creation of this group, the Moline Woman's Suffrage Association ("Female Suffrage Society").

28 Ryan.

29 Admittedly, it happened in June, during school vacation. But it's surprising that no reflections on it appear when classes resume.

30 The Augustana Synod was particularly well known for its then-advanced stands on social justice issues.

31 Lloyd Morris, qtd. in Boardman, 1.

32 Boardman, 16.

33 Boardman, 16.

34 *In the Company of Educated Women*, 157.

35 Clemence Dane, qtd. in Solomon, 158.

36 Solomon, 158.

37 "A Flapper Has the Last Word," *The Woman Citizen* 12 (June 1927), qtd. in Solomon, 157.
38 *Observer.*
39 "A Sense of Values," *Observer*, March 1921.
40 "A Woman Should Be," qtd. in *Observer*, March 18, 1926.
41 *Observer*, March 17, 1929.
42 Solomon, 170.
43 *Rockety-I* 1921, 160.
44 January 14, 1926, 1.
45 January 28, 1926, 1 and 6.
46 "What We Think," *Observer*, February 1926.
47 *Rockety-I*, 169.
48 Evald Papers, qtd. in Lennart Johnsson, "The Global Impact of Emmy Evald and the Women's Missionary Society," unpublished paper, 2006, 8.
49 Qtd. in Johnsson, 2.
50 Report...First International Woman Suffrage Conference Held at Washington, U.S.A., February 12, 13, 14, 15, 16, 17, 18, 1902.
51 Hearing before the select committee on woman suffrage, February 18, 1902 on the joint resolution (S.R. 53) proposing an Amendment to the Constitution of the United States, extending the right of suffrage to women.
52 *Mission Tidings*, June 1919, 9-12.
53 Gustav Andreen, unpublished letter to Gordon Keith Chambers, President of Rockford College, May 28, 1935, Gustav Andreen Papers.
54 Charlotte Odman, "A Great Leader Gone," *The Lutheran Companion*, January 1, 1947, 5.
55 "Among Ourselves," *Mission Tidings*, July 1935, 28.
56 *The Lutheran Companion*, September 16, 1937.
57 Gustav Andreen to Gordon Keith Chambers.
58 W. K. Fellows, head, Perkins, Fellows and Hamilton, Architects, Chicago, unpublished letter to Gustav Andreen and Members of the Augustana Building Committee, February 1, 1926, Gustav Andreen Papers.
59 Gustav Andreen Papers.
60 "The Greatest Call Today to the Augustana Women," pamphlet, Gustav Andreen Papers.
61 "A College Home for our Daughters," October 15, 1925, Gustav Andreen Papers.
62 "What We Think," October 15.
63 "Students Commend Board of Directors," *Observer*, September 6, 1926.
64 Gustav Andreen papers.
65 "Yours in the Master's Service: Emmy Evald and the Woman's Missionary Society of the Augustana Lutheran Church, 1892-1942," *Swedish Pioneer Historical Quarterly* 30 (July 1979). The history of the WMS has been extensively documented in various publications, such as *The Lutheran* and *The Lutheran Companion*, as well as in unpublished papers and correspondence.
66 Sharon Minter, great-granddaughter of Emmy Evald, telephone interview.
67 "Seventy-three Augie Girls Occupy Finely Furnished New Dormitory," September 13, 1928.
68 "Seventy-three Augie Girls..."
69 "About Our Churches," *Lutheran Companion*, January 28, 1959, 17.
70 Bergendoff, 167.
71 Fritiof Fryxell, personal interview.

72 Dora Cervin, Margaret Olmsted, and Ethel Anderson, unpublished "Tribute to Alma Johnson from Rock Island-Moline Branch of the American Association of University Women, February, 1959," 1.

73 Cervin, *et. al.*

74 Conrad Bergendoff, "In Memoriam Alma L. Johnson," *Augustana College Bulletin*, March 1959, 14.

75 Cervin *et. al.*, 1.

76 "About Our Churches."

77 Information for the Holmen sisters comes primarily from a series of conversations with Regina Holmen Fryxell and Fritiof Fryxell during the 1980s.

78 "Former Augustana vocal teacher remembered as American musical guru" [AP story], *The Dispatch and the Rock Island Argus*, June 19, 2003.

79 Clyde C. Walton, "Illinois Lives: The Prairie State Biographical Record" (Hopkinsville, Kentucky: Historical Record Association, 1969), 401.

80 "Former Augustana vocal teacher remembered as American musical guru."

Chapter 5
The Thirties: The Depression of Educated Women

1 Qtd. in Boardman, 103.

2 Qtd. in Boardman, 103.

3 Boardman, 138.

4 Frederick Lewis Allen, qtd. in Boardman, 137.

5 As many as 25,000 teachers and supporters participated in these protests. See Tracey Deutsch, "Great Depression," The Electronic Encyclopedia of Chicago (Chicago: Chicago Historical Society, 2005); John Newsinger, "A textbook protest," *Socialist Review* May 2009; *Chicago Tribune* March 22, 1933; Lyman B. Burbank, "Chicago Public Schools and the Depression Years of 1928-1937," *New Republic* 9 (1933), 365-381.

6 Boardman, 137.

7 Conrad Bergendoff, *Augustana...A Profession of Faith*, 174.

8 Bergendoff, 174.

9 Bergendoff, 174.

10 For an excellent discussion of Augustana's finances from 1935-1962 see Thomas Tredway, *A History of Augustana College, 1935-1975*, Chapter 5.

11 Woman's Club Minutes, September 13, 1933.

12 College Catalogues.

13 Solomon, 170.

14 *Rockety-I* 1927, 138.

15 Marjorie Nicholson, "The Rights and Privileges Pertaining Thereto," *Journal of the American Association of University Women*, April 1938, 138. See also, for instance, Dexter Merriam Keezer, "Where Are the Able Women Teachers?" *Journal of the American Association of University Women*, April 1938, 149-151.

16 Tredway, 21.

17 Tredway, 30.

18 An *Observer* article notes that "the two sexes do not enroll in the same proportion in the same subjects. Men enroll in science, math, and economics; women enroll in languages and English." But it rejects the idea that "the girls...take easier subjects" ("Are Augustana Girls Brighter Than Boys?" *Observer* January 27, 1927).

19 This terminology seems to suggest not only that faculty were expected to be male, but that when they were married, the spouse would inevitably be female.

20 Tredway, 21.
21 Nicholson, 140.
22 President's Report 1936-1937, 15.
23 President's Report 1936-1937, 14.
24 "House May Admit Augie Women to Membership," *Observer*, September 25, 1930.
25 "Dispense with the House Meeting This Evening," *Observer*, December 11, 1930.
26 President's Report 1936-1937, 15.
27 President's Report 1937-1938, 14.
28 "Letters to a College Girl," *The Lutheran Companion*, January 13, 1938.
29 Earle W. Gage, "Mothers of the World," *The Lutheran Companion*, May 5, 1838, 552.
30 Roald Tweet, personal interview.
31 Dorothy J. Parkander, "Henriette C. K. Naeseth," unpublished manuscript, 1.
32 Qtd. in obituary, *Argus*, November 27, 1987.
33 Unpublished speech, April 28, 2007.
34 *The Diary of Elisabeth Koren 1853-1855*, trans. David Nelson (St. Paul, Minnesota: Norwegian-American Historical Society, 1955), 114.
35 C. Naeseth, "Memories from a Little Iowa Parsonage," *Norwegian-American Studies and Records* 66, trans. Henriette Naeseth, 68.
36 C. Naeseth, 68.
37 Monroe was connected to the University of Chicago (the poetry room on the top floor of the old Harper library sported a large picture of her). Not only was she a practicing poet herself, but she was the moving spirit behind the University's prestigious *Poetry* magazine.
38 *A Poet's Life: Seventy Years in a Changing World* [1938], qtd. in *Poetry*, April 1938, 31.
39 Personal interview.
40 H. Naeseth, unpublished poem, June 1922.
41 *In the Company of Educated Women*, 158.
42 "Brief History of Grinnell College," *Grinnell College Alumni Directory* (White Plains, New York: Bernard C. Harris Publishing Company, Inc., 1997), iv.
43 Richard Yaki Arnell, Class of 1960, Grinnell College, personal interview.
44 H. Naeseth, "Kristian Prestgard: An Appreciation," *Norwegian-American Studies and Records* XV, 1949, 134.
45 Germany had sent in troops to occupy Norway and Denmark that month.
46 Unpublished letter, September 11, 1941.
47 Mildred Bakke, "Dr. Naeseth's Translation of Unset Book Successful," April 1942, 7.
48 As long as three decades after its publication, the book continued to be viewed as an "exemplary study" by scholars of ethnic theater, such as, for instance, Anne-Charlotte Hanes Harvey.
49 Gwin and Ruth Kolb, personal interview.
50 Tweet.
51 Tweet.
52 Parkander, 1.
53 Parkander, 3.
54 Parkander, 4.
55 Tweet.

Chapter 6
The Second World War: Girls and Women, Tasks and Possibilities

1   President's Report 1940-41, 3.
2   "War Memories," *Augustana College Magazine*, Summer 1995, 4.
3   Thomas Tredway, *Coming of Age*, 144.
4   1944, n. p.
5   Tredway, 146.
6   *Rockety-I* 1944, n. p.
7   Tredway, 147.
8   Tredway, 143.
9   Conrad Bergendoff, "The College and the War," *Augustana College Magazine*, Summer 1995, 5.
10 *Rockety-I* 1943, n. p.
11 Qtd. in Faculty Minutes, January 7, 1941.
12 Bergendoff, "The College and the War," 5.
13 *Augustana Bulletin*, February 1943, 36.
14 Bergendoff, "The College and the War," 5.
15 Faculty Minutes, March 11, 18, and 25, 1942.
16 Qtd. in Bergendoff, "The College and the War," 5.
17 Faculty Minutes, 1942-1943. Grant Olson, Class of 1943, for example, called up in the spring of 1943, was "close enough," he said, that the faculty graduated him. He went on to serve in intelligence, and was later an early recruit to the postwar C.I.A. (He married his Augustana sweetheart, Norma Erickson, after serving in the O.S.S.) (Kai Swanson).
18 Catalogue, 1944-1945.
19 See Chapter 2, "The Augustana Plan," *Coming of Age*.
20 See, for example, Olive C. Carmichael, "The University and the Community," *Association of American Colleges Bulletin* (May 1940), 261-266. Carmichael was chancellor of Vanderbilt University.
21 Tredway, 43.
22 Board Minutes, February 8, 1945, qtd. in Tredway, 43.
23 Qtd. in Tredway, 47.
24 Compare Carmichael: "…an intellectual and social perspective without an understanding and appreciation of spiritual values, results in an incomplete personality…."
25 Bergendoff to [Georg] Dellbrugge, January 16, 1961, qtd. in Tredway, 48.
26 Tredway, 72.
27 Dora Cervin, qtd. in Tredway, 73.
28 President's Report, 2-3.
29 *Augustana College Magazine*, Summer 1995.
30 Student Handbook, 1943-1944, 6.
31 Bergendoff, "The College and the War," 6.
32 Catalogue, 36.
33 Olive Johnson Schwiebert, Dean of Women 1946-1948, personal interview.
34 Tredway, 73.
35 Catalogues, 1941-1945.
36 Tredway, 73.
37 Faculty Minutes, November 17, 1942.
38 Catalogue, 1942-1943.
39 Faculty Minutes, October 22, 1943.
40 Student handbook, 1943-1944, 6.

41   President's Report 1942-1943, 19.
42   Charlotte Erickson, "Some Reminiscences about Life at Augustana, 1941-1945," *Augustana College Magazine*, Summer 1995, 7.
43   Bergendoff, "The College and the War," 6.
44   Bergendoff, "The College and the War," 6.
45   Albert Eddy, qtd. in *Observer*, February 14, 1946, 4. See also Richard B. Powers, "The U.S. Army Corps' Invasion of Augustana," *Augustana College Magazine*, Summer 1995.
46   "The U.S. Army Corps' Invasion of Augustana," 17.
47   Qtd. in V. R. Pearson, "Augustana Returns the Salute," *Rockety-I* 1944, n. p.
48   *Rockety-I* 1944, n. p.
49   Polly Fehlman, Class of 1946, telephone interview.
50   Gustavus Adolphus College board member, qtd. in Tredway, 149.
51   "Augustana Returns the Salute."
52   Erickson, 7.
53   President's Report 1942-1943, 19.
54   Betsey Brodahl, Class of 1944, personal interview.
55   Negley Harte, Senior lecturer, University College, London, obituary, *The Independent*, 16 July 2008.
56   Roy Sturguss, former student, London School of Economics, *The Independent*, 18 July 2008.
57   "Augustana Returns the Salute."
58   *Rockety-I* 1944, n. p.
59   Lacy, *Augustana College Magazine*, Summer 1995, 4.
60   Student Handbook, 1943-1944, 6.
61   "A Revolution in American Education," *Augustana College Magazine*, Summer 1995, 12.
62   *Rockety-I* 1945, 92.
63   Lacy, 4.
64   *Rockety-I* 1944, n. p.
65   *Rockety-I* 1944, n. p.
66   *Rockety-I* 1944, n. p.
67   *Rockety-I* 1941-1946.
68   *Rockety-I* 1946, n. p.
69   *Rockety-I* 1946, 15.
70   North Hall was a Victorian house located to the east and north of today's Carlsson Evald Hall in pre-Bergendoff Hall days. The building has since been razed.
71   *Rockety-I* 1946, n. p.
72   Dorothy J. Parkander, Class of 1946, personal interview.
73   Catalogue, 1941-1942, 44.
74   Schwiebert interview.
75   Student Handbook, 1941-1942, 30.
76   Student Handbook, 1944-1945, 37.
77   Student Handbook, 1940-1941, 34, and in others succeeding.
78   November 5, 1936, qtd. in Tredway, 73.
79   Schwiebert interview.
80   Jamie Nelson, personal interview.
81   *Rockety-I* 1945, 21.
82   Wolfgang Saxon, "Adda Bozeman Barkhuus, 85, Expert in International Relations," *The New York Times*, December 10, 1994.
83   *Sarah Lawrence Magazine*.
84   "Bozeman Writes Book Concerning World Relations," *Observer*, September 22, 1949.

85 Ann Boaden, notes from Brodahl Retirement Program.

86 Notes from Brodahl Building dedication program.

87 Brodahl, "Nebraska," *Augustana Swedish Institute Yearbook* 1966-67, 15.

88 Brodahl, "Nebraska," 16.

89 Brodahl, "Nebraska," 16.

90 Brodahl, "Nebraska," 22.

91 Brodahl, "Nebraska," 21.

92 Brodahl, "Nebraska," 22.

93 Brodahl, "Nebraska," 17.

94 Julie Jensen McDonald, "Music, history, clothes—all part of her persona," *The Gold Book*, January 1996, 42.

95 Betsey Brodahl, personal interview.

96 Brodahl, interview.

97 Brodahl, interview.

98 McDonald, 42.

99 Brodahl, interview.

100 Tredway, 237.

101 Brodahl, interview.

102 Brodahl, interview.

103 Brodahl, interview.

104 Brodahl, interview.

105 Much of the information in this portrait comes from conversations with Dr. Parkander over a span of years.

106 Anthony K. Stoutenburg, "Twelve of Augie's Most Powerful People," *Observer*, January 23 and February 4, 1981.

107 See, for example, the comments of fifty-year anniversary classes.

108 Interestingly, her own student Karin Youngberg became the third occupant of that chair.

109 Dorothy J. Parkander, personal interview.

110 *Observer*, March 19.

111 November 19, 1953.

112 William G. Karlblom, Class of 1969, unpublished letter.

113 *Observer*, February 24, 1944.

114 "Miss Dora Carlson Is Girls' New Dean," *Observer*, September 13, 1928.

115 President's Report 1942-1953, 19.

116 President's Report 1942-1943, 19.

117 "Dean Cervin Recalls…," *Observer*, May 16, 1946.

118 "Dean Cervin Recalls…," 2.

119 President's Report, 1943-1944, 5.

120 President's Report, 5.

121 "Dean Cervin Recalls….," 2.

122 President's Report, 1945-1946, 9.

123 President's Report, 9.

124 Virginia Penniston Wheeler, e-mail to the writer, November 17, 2009.

125 Nancy and Dale Huse, e-mail to the writer.

Chapter 7
Balancing On the Threshhold: Post-War and the Fifties

1   "Educate a Woman," *Association of American Colleges Bulletin*, December 1942, 525.
2   Susan M. Hartmann, *The Home Front and Beyond: American Women in the 1940s* (Boston: Twayne Publishers, 1982).
3   "A Revolution in American Education," *Augustana College Magazine*, summer 1995, 12.
4   Brodahl, 12.
5   Brodahl, 12.
6   Dorothy J. Parkander, unpublished speech, Augustana Historical Society, November 1985, 1.
7   Parkander, 1.
8   Parkander, 1.
9   Qtd. in Thomas Tredway, *Coming of Age*, 33.
10 Brodahl, personal conversation.
11 Brodahl, "A Revolution in American Education," 12.
12 Tredway, 50.
13 Conrad Bergendoff, "The College and the War," *Augustana College Magazine*, Summer 1995, 6.
14 *I.e.*, "preference was given to local students, in the upper half of their graduating class, and to upperclass persons who had been Augustana students before the war. Vets with good service records but high school transcripts in the lower half of their classes were given examinations to determine whether they would be admitted. We discouraged transfers unless they came from junior colleges" (Brodahl, "A Revolution in American Education," 12-13).
15 Brodahl, "A Revolution in American Education," 13.
16 Henriette C. K. Naeseth, chair of the Humanities Division and of the English Department, was largely responsible for this exam. Her work was featured in *College English* and commanded interest from a wide variety of colleagues nation-wide (Dorothy J. Parkander, personal interview).
17 Faculty Minutes, 1950-1959.
18 See, *i.e.*, March 13, 1952.
19 Faculty Minutes, September 25, 1952.
20 Faculty Minutes, September 19, 1957.
21 Bergendoff, "The College and the War," 6.
22 Bergendoff, "The College and the War," 6.
23 Tredway, 49-50.
24 Ann Boaden, "Weighing the Stars and Hearing the Word: Conrad Bergendoff's Idea of Christian Higher Education at Augustana College and Theological Seminary," *Aspects of Augustana and Swedish America: Essays in Honor of Dr. Conrad Bergendoff on His 100th Year* (Rock Island: Augustana Historical Society, 1995), 90.
25 "Dr. Bergendoff's Inaugural Address," *Observer*, October 1, 1936.
26 Arnold Levin, personal letter to the writer, June 27, 2006.
27 Levin.
28 *Rockety-I*, 30.
29 *Rockety-I*, 182-183.
30 One notable exception is editorship of *Saga*, Augustana's literary-art magazine, which was typically assumed by women and men alike. Interestingly, *Saga's* creator and advisor was a woman professor, Dr. Henriette C. K. Naeseth.

31 Charles Rushing, "Rushing Around Campus," *Observer*, October 5, 1950.

32 Rushing.

33 "Words of Wittenstrom," February 19, 1953.

34 Richard Collins, personal interview.

35 September 24, 1953.

36 Edith Friske, Class of 1951, for example, was elected to both Phi Beta Kappa and Aglaia, the forerunner of Mortar Board, honorary society for senior women who excelled in both scholastic and extra-curricular endeavors.

37 On a lighter note, the famous—or infamous, depending on your perspective—panty raid of 1949, generating nation-wide publicity, left college and synod alike scrambling to retrieve Augustana's reputation as a serious academic institution. While dismissing this "foolish prank by a few" as a misrepresentation of the majority who hadn't participated, still President Bergendoff found the incident distasteful and damaging (see Tredway, 77-78).

38 Tredway, 78-79.

39 See Tredway, Chapter 3, "And the Dance Went On."

40 Tredway, 86.

41 Faculty Minutes, December 11, 1952.

42 Tredway, 89.

43 Qtd. in Boaden, "Weighing the Stars....," 91.

44 Boaden, 90-91.

45 Tredway, 62.

46 Qtd. in President's Report, 1952.

47 *Rockety-I* 1952, 10-12.

48 *Rockety-I* 1953, 12.

49 *Rockety-I* 1950, n. p.

50 President's Report, 1952.

51 The college now found itself in the interesting situation of recruiting men—a problem that would have surprised Hasselquist. Tredway notes that one reason for the "growing percentage of women" at colleges like Augustana was that small liberal arts schools offered the kinds of fields that still attracted more women than men: elementary education, nursing, speech correction (Tredway, 74).

52 President's Report 1953, 2-3.

53 The idea of "introducing a home economics department," along with a chair in domestic science offered by the Augustana College Endowment Society, had been abandoned, but the idea that "certain courses would be desirable, as in home-making" (President's Report 1954, 2-3), seemed a hard one to surrender.

54 Tredway, 74.

55 For the record, D. A. and Charlie never actually went head-to-head with Yale, since the latter had fallen in earlier rounds. Still, Augustana's team did come out ahead of Yale that year.

56 Gloria and Arnold Levin, personal letter to the writer, April 11, 2006.

57 Peggy Anderson, Class of 1960, telephone interview, November 11, 2002.

58 Levin.

59 Qtd. in *Observer*, January 11, 1951.

60 Information for this profile comes from a personal interview conducted with Dr. Neely for the article "Plants and Places: A Profile of Dr. Florence Neely," *Augustana College Magazine*, April 1980.

61 Vicki Romano, qtd. in Ann Boaden, "Plants and Places," 13.

Chapter 8
Forging Bonds: Women's Groups

1 "Augustana Endowment Society" was the name initially adopted. Members later changed it to "Augustana College Endowment Society," to reflect its focus on the needs of the college exclusively rather than on both college and seminary because "it was felt that the seminary had its own endowment" (Lillian Nelson, *The Augustana College Endowment Society*, Esbjorn Bicentennial Newsletter of The Augustana Historical Society, Fall 2008, 8).

2 Esther Andreen Albrecht, "Endowment Society," unpublished manuscript, 1, Endowment Society Papers.

3 Albrecht, 6.

4 Conrad Bergendoff, *Augustana...A Profession of Faith*, 205.

5 Conrad Bergendoff, "A Memorable Event," *The Lutheran Companion*, February 1943, 205.

6 Nelson, 3.

7 Andreen, President's Report 1929, qtd. in Nelson, 7.

8 Nelson, 4.

9 She also spells her name "Marguerite." See "Fairview Hall: Mother's Family Business."

10 Qtd. in Wickstrom, "Purchase of Double Stucco House by College Recalls Old Fairview Academy."

11 Endowment Society Papers.

12 Bergendoff, "A Memorable Event," 205.

13 Qtd. in Nelson, 10. Lael Erickson's daughter, Dr. Charlotte Erickson, famously took her mother's advice to "expand": she achieved international renown for her scholarship on immigration history. See Chapter 6.

14 Nelson, 11-12.

15 Minutes, October 1 and 15, 1928.

16 Minutes, September 19, 1928.

17 So renamed, without explanation, in the 1940 Minutes. The fact that in that year delegates from Augustana attended a state conference, the Illinois Association of Women's Leagues, may, however, account for the change.

18 Herself a student leader in her college days, and an extraordinary teacher and mentor to students for more than four decades.

19 December 1937.

20 Minutes, February 9, 1837.

21 A story in the *Rock Island Argus*, covering the 1948 mock Republican Convention sponsored by the Women's League, reports that one male student, acting "as chairman of a resolutions committee,...brought in a platform which included some humorous planks, such as a demand by the government of a Swedish pioneer centennial commemorative stamp and 'equal rights for women'" ("Augustana Students, Right Since 1932, Give G.O.P. Nomination to Vandenberg," *Rock Island Argus* April 10, 1948). Who found the latter plank "humorous"—the students or the *Argus* reporter—and why, isn't clear.

22 Editorial, November 12, 1951.

23 Minutes, 1962-1963.

24 Though the terminology changed—women became "Mary Smith"—it wasn't until the seventies that one feminist faculty member boldly proclaimed, "I'm not Mrs. 'John' anybody!" ("John" is not the real name.)

25 Margaret Tweet, personal interview.

Chapter 9
The Challenge for a Chance: Women's Athletics

1 "The Co-ed Team," *Observer*, March 1917.
2 According to Lynn Sanders of the University of Virginia, as recently as 2000 396 complaints were filed with the Department of Education alleging sex discrimination in violation of Title IX (qtd. in Kathy Veroni, "The Rich History and Tradition of Women's Athletics at Western Illinois University: A Partial History," Western Illinois University Website).
3 *In the Company of Educated Women*, 103.
4 Qtd. in Solomon, 103.
5 Augustana, in fact, had a special connection with Amelia Earhart. An ad for Lutheran Mutual Life Insurance Company, featured in the *Observer* (October 5, 1950), cites Earhart as one in a series of "famous Lutherans" (she's Number 10).
6 Anderson, "Augustana Fifty Years Ago through a Co-ed's Eyes," 11.
7 Catalogue, 1899-1900, 71.
8 *Augustana…A Profession of Faith*, 128.
9 *Augustana…A Profession of Faith*, picture following 172.
10 *An Historical Survey of the Augustana Campus*, Revised edition (Rock Island: Augustana Historical Society, 1992), 47.
11 Bergendoff, 65.
12 Bergendoff, 150.
13 "General News," *Observer*, September 1919.
14 Helen Collins, "Physical Education for Women," *Rockety-I* 1923, 212.
15 "Girls' Athletics at Augustana," *Rockety-I* 1922, 188.
16 Salaries, of course, reflected these discrepancies. For example, in 1926, after completing her B.A. degree, Anne Greve received $1,200 as "Instructor in the Women's Gymnastics and Swimming" (though she in fact did more than this; her duties, specified in 1924, were to teach 8 hours or more per week and supervise all girls' activities), while the Director of Athletics, Arthur Swedberg, earned $2,300 (Board Minutes, February 11, 1926). However, salary comparisons based on dollar amounts alone can be misleading. Other variables entered into the calculations: faculty rank, based on academic credentialing; teaching and coaching loads.
17 Catalogue, 1922-1923, 133.
18 Catalogue, 1916-1917.
19 *Rockety-I* 1923, 202.
20 *Rockety-I* 1923, 202.
21 Maude Adams, Class of 1924, *Rockety-I* 1924, 125.
22 Adams, 125.
23 Indiana University Website.
24 *Rockety-I* 1936, 98.
25 1928, 133.
26 1932, 153.
27 "Augie Girls," *Rockety-I* 1928, 127.
28 "Augie Girls," 153.
29 *Rockety-I* 1929, 149.
30 *Rockety-I* 1929, 149.
31 *Rockety-I* 1929, 149.
32 *Rockety-I* 1933, 144.
33 "Girls' Athletics," *Rockety-I* 1934, 70.

34 *Rockety-I* 1926, 169.
35 *Observer*, March 12, 1931.
36 "Professors' Wives Excel Their Mates in Aquatic Sports," *Observer*, January 27, 1927.
37 Qtd. in Kai Swanson, "From Dome to Dome," *Augustana College Magazine*, Spring 2005.
38 *Rockety-I* 1934, 70.
39 *Rockety-I* 1934, 70.
40 Harold Sundelius, former Academic Dean, Augustana College, personal interview.
41 *Rockety-I* 1936, 98.
42 "Kat's Banquet Is a Meowing Success," *Observer*, April 26, 1937, Brissman Scrapbook.
43 "Kat's Banquet."
44 "Kats Visit in Andreen," *Observer*, Brissman Scrapbook.
45 Brissman Scrapbook.